Through Amazonian Eyes

Emilio F. Moran

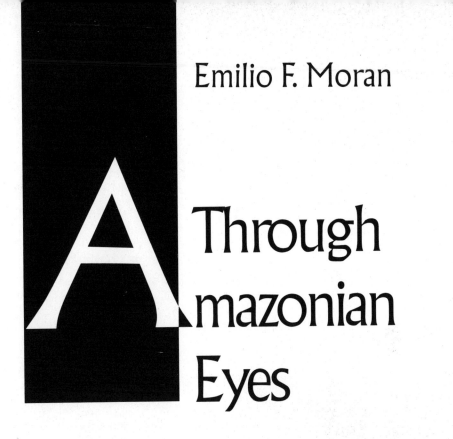

Through Amazonian Eyes

The Human Ecology of Amazonian Populations

University
of Iowa Press
Iowa City

University of Iowa Press,
Iowa City 52242

Copyright © 1993 by the
University of Iowa Press

Printed in the United States
of America

Design by Richard Hendel

Printed on acid-free paper

Library of Congress Cataloging-in-Publication Data

Moran, Emilio F.

[Ecologia humana das populações da Amazônia.
English]

Through Amazonian eyes: the human ecology of
Amazonian populations / by Emilio F. Moran.

p.   cm.

Rev. and updated translation of: A ecologia humana
das populações da Amazônia.

Includes bibliographical references (p.   ) and
index.

ISBN 0-87745-417-5 (cloth), ISBN 0-87745-418-3
(paper)

1. Human ecology—Amazon River Region.
2. Indians of South America—Amazon River
Region.   3. Human ecology—Brazil.   4. Man—
Influence on nature—Amazon River Region.   I. Title.

GF532.A4M6713   1993   93-1148

304.2′0981′1—dc20   CIP

97 96 95 94 93 C 5 4 3 2 1
97 96 95 94 93 P 5 4 3 2

To my daughter

EMILY VICTORIA MORAN

whose actions, drawings, and

special appreciation for plants

and animals continuously

remind me how important it

is to conserve the environment,

so that the imagination of

future generations can be

stimulated by its awesome

beauty and complexity

Contents

Preface, xiii

Acknowledgments, xvii

1   Amazonia: People and Environment, 1

2   Blackwater Ecosystems, 35

3   Upland Forests, 57

4   Floodplains, 85

5   Savannas, 117

6   Human Ecology as a Critique of Development, 141

Notes, 163

Bibliography, 169

Index, 227

Tables

1   Distribution of Soils in the Humid Tropics, 12

2   Common Constraints in Soils of the Humid Tropics, 12

3   Types of Vegetation in the Amazon Basin, 25

4   Soil Types in the Amazon Basin, 66

5   Mean Returns from Hunting and Fishing, 79

6   Returns with Various Fishing Techniques at Itacoatiara, 102

7   Comparison of Hunting and Fishing Efficiency, 111

8   Use of Biotopes of the Upper Floodplain, 113

9   Soils and Vegetation of the Savannas, 123

10   Characteristics of Savannas, 125

11   Xavante Height and Weight Measures, 135

12   Appropriate Management Strategies, 147

Figures

1   Map of the Legal Amazon and the Amazon Basin, 3

2   Impact of Epidemics on Age and Sex Distribution, 5

3   Rubber Exports from Belém, Pará, 1847–1915, 6

4   Catch-up Fertility Following Epidemics among the Suruí Indians, 8

5   Areal Extent of the Humid Tropic Biome, 10

6   Variation in Rainfall in Amazonia, 10

7   Soil Order Map of Amazonia, 13

8   Area-Species Association, 16

9   Biomass Distribution in Tropical Forests, 20

10   Amazon Basin Habitats, 21

11   Water Cycling, 22

12   Water Recycling, 23

13   Whitewater, Blackwater, and Clearwater Watersheds, 23

14   Mosaic of Vegetation in the Tapajós Basin, 26

15   The Rio Negro Basin and Its Affluents, 37

16   Vegetational Gradient in the Rio Negro, 39

17   Association of Location with Fishing Success, 49

18   Height-for-Age Growth Rates in the Rio Negro and Rondônia, 51

19   Cross Section of a Terra Firme and a Várzea Forest, 64–65

20   Species of Vegetation Indicative of Good and Poor Soils for Agriculture Identified by Amazonian Caboclos, 74

21   Agricultural Calendar of the Suruí Indians, 77

22   Map of the Floodplains of the Amazon Basin, 87

23   Dendritic River System with Oxbow Lakes, 89

24   Floodplain Biotopes, 91

25   Vegetation in Floodplain Lakes, 93

26   Vertical Zonation in the Floodplain, 99

27   Fishing with Seine Nets, 101

28   Fishing with Baited Trotlines and Drifting Deepwater Gillnets, 103

29   Conical Fish Trap, 104

30   Dolphin/Fisheries Interactions, 106

31   Biotopes in an Upper Floodplain Region, 108–109

32   Use of a Managed Lake in the Upper Amazon, 110

33   Upland Savannas of Amazonia, 119

34   Biomass Productivity of Savannas, 124
35   Gê and Xinguano Ecological Differences, 128
36   Biotopes of the Kayapó Gorotire, 133
37   Islands of Resources in Gorotire, 134
38   Development Activities in the Amazon Basin, 152–153

Preface

Since 1985 citizens all over the planet have become concerned with the fate of the Amazonian tropical forests. After many years of scholarly research on changes taking place in the Amazon Basin, the media finally began to give headlines to the images from satellites and scholarly analyses and to recognize the scale of the problem, reaching a peak in 1987 when seven thousand individual land areas were burned in one day in Amazonia. Several states of Amazonia have already had up to 26 percent of their forested land cut. This concern became a focus of worldwide attention at the Earth Summit, the United Nations Ecology and Development meeting in Rio de Janeiro, Brazil, in June 1992. The confrontation between conservation and "development" which each nation and people face within their boundaries each day became a multinational battle over the fate of the earth. The concrete outcomes of that summit were not many, but it is unlikely that concern for the role of forests in the health of the planet will ever be belittled again, and ecology has now become a matter not only for scientists and advocacy groups within nation-states but for political groups everywhere. Moreover, one important result of the Earth Summit was that it moved ecology and conservation away from a focus largely on plants and animals. The importance of the human condition—health, education, and income—in the achievement of a balanced relationship with the other species of the planet was recognized and will lead ecological study toward more comprehensive understanding of how *human* ecosystems work.

In these final years of the twentieth century we live with an omnipresent worry: will the Amazonian forests survive the current deforestation trends? Will the native populations survive the spread of introduced diseases and the expropriation of their traditional territories? Will the promise of biotechnology ever be achieved, given the rates of genetic losses we are currently experiencing? Will the sciences of medicine and pharmacology find new chemical substances in the forests of Amazonia to cure diseases heretofore incurable or unknown? Will we learn to use, rather than thoughtlessly destroy, the thousands of tropical species that we now consider without value? Will we invest in agronomic research in order to find ways to achieve sustainable ways of cultivating parts of the humid tropics?

The Amazon region's resources have been exploited thus far in ways that are inappropriate for the characteristics of that biogeographic and human province. One of the consequences of the demographic disaster of the six-teenth century was the loss of the knowledge of the large-scale populations that inhabited the rich floodplains of the Amazon, devastated by the diseases brought by the Europeans. The Europeans and their descendants introduced systems of resource use that ignored the characteristics of the environment.

The Amazon has the capacity to sustain sizable populations; but for this potential to be achieved, it will be necessary to change the current forms of resource use and development. It will also be necessary to recognize that the Amazon must not be treated as a homogeneous region. It is neither "green hell" nor "paradise." The Amazon is an ecological mosaic where one finds a rich variety of flora and fauna, soils of all kinds, and significant climatic differences. The native populations of Amazonia recognized this heteroge-neity long ago, and it will be necessary for contemporary populations to begin to realize the difference that this recognition can make to the way we think about and treat this vast region.

The Amazon Basin is neither a demographic nor a cultural vacuum. Liv-ing in this lush green world are Indian and peasant populations that have grown familiar with the special character of their local habitats. If we are to contribute to balancing the use and conservation of this habitat, it will be necessary to begin with an appreciation of the knowledge that these local populations have about their environment. The Amazon includes a very large number of ecosystems, each related to the other, each having a distinct natural history, unique geophysical and chemical characteristics, and hu-man populations that differ in their history, demography, social and political organization, and view of nature. These differences result in part from the process of adaptation of these populations to the variability present within Amazonia and in part from their individual cultural histories. Human be-ings are embedded in a historical context, and their future is shaped by these highly particular experiences.

In this book I hope to introduce the reader to the range of human and ecological diversity present in the Amazon Basin. To do so it will be funda-mental to begin with the knowledge of the Indian and peasant populations of the region. Recent migrants to the region lack the necessary familiarity with the environment that can give us guidance on how best to adjust to the characteristics of the region. Migrants always attempt to reproduce their knowledge in a new region without regard for the special character of the habitat. We *can* learn from the many mistakes they have made and from the serendipitous successes they have experienced in trying to find workable strategies for resource use.

The following chapters introduce the reader to a number of ecosystems of the Amazon, to their ecological characterization, and to some of the human strategies of resource use that seem to represent workable approaches to the environment. The Amazon is far more diverse than the dichotomy made between terra firme (uplands) and várzea (floodplains) would suggest. We can compare seasonally flooded savannas with savannas that are well-drained. We can compare mature upland forests with anthropogenic forests that look "virgin" but have had prolonged human occupation. Each ecosystem offers opportunities as well as limitations. Each has unique characteristics that can be either used advantageously or resisted. Native peoples not only adjust to the environment but also actively modify the environment to enhance features that would result in greater long-term value to them. The view that native peoples of Amazonia are "backward" must be replaced by an attitude of respect for their stewardship of that region. The view that they are "noble savages" is no less off the mark. Native peoples vary a great deal among themselves. They do not agree about how to treat nature. Nevertheless, the imprint they have left on the forests has been far less destructive than that of outsiders despite their use of the region for millennia compared to the relatively recent arrival of Europeans in the region. The final chapter examines how we might be able to move from human ecology as a diagnostic tool to understanding its value for the design and implementation of a balance between use and conservation.

This introduction to the complexity of Amazonia is just the beginning of a long-term task. Amazonia is far more complex than could be outlined here. We have to begin with humility and a willingness to learn from the people of the region. One of the principal objectives of this book is to show that the traditional inhabitants of Amazonia (the Indians and the caboclos) exhibit greater understanding of the diversity of Amazonia than do most outsiders. There are strategies of resource use that do not destroy the structure and function of the ecosystem. Are we ready to learn?

Acknowledgments

This book appeared in an earlier form in Portuguese (*A ecologia humana das populações da Amazônia*, published by Editôra Vozes of Brazil in October 1990). In preparing the English revised edition, I have taken the opportunity to update the book. Although I normally write my books and articles in English, rather than in Spanish or Portuguese, I wrote this one in Portuguese first because I felt strongly that this synthesis should make its way as quickly as possible into the hands of the people most directly affected by its subject. Curiously, it has been easier to read about the environmental crisis in Amazonia in English, French, and German than in Portuguese or Spanish. In addition to the Portuguese edition, a Spanish translation of this work is available from Fondo de Cultura Económica in Mexico. The apparent greater interest of outsiders in the Amazon has already begun to change. Brazilians, rich and poor alike, have been awakened to the crisis in their midst and have begun to respond to it. Latin Americans living in countries with Amazonian territories (Ecuador, Peru, Bolivia, Colombia, Venezuela, the Guianas) likewise have begun to claim their proper place in the international discussions about "the fate of the forest"—rather than letting outsiders define the terms of the debate. Latin American environmental organizations have begun to proliferate and flourish—despite the worldwide economic crisis and the fear of violence against those who try to protect the forest from its destroyers. Incipient Green parties work toward conservation and awareness, mainstream parties have begun to address the concerns of local populations, and other groups focus on particular endangered parts of the Amazonian environment. Indigenous peoples have become increasingly effective in mobilizing media and public support for their struggle to have territories demarcated and protected. Ultimately, people everywhere should assist the populations of the Amazon region to develop their own strategies of resource use and conservation, rather than rely on ready-made solutions. The latter work no better in environmental matters than they do in efforts to promote economic development.

The task of writing this book was assisted by a large number of individuals and institutions. I wish to thank the Goeldi Museum in Belém and the Fulbright Commission, which made it possible to take time off from my full-time academic obligations in the United States to devote time to conceptualizing and beginning to write this book. I also thank Indiana University for providing a sabbatical leave that permitted me to go to Brazil during this period of research and writing. Without a fellowship from the John Simon Guggenheim Memorial Foundation and a year-long period of residence at the Institute for Advanced Study at Indiana University the manuscript could not have been completed. Several colleagues at the Goeldi Museum read early versions of the manuscript and corrected many of its imperfections. Among them I want to thank especially Dr. Walter Neves, coordinator of the Human Biology Program, and Dr. William Balée, then coordinator of the Ecology Program and now on the faculty at Tulane University. Dr. Ana Anderman of the Fulbright Commission read several chapters and provided corrections. Anonymous readers for the University of Iowa Press provided numerous suggestions for this English edition.

I also benefited a great deal from the comments of colleagues at the University of Brasília, especially Gustavo Ribeiro and Waud Kracke. I gained insights from discussions with Professor Mercio Gomes of the University of Campinas. I had the good fortune to come to know Professor Renate Viertler of the University of São Paulo and Professor Irmhild Wust of the University of Goiás, who offered numerous suggestions that gave the manuscript a more effective focus. Professor Dennis Werner, of the University of Santa Catarina at Florianópolis, provided me with a very thorough commentary on the first draft, for which I am immensely grateful. Mr. John Hollingsworth, of the Geography Department at Indiana University, prepared the illustrations.

Many colleagues read parts of the manuscript and offered valuable suggestions, among them: Carlos Coimbra, Jr., Eduardo Góes Neves, Branca Egger Moellwald, Ricardo Ventura Santos, Jonathan Hill, Darna Dufour, Jean Jackson, Nigel Smith, and Robert Goodland. The inevitable mistakes are the sole responsibility of the author.

The first readers of the manuscript were the students enrolled in the course I taught in 1989 at the Goeldi Museum on the Human Ecology of Amazonian Populations. I want to thank them all, especially those who took the time to make useful and detailed suggestions: Eduardo Brondízio, Claudia Montezuma Firmino, Jean Philippe Boubli, Hilton Pereira da Silva, Dirse Clara Kern, Fábio de Castro, Cintia Jalles, Cristina Senna, Eduardo Góes Neves, Maria Christina Leal Rodrigues, Luis Donisete Benzi Grupioni, Rui Sergio Sereni Murrieta, Christiane Lopes Machado, Maria Clara da Silva, Renato Kipnis, Andréa Siqueira, and Lucila Pinsard Viana. It was a marvelous group of students, representing nearly every imaginable discipline, who understood from the outset the importance of human ecology to the future of the Amazon. Students in my course on the Amazon in Crisis: Ecology and Development, taught at Indiana University in winter 1991, provided feedback on the revised English edition of the manuscript, for which I am grateful.

I would like to invite the reader to contribute actively to the more rational and less destructive use of the Amazon. To get there we must begin by respecting the native people of the region.

Through
Amazonian
Eyes

1

Amazonia: People and Environment

The Amazon's ecosystems and their native populations are threatened with extinction today. Deforestation, epidemic diseases, inappropriate development policies, and a lack of regard for the quality of life on our planet can be listed among the forces responsible for the current situation. The changes that deforestation of the greatest rain forest on earth might bring about in the planet's hydrologic cycle and climate, while not fully established, can easily be guessed: drying of areas to the south of the basin that currently produce the second largest crop of soybeans in the world; desiccation of the moist forests in the eastern Amazon, an area with some of the best soils; increased flooding along productive areas of the seasonally flooded valley—not to speak of carbon dioxide accumulation in the atmosphere exacerbating global warming. The decimation of native peoples is serious not only because of the loss of their knowledge of the Amazon but because it shows so little regard for fellow human beings. The destruction of the forest and its native peoples constitutes not only a reduction in biotic and cultural diversity but the effective impoverishment of every single person still to be born.

It is not easy to define the Amazon or Amazonia. At times it is defined simply as the drainage basin, or the Amazon Valley, with all its affluents—an area of about 4 million square kilometers in Brazil alone (fig. 1). This biogeographical region is, if anything, too big to discuss meaningfully in its entirety. Rather than divide it into smaller, more coherent units, the tendency has been to make it even larger. Other commonly used definitions have added political-economic criteria, such as that used in Brazil when referring to the "Legal Amazon." According to the latter, large areas of the Brazilian Plateau are also considered part of the Amazon—with the objective of giving access to special tax exemptions—expanding rather than restricting the scope of the Amazon to a region of over 5 million square kilometers (fig. 1). Whichever definition is used, each one embodies a reality which is not only that of a physical environment but also a human environment with a social, political, and economic history. The recent tendency to rely on political-economic definitions rather than on hydrographic ones serves to remind us that any solution to the environmental crisis of Amazonia must deal with the social, political, and economic dimensions of that crisis.

Brazil's Legal Amazon includes an area 1 million square kilometers larger than the drainage basin (Benchimol 1989: 15), an area roughly half of Brazil's total territory. The total drainage basin is about 6 million square kilometers. In comparative terms, the area occupied by the Amazon is equiva-

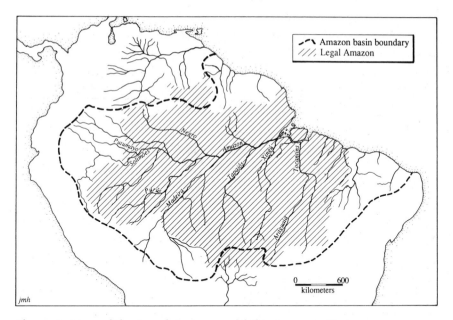

Figure 1. Map of the Legal Amazon and the Amazon Basin.

lent to the continental United States or to both Eastern and Western Europe combined (without the former Soviet Union). The Amazon is a region not only of rain forests. It also has seasonal forests, flooded forests, savannas of various types, montane forests, and palm forests. The rivers have very distinct qualities, some with clear, limpid waters and others with a muddy appearance, reflecting important differences in the amount of alluvium they transport. Contemporary governments act as if the Amazon was all about the same, forgetting the importance of adjusting human activity to the limitations and opportunities presented by the physical environment—or over-looking the need to be ready to spend inordinate levels of resources to get around those conditions. Policy makers have forgotten the physical environment as well as the people who had a prior claim to those lands and who have a long-term familiarity with the Amazonian environment.

Current evidence suggests that the ancestors of contemporary indigenous peoples have inhabited the Amazon Basin for at least 12,000 years (Roosevelt 1989: 3). They may be among the first to have produced ceramics in the New World 6,000 to 8,000 years before the present (Roosevelt 1987). By 5,000 years ago they seem to have had a set of domesticated crops and art forms very similar to those of contemporary indigenous populations. By 2,000 years ago there is evidence of the rise of larger settlements with more complex political organization and art forms such as polychrome pottery.

These appear to have been more common in the more fertile areas of the floodplain and to have been supported by the cultivation of manioc and cereals such as corn (ibid.).

The heterogeneity of the populations that inhabit the Amazon reflects the diversity of the physical environment and their diverse historical experience (Oliveira 1988: 66). The European explorers of the sixteenth century found an Amazon with large populations inhabiting the banks of the larger rivers, capable of organizing themselves in self-defense and of conquering territory (Roosevelt 1989; Porro 1989; Whitehead 1989). Chroniclers of the time describe the existence of chiefdoms capable of mobilizing thousands of warriors and of offering an abundance of food to visitors, with towns extending for hundreds of kilometers along the riverbanks (Carvajal 1934; Cruz 1885; Herrera 1856; Simon 1861; Porro 1989; Myers 1989; Whitehead 1989). According to ethnohistoric sources, the land of the Omagua in the sixteenth century included between twenty-three and thirty-four villages along a 700-kilometer continuous stretch of riverfront, from the Lower Napo River to the mouth of the Javarí and Içá rivers (Myers 1989: 6). Some of these villages are estimated to have had at least 8,000 inhabitants (Porro 1989: 7). The Omagua population persisted until the seventeenth century, although its numbers declined and its settlements covered by then only 300 kilometers of riverfront (Porro 1989; Myers 1989). There is evidence, too, for pre-Columbian chiefdoms in the upland forests of the Amazon, which Whitehead (1989: 9) suggested depended more on control over regional commerce than on local habitat productivity to sustain their complex polities. The Caripunas, or Aruacas, for example, seem to have dominated the commerce in wooden weapons and carvings. Such a system of regional exchange depended on numerous populations scattered over a large territory in the interfluves and less visible from the waterfront; they declined more rapidly than those of the floodplain (Whitehead 1988, 1989: 17–18).

These floodplain populations were quickly decimated by the epidemic diseases brought by the Europeans: measles, the common cold, whooping cough, and influenza. Disease proved to be one of the most powerful weapons of conquest. Historians and archaeologists estimate that the populations of the floodplain declined by 50 to 95 percent in the first century of contact (Denevan 1976; Myers 1973). The Omagua, referred to above, saw their population reduced by 70 percent in the first century of contact (Porro 1989: 8). The impact of these epidemic diseases is repeating itself once again as populations that had managed to remain relatively isolated deep in the interfluvial forests are now reached by miners, farmers, and others seeking

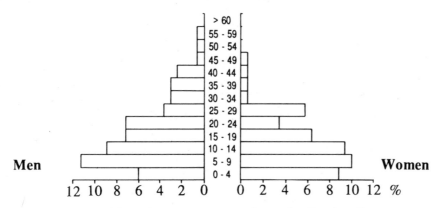

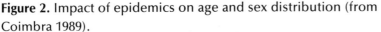

Figure 2. Impact of epidemics on age and sex distribution (from Coimbra 1989).

to gain access to the region's resources. The Suruí of Rondônia, for example, lost about 75 percent of their population in the first decade after initial contact in the late 1960s. Figure 2 illustrates the impact of epidemic disease on the age-sex structure of the Suruí Indians of Rondônia some ten years after the arrival of epidemics through close contact with national society. Note the abnormally lower population in the 0 to 4 age cohort and the low and unbalanced population in the over-30 cohorts, especially among women. During epidemics, there is not only high mortality but also a drop in fecundity (Coimbra 1989; Feldman 1977: 29; Peters 1980; Netter and Lambert 1981), compounding the demographic collapse and crimping the pyramid in telling ways. European diseases were a powerful weapon five hundred years ago. Even today disease is serving the interests of those who want to take over the region's resources.

In the sixteenth and seventeenth centuries the principal impact on the indigenous people came from epidemic diseases, the presence of the missionaries, and the wars of conquest along the major rivers (Fritz 1922; Chaumeil 1981; Chantre y Herrera 1901; Figueroa 1904; Uriarte 1952; Hemming 1978). By the beginning of the eighteenth century the demographic situation seemed to have stabilized, the missionaries had gained control over the bulk of Indian labor, and the civil authorities complained that the occupation of the New World would be hampered unless they got greater access to the labor of the native population (Kiemen 1973; Mörner 1965).

By the mid-eighteenth century all that was to change. This period was dominated by the figure of the marquis of Pombal, whose state-building efforts brought him into conflict with the church. He expelled the Jesuits,

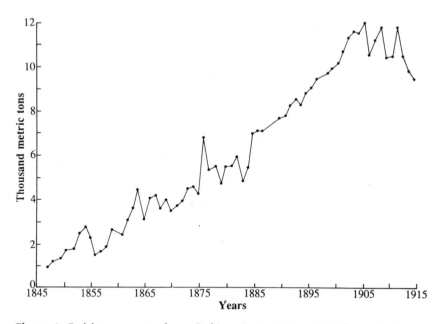

Figure 3. Rubber exports from Belém, Pará, 1847–1915 (from Anderson 1976: 61).

the leading figures in missionary activity of the time, and replaced them with "the Directorate," which made Indian labor available to civil authorities in Directorate villages created to replace the Jesuit missions. The consequences of the Directorate (explored in great detail by Anderson 1976) were the emergence of the first cities in the Amazon; the development of a new regional culture that mixed Portuguese and Indian knowledge, which we have come to call caboclo culture (Wagley 1953; Moran 1974; Parker 1988); and the definitive defeat of the Brazilian Indians (Hemming 1987). Moreira Neto (1988) showed that Amazonian populations in some places managed to keep up their numbers until the time of the Directorate. After this dismal social experiment, the native peoples never recovered and have remained a minority of the region's population rather than the majority which they had been.

When the rubber era began in the middle of the nineteenth century the native peoples were already a minority. The mad search for rubber led to the violent expulsion of native peoples from their territories. The expansion of rubber exports from Belém (fig. 3) gives a clear indication of the speed of the process, without giving an inkling of the violence in human relations that attended such an accomplishment. Instead of being a necessary, even essential, labor force, as they had been up to this point, the Indians began to be seen as an obstacle to the region's development, and outside labor was brought to take on productive tasks (Weinstein 1983; Oliveira 1988: 68). Darcy Ribeiro (1970) estimated that 88 ethnic groups disappeared in the period between 1900 and 1957 in the Brazilian Amazon. Today only 220 ethnic groups survive, with a total population of about 230,000, 60 percent of them living in the Brazilian Amazon (Gomes 1988: 24).

Fortunately, there is evidence of rapid population growth among some groups who have already gone through the devastating experience of epidemics and who have gained access to health services. The future of some Amazonian populations looks brighter than it did a few years ago despite the persistent problems that remain: constant defense of their territories, inadequate provision of health care, and how to coexist with the national society (Gomes 1988). Following a major decline in fecundity and mortality, a population may undertake a period of catch-up fertility, which is what Coimbra (1989) observed among the Suruí. Figure 4 illustrates the rapid increase in the number of children in the 1984 and 1988 censuses despite high child mortality. Between these two censuses the population grew at an annual rate of 5.6 percent, which would permit it to double every fourteen years and is one of the highest rates of growth ever recorded in a human population. Given that the Suruí are recovering from 75 percent mortality from the first decade of epidemics (Meireles 1984: 105), such rates are entirely justified to ensure their biological survival.

Disturbing events such as the invasion of Yanomamo lands by gold miners and attempts to create a dispersed reservation system continue to create situations which threaten the biological and cultural existence of native peoples. The persistence of these efforts reminds us that for every group doing better there are several others experiencing severe biological or cultural losses.

In spite of all these threats, some groups such as the Suruí and the Kayapó are recuperating from near-extinction—and some are resisting and becoming politically savvy in their struggle against those who would prefer to have them invisible or dead. Not only do these people have a right as human beings to live, but their expertise is necessary to the future development of the region (Correa 1990; Dufour 1990; Posey and Balée 1989; Ribeiro and Ribeiro 1986). The Indian and caboclo cultures of the Amazon have adjusted to the physical environment and to the powerful external forces that

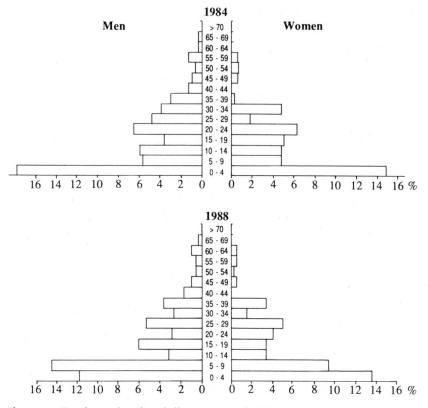

Figure 4. Catch-up fertility following epidemics among the Suruí Indians: 1984 (above) and 1988 (below) (from Coimbra 1989).

act within it. The degree of adaptation that each one may have achieved at a given moment will vary, as a function of historical, social, political, and economic forces that may have influenced it. The forms of management of one society may be not so much attuned to the physical environment as to the market forces of Brazilian society, while another ethnic group may have sophisticated forms of environmental management coming out of long-term experience and resistance to changing their use of resources despite the pressures from missionaries, government agents, and traders. One of the important objectives of human ecology is to discover those long-term practices that permit use with conservation (Correa 1990). The adaptive strategies of Amazonian populations constitute riches that human ecology, and society, ought to value since they offer examples of how to balance use with conservation of the richest realm of nature. The following sections examine just how diverse this area can be.

Ecosystems of the Humid Tropics

The Amazon is the largest extant portion of the humid tropics, which tend to be defined in terms of their hyperhumid and warm temperatures year-round.[1] The humid tropics form a greenbelt around the earth (fig. 5) that covers 10 percent of the planet's surface or an area of about 1,500 million hectares (Sánchez et al. 1982: 821). They are not a continuous belt of forested land, as many think. One-fifth is made up of tropical savannas (ibid.). There are areas of seasonal forests, as well as evergreen pluvial forests. Along the floodplain, remarkably, forests are found, despite being flooded for half the year (Goulding 1990). The Asian and African rain forests have been severely reduced since World War II, with less than 25 percent of them still standing in some areas. The South American rain forests are the largest, with one-third the total area (Nicholaides et al. 1985). Deforestation has also begun to be felt in the great South American rain forests (i.e., Amazonia), with rates of loss in excess of 40,000 square kilometers annually.

While the average annual temperatures in the humid tropics vary by less than 2 degrees C (24 to 26 degrees C), the daily maximum and minimum temperatures can fluctuate as much as 15 degrees C in one day. There is said to be a rainy season and a dry season, but regional differences are significant. In some areas the dry season may be less than two weeks, while elsewhere it may last four months. Months with less than 100 millimeters of rainfall may elicit leaf dropping as extensive as in temperate zones during autumn. Outsiders have sometimes characterized the difference between the dry and the wet season as "in the dry season it rains every day, while in the wet season it rains every day all day." This view is more folklore than scientific observation. Relative humidity fluctuates between 75 and 100 percent annually, a factor that makes the temperatures feel far warmer than they in fact are. The high humidity renders the cooling of skin through evaporation ineffective, particularly when clothes become soaked. Ambient temperatures feel like they are usually over 35 degrees C when in fact they are commonly in the 24 to 30 degree range. On average, the humid tropics receive two times more solar radiation than the poles (Barry and Chorley 1970: 33). Atmospheric circulation carries 80 percent of the heat from solar radiation to other areas, thereby avoiding excessive overheating of the tropical regions (Stella 1976: 152). The biggest cause of variability in insolation in the Amazon Basin is the degree of cloud cover. The mean solar radiation for the basin is 400 calories per square centimeter per day (Salati 1985: 21).

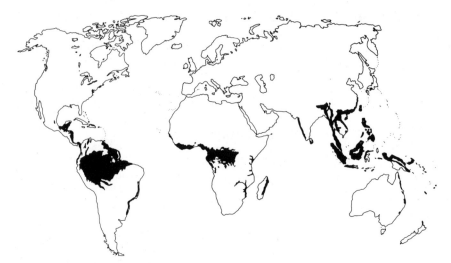

Figure 5. Areal extent of the humid tropic biome.

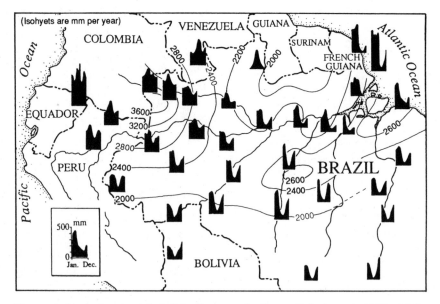

Figure 6. Variation in rainfall in Amazonia (from Salati et al. 1978: 204).

One of the basic parameters in understanding ecosystem structure and function is climate. Climate affects organic decomposition, nutrient cycling, seasonality, leaffall, and many other ecosystem components. Amazonian climate was cited for some time as one of the reasons for the region's underdevelopment. Allusions were made to its high heat and humidity, "excessive" rainfall, and "lack of seasonality." Climate still looms as one of the alleged problems the region poses for outsiders.[2]

The number of climatological stations in Amazonia is sorely insufficient, and more attention to climatic data is needed in future studies if we are ever to be able to take proper accounting of the role of climate in human decisions. Until such time as more inclusive data are available for the immediate area under study, it may be wise to seriously collect the ethnoecology (i.e., the folk knowledge) of climate prediction, which represents long-term observations by local people (cf. Stigter 1986), and to take the data from distant collecting stations of only a few years' duration with a dose of skepticism. Figure 6 gives an idea of the great variation from place to place in total precipitation and in its seasonal distribution in Amazonia.

Soils

The soils of the humid tropics are generally considered to be poor, leached, acid, with little horizon differentiation in the profile, and capable of producing for only a couple of years before being abandoned due to fertility decline (McNeil 1964). As a generalization this may be true, but one should not forget that there is considerable variation in soil quality within the humid tropics. In fact, the humid tropics include some of the poorest and some of the richest soils in the world (Sánchez 1981: 347). Table 1 summarizes the distribution of soil types by continents. It is clear that the South American area has more chemically poor soils (81 percent) than the Asian humid tropics (38 percent) and fewer medium- to high-fertility soils (7 percent and 33 percent, respectively). But the American humid tropics have fewer erosion problems due to steepness and a higher frequency of deeper soils (table 2). In other words, the Amazonian region is nutrient-limited, while the Asian tropics are more commonly limited by geophysical factors.

Three soil types predominate in the humid tropics: oxisols, ultisols, and alfisols. The most common are the oxisols, characterized by an oxic horizon (consisting of hydrated oxides of iron and aluminum). When the conditions that create an oxic horizon are accompanied by a fluctuating water table, plinthite (the technical term for the irreversibly hardened material known

Table 1. *Distribution of Soils in the Humid Tropics*

	Americas %	Africa %	Asia %	Total %
Acid soils of low fertility (oxisols, ultisols)	81	56	38	63
Soils of medium to high fertility, well-drained (alfisols, vertisols)	7	12	33	15
Poorly drained soils (aquepts)	6	12	6	8
Extremely poor and sandy soils (spodosols)	2	16	6	7
Shallow soils (lithic entisols)	3	3	10	5
Organic soils (histosols)	1	1	6	2

Source: Adapted from Sánchez 1987.

Table 2. *Common Constraints in Soils of the Humid Tropics*

	Americas %	Africa %	Asia %	Total %
Low levels of nutrients	66	67	45	64
High aluminum saturation	61	53	41	56
High phosphorus fixation	47	20	33	37
High acidity, not tied to aluminum	11	22	33	18
Slope over 30%	18	5	33	17
Poorly drained	11	14	19	13
Low cation exchange capacity	8	20	5	11
Shallowness	7	4	12	7
No limitations	3	2	2	3

Source: Adapted from Sánchez 1987.

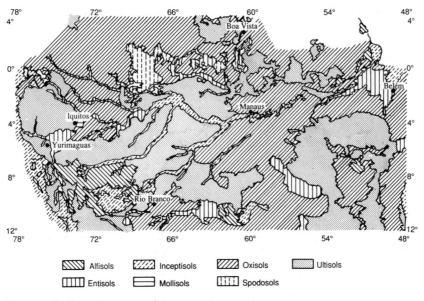

Figure 7. Soil order map of Amazonia.

more commonly as laterite) is formed. It may be found in only 2 to 6 percent of the humid tropics and is less widespread than commonly thought (Sánchez et al. 1982; Sánchez and Buol 1975; Sánchez 1981). The ultisols are dystrophic soils (soils with low base saturation in contrast to eutrophic soils) with a clayish B horizon, more leached than the alfisols and occupying a more stable position in the landscape. They are common throughout Amazonia. The main difference between the oxisols and ultisols is the increase in the percentage of clay with depth in the ultisols, an increase not found in the oxisols. Thus, the physical characteristics of ultisols are less favorable than those of oxisols, not only because of the increase in clay with depth but also because they tend to occupy steeper areas. Alfisols are found in less leached areas of the humid tropics and derive from basic rocks such as basalt. The oxisols and ultisols predominate in the American tropics, where they make up 82 percent of the soils. The alfisols and alluvial soils occupy as much as 33 percent in the Asian tropics, in contrast to only 7 percent in the American tropics. Figure 7 illustrates the distribution of these soil orders in the Amazon Basin.

Amazonian soils have been the focus of controversy for a good part of this century. Late nineteenth century travelers' opinions that the soils of the region must be very rich given the lushness of the vegetation were followed by a severe attack suggesting that they were so poor that they could not support complex cultures or intensive cultivation. No one has stated this latter view more coherently and firmly than Betty Meggers. In her now classic article of 1954 she set out to demonstrate that the poor and acid soils of the humid tropics could only support small-scale societies living by swidden cultivation because soil fertility could only be sustained from the nutrients released by the slash-and-burn method of cultivation. It did not take long for critics of this view to appear. Carneiro (1957) suggested that the Kuikuru Indians of the Upper Xingú could sustain populations of up to two thousand people over the long term with a manioc-based swidden system without requiring village movement. For him, the limiting factor was not the fertility of the soils but weed invasion. This suggestion turns out to be correct—for very rich soils. In the better soils (alfisols, for example) the vigor of weed invasion is greater than in acid, nutrient-poor soils, where soil fertility becomes a limiting factor first (Sánchez et al. 1982). Other critics, such as Ferdon (1959), pointed to the dynamic nature of soil management. Thus, soil limitations can be corrected through the addition of organic matter, mulches, and irrigation. Recent studies tend to emphasize that the soils of the Amazon are among the richest and the poorest in the world, with many soils along the middle of such a fertility continuum. Research in the area must include an understanding of this soil patchiness in order to analyze the variability.[3]

Flora

The high insolation and humidity of the humid tropics favor a high biomass productivity. Plant biomass productivity in tropical moist and rain forests is among the highest of any terrestrial ecosystem. For the humid tropics as a whole, the mean has been estimated to be 23.9 tons per hectare per year, much higher than the mean of 13 tons for temperate forests (Farnworth and Golley 1974: 81–82). Standing biomass is about 450 tons per hectare compared with 300 tons for temperate deciduous forests (Whittaker and Likens 1975; see also the syntheses in Golley 1983 and Lieth and Werger 1989).

The large volume of litterfall and plant biomass that drops to the ground is rapidly recycled, thanks to the action of mycorrhizae (fungi) that help to transfer nutrients back to the vegetation. Thus, the richness of plant biomass is commonly sustained not by rich soils but through very effective processes of decomposition (Swift and Anderson 1989) and nutrient recycling (Jordan 1985). Stark (1969) estimated that 5.4 grams per square meter of leaffall were mineralized per day, close to the daily primary productivity of 6.0 grams. This means that the rain forest produces an amount of total biomass barely greater than the amount it decomposes, thereby maintaining a recycling process that yields a small net output to organisms higher up on the food chain. Stark and Jordan (1978) demonstrated that 99.9 percent of the calcium and phosphorus was absorbed by the vegetation and that a mere 0.1 percent escaped the nutrient-capture mechanisms in the immediate vicinity of the tree. This efficiency in nutrient capture was possible due to the recycling capacity of the fine above-ground rootmat and associated mycorrhizae. This process is more efficient in some parts of the humid tropics than in others. In general, the more nutrient-limited the ecosystem, the tighter will be the nutrient-conserving mechanisms.

One of the most notable aspects of the tropical moist and rain forests is their biotic diversity and the small number of individuals of a species per hectare. Janzen (1970) explained this phenomenon as a result of the effect of the host-specific herbivores that foraged in the vicinity of a tree, a process that favored survival of individuals at greatest distance from the seed-producing tree. There can be considerable differences in the number of species per hectare: in one sample hectare in Barro Colorado Island in Panama only 55 tree species were found, in contrast to 207 species near Manaus, Brazil (Gentry 1992), even though the Barro Colorado Island site was more fertile.

The larger the area sampled, the greater the number of species found. This indicates that we still have not discovered an appropriate sample size at which the number of species stabilizes. Figure 8 illustrates this situation. Thus, estimates of number of species per hectare cited by various authors should be taken with the caution that the number of species may be a function of the size of the areas sampled as much as an indication of species richness per se. What we face here is the endemism of species in Amazonia, a problem studied with great intensity in Hawaii but still poorly understood in Amazonia.

The number of plant species is impressive. Klinge et al. (1975: 119) found more than six hundred species per hectare, although this number is uncommonly high. Jacobs noted that the number of species more commonly fluctuates between eighty and two hundred per hectare (1988: 79). Given the small number of individuals per hectare, in any given local area there must be a large number of species that survive in a fragile state of disequilibrium. Such disequilibrium is a function of differential mortality, opportunistic reoccupation of openings when tree falls occur, climatic changes, and the behavior of dispersing species (Connell 1978: 1309). Species diversity in the humid tropics seems, therefore, to result more from small-scale disequilib-

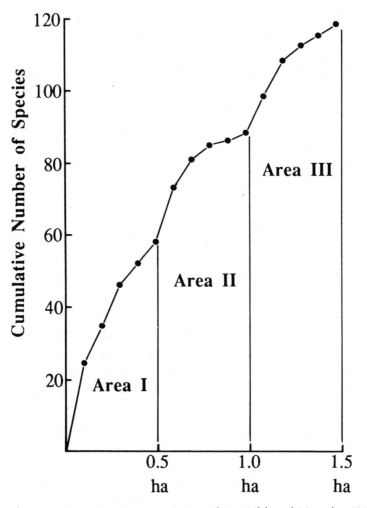

Figure 8. Area-species association (from Uhl and Murphy 1981: 224).

riums and perturbations than from long-term stability and equilibrium conditions (Colinvaux et al. 1985). The challenge to sampling which these conditions present has not been entirely solved.[4]

   Although some trees reach a height of 90 meters, it is more common to find them in the 20 to 50 meter range. The girth is generally modest, with a diameter at breast height averaging between 25 and 45 centimeters. Opinions vary as to whether there exist "stories" in the forest that are well defined. The number of studies focusing on the presence or absence of strata is still small. The differences of opinion may be a result of the particular character of the areas studied and of the research methods used. In areas of

very poor soil, for example, it is common to find majestic trees with but-
tresses that provide them with structural support and then a second layer of
smaller trees.

Richards (1952) is responsible for the traditional view that there are three
clearly defined strata. More recent studies by Halle et al. (1978: 333) have
shown that the forest is in a continuous process of renovation and senes-
cence—with periods when more or less well defined strata may be observed
and periods when they cannot be seen (Rollet 1978).

The moist and rain forests are perceived to be evergreen. However,
growth and flowering are periodic and for many species seem to be indepen-
dent of annual seasonality. Some species shed their leaves during dry periods, much as deciduous trees lose their leaves in temperate zones in winter,
while others gain and lose leaves continuously. Thus, the tropical moist and
rain forests do not have a clearly defined flowering and fruiting season.
Some species follow an annual cycle, while others may fruit only every two
or four years. This presents an interesting problem for animals who consume the leaves and fruits of trees, including humans. It requires very detailed ethnobotanical knowledge and dispersal over a large territory to exploit preferred species. A certain degree of nomadism helps to exploit the
widely dispersed resources, an effective strategy only when population numbers are small per unit area. The variability in flowering and fruiting also
provides a supply of food year-round that need not be stored, which would
be necessary if harvests were strongly seasonal. Storage would constitute a
problem in the humid tropics, where preservation is often difficult.

In the rain forests, plants have developed effective ways to control predation. In Barro Colorado, the animal populations are regulated by the
cycles of abundance and scarcity (Leigh 1975: 82). Often the tree seeds have
a thick shell to protect them. The hard endocarp protects the seeds, while
the mesocarp provides food for rodents who act as dispersal agents (Smith
1974a). Many species are important agents of pollination, dispersal, and
recycling (Fittkau and Klinge 1973). Dispersal agents like the agoutis (*Dasyprocta* sp.) may hide and store nuts, forgetting where they have put them
and thereby helping with species dispersal (Alho 1988: 43).

In areas limited in nutrients, one finds numerous plant defenses against
herbivory. The next chapter discusses these mechanisms in greater detail. In
general, in such areas plants have secondary chemical compounds, many of
them toxic, that reduce herbivore pressure and total animal biomass (Janzen
1974).

One of the main reasons for the attention to the deforestation of Amazonia is the loss of species—particularly losses of plants, given their basic role on the planet as the converters of solar energy into biomass and as sources of food for all other components of the food chain. The diversity of floral species is believed to offer important resources that will be needed to cope with future human needs.

Fauna

Some scholars concerned with explaining the apparent lack of development of complex social and political systems have argued that it was not soil quality but the availability of game that kept the size of settlements small in Amazonia (Lathrap 1968). The discussion was then taken up by Gross (1975), who suggested that the consumption of animal protein varied between 15 and 63 grams per capita per day and that it was necessary to relocate settlements to maintain such levels. Implicated in this process of village mobility was the taboo against hunting some of the larger mammals, as noted by Ross (1978), because their incidence was so low that it was more effective to focus cultural attention on smaller game than on large game. A whole generation tried to prove or disprove this proposition, each arguing from site-specific data the rightness or correctness of the formulation (e.g., Beckerman 1979; Chagnon and Hames 1980; Hames, 1980; Vickers 1979; Hill and Hawkes 1983; Yost and Kelley 1983; see reviews in Johnson 1982, Sponsel 1986, and the thoughtful reassessment in Beckerman 1989).

Despite a now considerable body of information, we still do not have systematic studies of animal biomass production in a variety of ecosystems of Amazonia. One study pointed out that it was precisely the meat yield of tapir and peccaries which accounted for the bulk of the meat hunted in the western Amazon (Vickers 1984) and that taboos are specific to ethnic groups and need to be explained in microecological, rather than regional, terms. Vickers also noted that the meat yields drop in tropical forests at 600 meters above sea level, as one should expect in montane forests—and that yields are higher in the lowland forests. Another careful analysis seems to suggest what may be behind the assumption of low faunal availability: of the forty-one most hunted species in an area of the Venezuelan Amazon, 39 percent were of less than 5 kilograms total weight, 73 percent were nocturnal, 54 percent were solitary, and 44 percent were arboreal (Sponsel 1981).

The lack of long-term studies continues to limit human ecological formulations of how people use faunal resources. In small-scale populations, the results of a single year of data may represent an outlying point in a long-term average which cannot be estimated from a single year's data. This deficiency has begun to be corrected by Vickers' documentation of hunting returns in a Siona-Secoya village in northeastern Ecuador over a ten-year period. His data suggest that some species were being depleted locally (e.g., wooly monkey, curassow) while other species such as peccaries, tapir, deer, rodents, and reptiles did not show evidence of such depletion (Vickers 1988). More studies of this sort are needed.[5] To this day, there is an excessive dependence on the two studies of animal biomass made in the neotropics: one in Barro Colorado Island, Panama (Eisenberg and Thorington 1973), and the other near Manaus, Brazil (Fittkau and Klinge 1973). The study by Fittkau and Klinge, for example, may seriously have underestimated animal biomass (Eisenberg and Redford 1979; Eisenberg et al. 1979; Emmons 1984).

Species diversity characterizes moist and rain forests. In the 15.5 square kilometers of Barro Colorado, Panama, more than 20,000 species of insects have been documented, compared to a few hundred in all of France. Insects are very important in the recycling of nutrients as sources of protein and fat appreciated by Amazonian populations.

The fauna represents a small fraction of the total biomass of the tropical forest. Fittkau and Klinge (1973) calculated that the plant biomass was of 900 tons per hectare, whereas the animal biomass was only 0.20 ton. This is not only a reflection of the laws of thermodynamics but also a result of the low amounts of net productivity made available by the green plants to the herbivores and carnivores. Figure 9 illustrates the distribution of biomass in one site and its cycles. However, the number of biomass studies is very limited, and there may be important differences in ratios from site to site.

Most of the animal biomass is made up of invertebrates that live in the soil, as part of the decomposing component of the ecosystem. The vertebrate fauna is predominantly arboreal (40 to 70 percent of species), given the more favorable conditions of the upper canopy (Eisenberg and Thorington 1973). Fruit-eaters require a territory twenty-five times larger than leaf-eaters to maintain themselves in tropical moist forest (Milton 1981b: 538).

The Ecosystems of the Amazon Basin

The Amazon shares with the rest of the humid tropics high solar radiation, uniformly high temperatures, high rainfall and humidity, and rich spe-

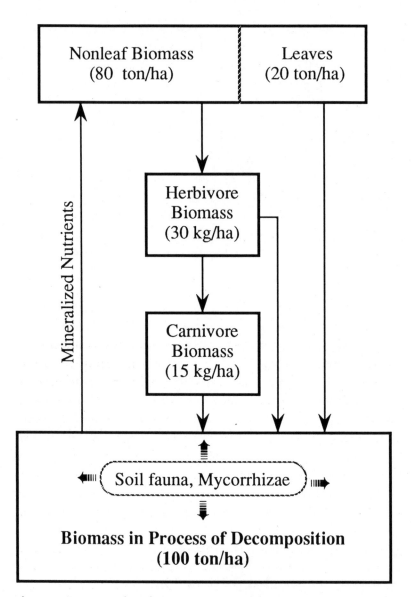

Figure 9. Biomass distribution in tropical forests (adapted from Fittkau and Klinge 1973: 11).

cies diversity. Despite the growing recognition of the diversity that the Amazon Basin encompasses, discussions of the region by both scholars and policy makers tend to treat the region in homogeneous terms which hardly differentiate between the Amazonian and the African and Asian rain forests—not to speak of differences within the Amazon Basin itself. Indeed,

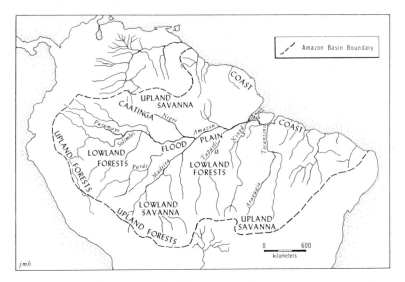

Figure 10. Amazon Basin habitats.

the Amazon is so different from the temperate and subtropical regions in which most scientists and bureaucrats live that it is not surprising that to them it is all hyperhumid, hot, and luxuriously green. If any distinction is made, the tendency has been to overrely on a simple dichotomy between terra firme, or uplands, and várzea, or floodplains. This duality fails to distinguish between very fragile regions within the terra firme and regions with greater resilience or between areas with relatively high plant and animal biomass productivity and areas much more limited. The várzeas make up about 2 percent of the Amazon Basin, an area of approximately 64,000 square kilometers, but their importance to human populations is disproportionate to their areal extent (Sternberg 1975: 17). The other 98 percent of the basin, or terra firme, has only recently begun to be differentiated as including not only moist and rain forests but also well-drained and poorly drained savannas, anthropogenic forests, and montane forests (Moran 1990 and fig. 10).

   The Amazon, as the largest area of extant rain and moist forests, is responsible for large amounts of water vapor recycling in the atmosphere. One of the important findings from research in the past decade has been the demonstration that half of the rainfall within the Amazon Basin is the result of internal recycling by the forests (fig. 11). Thus, the vegetation contributes just as much as does the moisture coming into the basin from oceanic evaporation, previously considered to be the dominant factor in the

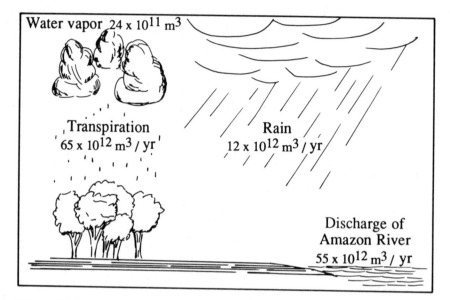

Water vapor 24×10^{11} m^3

Transpiration
65×10^{12} m^3 / yr

Rain
12×10^{12} m^3 / yr

Discharge of
Amazon River
55×10^{12} m^3 / yr

Figure 11. Water cycling (from Salati 1985: 43).

regional hydrologic cycle (Salati 1985: 31). The role of the vegetation is fundamental—75 percent of the rainfall returns to the atmosphere through evapotranspiration (fig. 12).

Rainfall is highly variable within the basin both in total amount and in seasonal distribution (fig. 6). Rainfall tends to be higher in the areas oro-graphically affected by the Andean mountain chain, where rainfall can be as high as 5,000 millimeters annually and with virtually no dry season. By contrast, the eastern Amazon of Brazil receives as little as 1,700 millimeters of rainfall annually, with a marked dry season of about four months, and supports a seasonal moist forest rather than rain forest vegetation.

Three types of rivers draining Amazonian watersheds have been de-scribed: whitewater, clearwater, and blackwater rivers (Sioli 1951). White-water rivers originate in the Andes and carry sediments of high fertility which they deposit downstream during the flood season. Clearwater rivers drain areas of the Brazilian Plateau and the Guiana Plateau and carry sedi-ments of medium to low fertility from those ancient leached formations (fig. 13). Finally, blackwater rivers drain areas with a predominance of white sand soils extremely acid and poor in nutrients and are covered with vege-tation containing unusually high levels of tannins and other secondary com-pounds. The black color of the water comes from the large amounts of un-decomposed organic matter and dissolved chemicals from the vegetation.

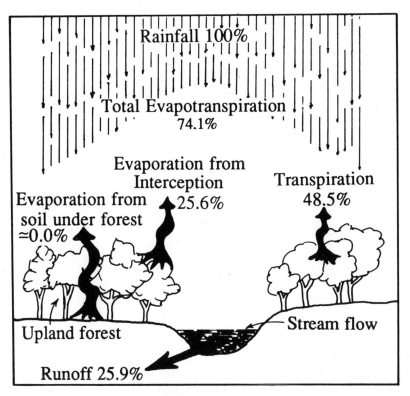

Figure 12. Water recycling (from Salati 1985: 40).

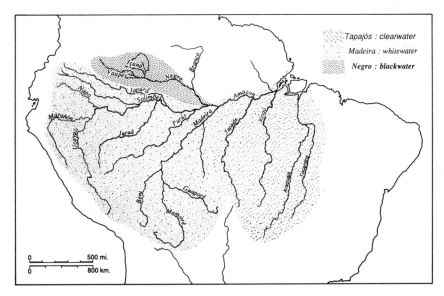

Figure 13. Whitewater, blackwater, and clearwater watersheds.

Areas drained by blackwater rivers need to be treated separately from other parts of the Amazon. The extreme poverty of these areas is atypical of the basin as a whole. Smith (1979) has noted that blackwater lakes have a fish productivity fifteen to nineteen times lower than lakes fed by whitewater rivers. As the next chapter shows, blackwater basins have a variety of vegetational covers but are clearly on the extreme of a continuum from rich to poor. Many of the mechanisms that support its rich biotic life are particularly fine-tuned and fragile when perturbed by human activities.

The rich diversity of the Amazon flora has given rise to numerous theories to explain its occurrence. Until the middle of this century it was presumed that long-term climatic stability lay behind the richness in species. This theory led, in turn, to the "Pleistocene refugia" theory, which suggested that a drying of the continent during the Pleistocene led to a constriction in forest areas and that this separation created islandlike conditions that favored speciation (Haffer 1969; contributions in Prance 1982). More recently, Colinvaux et al. (1985) proposed that a wide variety of different disturbance processes throughout the basin have created ever different conditions for survival and speciation. Some of these processes are ancient, while others are recent and continuous.

In an area as large and diverse as the Amazon, vegetational differences must be incorporated into any efforts to explain how human populations in the region cope with life. With every year that passes, the number of distinctions made by biologists increases. Table 3 summarizes a recent synthesis of the vegetation types found in Amazonia. In reality, these differences in flora occur within a true ecological mosaic that is both a constraint and an opportunity for human populations. Figure 14 illustrates a mosaic found in an affluent of the Tapajós, a clearwater river of the southern bank of the Amazon. The proportions of these mosaics will vary from place to place, as a function of past and present uses by human populations, topography, and edaphic characteristics.

More Than Just Terra Firme and Várzea

Despite the explosion of research in Amazonia over the past twenty years, which has shown just how variable the habitats there can be, comparative studies tend to aggregate findings within the terra firme/várzea dichotomy, thereby obscuring the variability present therein. Findings from one site are viewed as generalizable to the entire region, or, conversely, findings are presented as having unique site-specific characteristics. Most anthropologists

Table 3. *Types of Vegetation in the Amazon Basin*

Upland Forests of Terra Firme
  a. dense forests
  b. open forests
  c. liana forests
  d. caatinga or campina over spodosols
  e. bamboo forests
  f. palm forests
  g. dry forests
  h. premontane forests
Floodplains and Flooded Forests
  a. forests over clayish soils
  b. floodplain forests of the Lower Amazon
  c. floodplain forests of the Upper Amazon
  d. forests of the estuary
  e. pantanal of the Rio Branco
  f. flooded forests in blackwater rivers
Upland Savannas of Terra Firme
  a. campo sujo
  b. campo cerrado
  c. cerrado
  d. cerradão
  e. campo rupestre
  f. savanna of Roraima
  g. coastal savanna
  h. flooded savannas
Restricted Vegetation
  a. mangroves
  b. levees
  c. *buriti*-dominated areas (*Mauritia* sp.)

Source: Adapted from Prance 1978 and Pires and Prance 1985: 113.

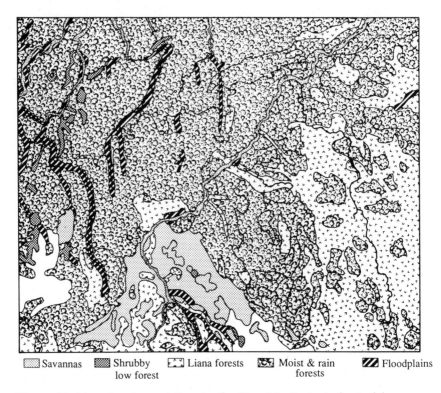

Savannas   Shrubby   Liana forests   Moist & rain   Floodplains
low forest   forests

Figure 14. Mosaic of vegetation in the Tapajós Basin (adapted from Prance 1978: 210).

accept the terra firme/várzea dichotomy and place data from areas as ecologically different as the Xingú Basin, the Rio Negro Basin, and the central Brazilian savannas into the same category of "terra firme adaptations" (or into the even more aggregating "lowland South America"). Thus, evidence from ecosystems with widely different soils, above-ground biomass, and moisture regimes is used to support radically opposing views explaining cultural development, village size, and population mobility. The distinction between terra firme and várzea glosses over important differences in Amazonia. But let us take one step back from this dichotomy and look at the characteristics of the Amazon and the humid tropics of which it is a part.

The persistence of the terra firme/várzea scheme is no accident. It is a dichotomy broad enough to be used across the biological and social sciences, allowing the integration of findings from each. It has considerable value in distinguishing areas enriched by Andean sediments and highly productive fisheries and areas less well endowed (Lathrap 1970; Meggers 1971). Any framework to improve on this dichotomy would have to be based on criteria that are meaningful across disciplines and that will allow us to make finer determinations than are possible at present.

The várzea needs to be differentiated into at least three distinct habitats: the estuary, the lower floodplain, and the upper floodplain. The estuary of the Amazon differs from the lower floodplain in the important role played by the daily fluctuations in the tides. Here we do not find the once-a-year fluctuation in river level found elsewhere but a twice-daily fluctuation in river level and a marked influence of salty water. The estuary runs from the mouth of the Xingú River to the island of Marajó at the mouth of the Amazon. This type of várzea is associated with clayish soils on which grow an abundance of palms adapted to the cycles of the estuary. The estuary fills up twice a day and supports an unusually high plant biomass that has less diversity in species than other areas of Amazonia. The estuary resembles a system experiencing constant early secondary succession, in which the system is thrown back to earlier stages by the dynamic of the river system. Among the species frequently found are *murumurú* (*Astrocarium murumuru*), *jupatí* (*Raphia taedigera*), *açaí* (*Euterpe oleracea*), *inajá* (*Maximiliana martiana*), *buriti* or *miriti* (*Mauritia* sp.), and *ubim* (*Geonoma* sp.).

These are restricted areas with very high carrying capacities when properly managed. A team of researchers from the Goeldi Museum in Belém (Anderson et al. 1985; Anderson and Ioris 1989) found intensive systems of agroforestry management supporting up to 48 persons per square kilometer. This relatively high carrying capacity is sustained chiefly by extractive activities which do not seem to disturb any more than 2 percent of the forested land. However, it would be a mistake to think that these activities can be replicated in nonestuary portions of the floodplain or in terra firme. The location of the estuary and the dynamic interaction of the sediments near the mouth of the Amazon River system give this area an enviable potential for these kinds of sustained-yield extractive activities. By contrast, agriculture in the estuary is more difficult and less productive than extractive activities (Lima 1956; Anderson and Ioris 1989).

Archaeological investigations suggest that complex systems of water management may have been in place prehistorically, especially on Marajó Island (Roosevelt 1989, 1991). Nevertheless, archaeological investigations will need to be far more detailed to understand the techniques practiced in prehistory, the social organization that permitted the application of those techniques, and the results of those efforts in terms of carrying capacity and sustainability. The depopulation of the floodplain that followed upon the contact between European populations and native Amazonians after 1492 removed the know-how, and the population pressure, that justified and made possible intensive uses of the estuary. Only with the recent growth of Amazonian cities like Belém have we begun to see dense populations of traditional caboclos once again undertake intensive production systems to supply the demands of the urban market for products such as *açaí*.

A second type of várzea occurs upstream and is known as the lower flood-plain or Lower Amazon. This is the area described most often as typical of the floodplain, with annual deposition of alluvium rich in nutrients from the young Andean mountains, a pH near neutral, and a high fish biomass (Junk 1984: 215). Despite its high potential, the benefits of which supported very large pre-Columbian populations such as the Omagua (Myers 1989), the lower floodplain has not been fully exploited for several centuries. The highly variable annual flood levels make control of the water system diffi-cult and costly. Camargo estimated the extent of the Lower Amazon as 64,000 square kilometers (1958: 17), an area equivalent to 1.6 percent of the Brazilian Amazon.

The Lower Amazon is characterized by a highly dynamic morphology, where rivers continuously cut and modify the landscape, annually carrying whole riverbanks which are deposited downstream as sediment (Sternberg 1975: 17–18). The rhythm of the annual floods affects everything because of its scale. The Amazon and its tributaries drain an area of 4 million square kilometers and carry a volume of water equivalent to 20 percent of the total volume of potable water on the earth.

The third kind of floodplain is known as the upper floodplain or Upper Amazon. This is a highly variable area in environmental characteristics, depending on the geological areas from which its sediment is derived. A recent research report on the alluvial soils of the Upper Amazon concluded that floodplain soils are significantly diverse in chemical and physical prop-erties. Soils with headwaters in the Eastern Peruvian Cordillera (e.g., Río Mayo) are generally of high base status and pH values (6.5 to 8.5). Those developing in sediments eroded from the calcareous sedimentary deposits on the Andean foothills of both Ecuador and Peru (e.g., Río Cashiboya) tend to be slightly acid (5.0 to 6.5) but present no serious chemical or min-eralogical problems. By contrast, floodplain alluvial soils originating in the eastern portion of the Peruvian Basin (e.g., Río Yavari watershed) tend to be strongly acid (4.0 to 5.0) and have levels of aluminum saturation exceeding 85 percent (Hoag et al. 1987: 78–79). In those areas of the Upper Amazon with high acidity, lower nutrient content, and high aluminum saturation, we would expect to have lower population densities than in other parts of the same Upper Amazon, due to lower potential crop productivity.

It has been common in the terra firme/várzea dichotomy to emphasize the favorable conditions of the várzea. However, there are portions of the floodplain which are no better endowed than the stereotypical terra firme and some which are much less well endowed than relatively rich areas of terra firme. Furley (1979) has noted that the floodplains in the state of Rondônia, Brazil, tend to be very acid hydromorphic gleys which are of less agricultural value than the richer, high base status soils found in portions of the terra firme of Rondônia. A further element which differentiates the Upper Amazon from the Lower Amazon and the estuary is the importance of altitude and slope in human adaptive behavior. It is generally understood that above-ground biomass productivity declines with altitude in rain forests and this factor, in turn, affects animal biomass productivity and the productivity of hunting (Vickers 1984).

The terra firme, an area of over 4 million square kilometers constituting 98 percent of the Amazon Basin, contains a diverse array of habitats that grow in number each year as research accumulates. We could begin by distinguishing minimally between lowland savannas, blackwater ecosystems, upland forests, and montane forests of terra firme. Each of these ecosystems is internally differentiated.

Lowland savannas are characterized by seasonal inundation during the rainy season, followed by a marked drought season during the dry period. They are constrained agriculturally by extremely acid, low-phosphorus soils that when combined with the excellent drainage and low growing-season rainfall make agriculture very uncertain and of relatively low productivity. The lowland savannas, like most parts of Amazonia, are cross-cut by rivers; it is along these gallery forests hugging the banks of permanent rivers that the population has practiced horticulture. Populations are not as dense here as in the estuary, the Lower Amazon, or the more favored areas of the Upper Amazon. Because these savannas are midway between the rich coastal areas and the rich floodplain, they became the home of populations with substantial military capabilities, whose social organization includes elements that permit both population concentration and dispersion. They are among the most numerous populations of native Amazonians in Brazil (Gross et al. 1979; Posey 1985; Anderson and Posey 1985).

Blackwater watersheds have always attracted attention. These areas have a distinctive vegetation known variously as caatinga amazônica or campinarana—a type of xeromorphic vegetation which reminds one of the spiny scrub forests of northeast Brazil, rather than an Amazonian landscape. From the viewpoint of nutrients, these are the most limited and fragile regions of the Amazon (Jordan 1989; Jordan and Herrera 1981). Rainfall is high, soils are white sands of near-pure quartz that are extremely acid and devoid of nutrients, and plants have an unusually high content of secondary compounds that reduce herbivore pressure and nutrient losses. Plants have adaptations to droughts (e.g., sclerophylly or hard and leathery leaves) as well as to floods (e.g., above-ground root mat). Nutrients are recycled with a perfection rarely found elsewhere in Amazonia. Although total plant biomass in this ecosystem is comparable to that of other areas of terra firme and the humid tropics, nearly two-thirds of it is below-ground biomass, in the form of roots. Agriculture is not possible on the white sand soils of the region but occurs only in the patches of upland tropical forest on better soils and in the alluvial levees (Hill and Moran 1983). Even in these limited areas within the watersheds, agriculture is possible only through dependence on plants with evolutionary adaptations to low nutrients, acidity, high aluminum saturation, resistance to herbivore predation, and some drought resistance. The result is an unusual dependence in these areas on highly toxic varieties of manioc, very small settlements, and considerable hierarchy which structures the exploitation of resources and circulation of goods (Moran 1991).

Upland forests of terra firme is a catchall category which includes a wide variety of habitats. We should expect considerable differentiation in this enormous region in the years ahead with advances in research. In this region we find what appear to be anthropogenic vegetations such as liana, bamboo, *babaçú*, Brazil nut, and palm forests (Balée 1989). Forests in the eastern Amazon of Brazil fall under the category of tropical moist forests; as one moves west one finds increasing moisture levels and eventually areas of rain forest proper. The liana forests are estimated to cover over 100,000 square kilometers of the basin and are found near or on sizable outcroppings of high base status parent material and soils of medium to high fertility, in areas with a characteristic dry season, and associated with patches of anthropogenic black earths (terra preta do índio). These are the forests that Herrera (1985) called eutrophic, as compared with the oligotrophic rain forests of the nutrient-poor blackwater watersheds. The above-ground root layer is almost nowhere visible here, nor are the many other nutrient conservation mechanisms referred to earlier in reference to blackwaters. Agriculture in these areas can be sustained for longer periods, given the higher initial conditions of soil fertility and higher pH. In these areas abandonment of swiddens is more likely to result from weed invasion than from fertility decline.

The montane forests (montaña) have been the focus of study by many anthropologists. They are very different forests than those discussed heretofore, with lower tree biomass but more epiphytes. They have noticeably lower animal biomass, but the slightly higher frequency of soils of moderate acidity and fertility make agriculture a little more productive and certain than in the lowlands. Longstanding economic relations between montane forest and highland populations permitted higher carrying capacities here than elsewhere.

Amazonia through the Eyes of Native Amazonians

The rest of this book presents native approaches to dealing with the diverse resources and habitat characteristics of Amazonian environments. I will try to link native perception and forms of resource use with recent attempts to understand the ecology of the region through Western scientific methods. Emphasis is given to research based on native informants so that the native viewpoint emerges and is explained in terms familiar to Western science. This approach derives from the need to link native views on the use and conservation of nature with the specialized knowledge and sympathetic understanding of scientists who share a concern with the conservation of biodiversity and sustainable development.

Each society develops its own criteria through which it makes decisions about resource use. Autonomous societies, such as those found in Amazonia, will tend to have intimate relations with the habitat arising from their dependence on it for most of their needs. By contrast, societies with high degrees of specialization and economic interdependence will depend as much, or more, on adjustments to institutions which mediate environmental, economic, and political life. Thus, one of the reasons why one can confidently affirm that native Amazonians know their environment is their more direct interaction with it, in contrast to outsiders' highly buffered forms of interaction with the physical environment. Whether one is examining Amazonian or any other society, however, attention must be paid both to the direct interaction between the people and the environment and to the role of institutions and organization within which people act (Ellen 1982).

In promoting the value of native Amazonians' knowledge one should beware of "noble savage" or "conservationist" assumptions that one might impose on these populations. Indigenous peoples differ widely in their attitude toward nature. Various ethnic groups have different ideologies,[6] social organization and structure,[7] and perceptions of their environment.[8] If indigenous peoples are conservationists, it is a utilitarian version rather than a romantic or "liberal" version such as may be common in Western society. If native Amazonians conserve, it is because they still interact closely enough with their physical environment to understand that they have to be concerned with the impact of their actions upon the long-term productivity of their habitat. As a whole, native Amazonians are less dependent on imports from distant regions to support their levels of consumption. Instead, they are able to judge the cutting of the forests for what it is—a loss of future farmland, future wild game, wood and vine for house construction, medicinal plants, a comfortable place through which to move in search of other resources, and a beautiful wild landscape, the source of all life. But this situation is changing. Some groups have grown accustomed to consumerism, and with it they have begun to experience hard choices similar to those debated by nation-states at the Earth Summit in Rio de Janeiro, choosing between conserving nature and exploiting it beyond sustainable levels. Amazonia is not isolated from world political economic processes, and neither are native Amazonians.

Native Amazonians' health status before contact has been rated by physical anthropologists as generally good. Following contact with national society, they experience epidemic mortality, eventually stabilizing and then increasing their numbers. With greater integration into national society, indigenous societies are more affected by metabolic and chronic diseases.[9]

With changes in their relations with national society, the epidemiological and nutritional status of native populations has a tendency to decline (Ribeiro 1956; Cardoso de Oliveira 1968). This process has sociological (Cardoso de Oliveira 1978; Gomes 1988) and epidemiological dimensions. Generally, the rate of infant mortality goes up dramatically during contact, falling only after one or two decades. Fertility decreases during the epidemic or resettlement stages of contact and rises dramatically after a decade or two. This was the experience of the Suruí of Rondônia (Coimbra 1989), and these rate processes need to be tested for other populations of Amazonia.

The subsidies provided by the Brazilian Foundation for Indian Protection (FUNAI) and by missionaries during this stage gradually has led to the population's loss of autonomy and growing dependence on subsidies. The contribution of these new sources of nutrition has rarely been positive. Most often the products made available include refined sugar, table salt, and alcohol, associated with chronic and metabolic disorders such as goiter (Vieira-Filho 1981a) and diabetes (Vieira-Filho 1977). Efforts to sedentarize Amazonian populations, without improving their access to better medical attention, could result in the spread of serious illnesses such as Chagas' disease, which has never been reported for lowland South America but is endemic in the Andean region, as indicated by paleopathological finds in ancient Peru. Coimbra (1988) suggested that freedom from Chagas may be tied to the pattern of mobility and the type of housing materials used, which do not provide a favorable environment to the vector of the disease. This could change as people are restricted in their mobility and forced to sedentarize. Given the presence of the vector in their environment, the situation could become critical very quickly.

As this suggests, living close to nature has its perils—but no more than living close to Europeans and their descendants. Mistakes in the use of resources can bring about rapid death through poisoning or through lack of food or through expropriation. Lack of attention to proper hospitality and the feelings of others can lead to violence and quick justice. To get around these and many other perils, native societies have instituted varied social mechanisms that value elders (as repositories of knowledge), that assign responsibilities for different aspects of the food quest, that define social relations through complex naming, ceremonial, and kin terms, and that seek to provide a stable basis for human production and reproduction. These human strategies are a product of complex negotiations that reflect past experience, current conditions, and future expectations—within a varied mosaic of habitats. These varied habitats are the subject of the following chapters. How much of this diversity remains to be appreciated in the twenty-first century may well depend on how much we learn from native approaches to the use and conservation of Amazonian resources—and upon how respectfully nation-states treat this rich realm of nature.

2

Blackwater
Ecosystems

The stereotype of the Amazon as an environment characterized by soils too poor and acid to sustain cultivation for more than a year or two holds most true in what are known as blackwater river watersheds. Blackwater rivers can vary a great deal in growing conditions,[1] but in their more extreme forms they are among the poorest in the world. In nutrient content they are similar to rainwater (Sioli 1950, 1951). They occur in areas draining mostly white sand soils (spodosols) on which grows a xeromorphic vegetation that contrasts in both height and biomass with other areas of Amazonian terra firme. The vegetation reminds one more of the scrub forests of the arid Brazilian northeast than an Amazonian landscape. Other kinds of vegetation grow in these basins as well, including tropical upland forest on oxisols occupying higher ground. This tropical upland forest, however, is not as tall or productive as tropical upland forest elsewhere in Amazonia, where soils are less acid, less prone to waterlogging, and less depleted of nutrients (Medina et al. 1990: 51; Moran 1989).

Blackwater basins were of interest from the outset to the naturalists traveling in the Amazon (Wallace 1853; Humboldt 1852; Spruce 1908; Huber 1909), who quoted the early chroniclers in calling them "rivers of hunger." The largest blackwater ecosystem in the Amazon occurs in the northwest Amazon in the drainage areas of the Negro, Vaupés, and Içana rivers (fig. 15),[2] areas that have interested anthropologists because of the multilingual, linguistically exogamous patrilineal sibs found there (Goldman 1948, 1963; Jackson 1972, 1976, 1983; Hill 1983, 1984, 1989; Hill and Moran 1983; Moran 1991; Chernela 1983, 1986a, 1986b, 1989; Wright and Hill 1986, among others).

It is in regions such as the poorer kinds of blackwater ecosystems that we would expect to find the most elaborate and effective responses to environmental limitations in Amazonia. This is not to be confused with saying that one should expect greater diversity of adaptive strategies. As we will see, at the extremes of ecosystem productivity the range of effective responses is less, and thus one finds more consistency in responses. Indeed, this is the poorest area of the Amazon Basin. In the northwest Amazon we find sparse populations (ca. 0.2 or less than 1 person per square kilometer), some of them specialized in riverine life while others focus on forest and horticultural resources. Here we find dependence on bitter manioc in horticulture, with a near-absence of sweet varieties—in contrast to areas like the western Amazon where mainly sweet varieties are cultivated (Métraux 1949: 384; Steward 1948: 517; Steward and Métraux 1948: 542; Boom 1987: 45) or where the mix is more or less even (Carneiro 1957; Werner et al. 1979;

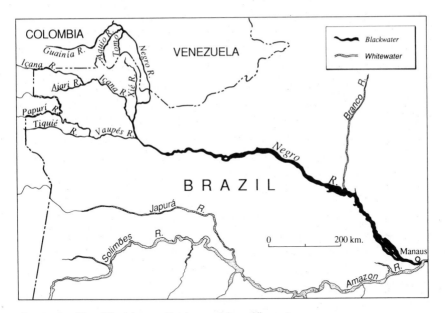

Figure 15. The Rio Negro Basin and its affluents.

Zarur 1979). Unlike other regions of the Amazon, in this area there is inherited control of river fronts, with rights vested in patrilineal sibs. Also unlike the rest of Amazonia, some communities delegate hunting to populations who are held in low esteem by the dominant fishing/farming populations. In a comparative study of South American populations, the Tukanoans of the Vaupés had the highest dependency on fisheries of any Amazonian group (Carneiro 1970, cited in Chernela 1989: 242). This is a situation in strong contrast to other areas of Amazonia, where hunting is said to be the preferred subsistence activity.

Use of these areas by human populations should interest us because they constitute the most demanding environmental conditions found in Amazonia. Many of the generalizations made about Amazonia's ecological limitations refer, in fact, to the extreme and unusual conditions found mostly in the Rio Negro Basin, the classic and most often studied blackwater ecosystem.

The limiting factors in this kind of Amazonian environment are deeply felt by all biological organisms. The extremely low level of nutrients, or oligotrophy, leads to responses that create difficulties for organisms exploiting such areas: organic matter decomposes more slowly because of the extreme acidity of the soils. Native plants have evolved high levels of polyphenols and other toxic substances that appear to reduce nutrient loss through herbivory but which require specialized processing to detoxify the plant material. The extreme cycles of flood and drought (generally lasting less than a week) have selected for plants with highly specialized adaptations to these conditions, in the form of unusually high root biomass and leaves that are either leathery or spiny. The poor optical resolution of the rivers makes techniques like the use of the bow and arrow in fishing less productive than elsewhere—fishing must rely more heavily upon large traps, which are costly to build and maintain. The investment in these large traps, as well as the scarcity of optimal locations, favors the development of territoriality. These areas require careful description by ecologists and ethnographers because, despite the presence of dominants in the vegetation, there is a high incidence of endemic species in these areas, due to patchiness and insularity, resulting in considerable species richness at the regional level (Anderson 1981: 205).

Characterization of the Environment

Blackwater ecosystems include a wide array of vegetation. But one type of vegetation occurs in this area with greater frequency than elsewhere in Amazonia: campina, or caatinga amazônica. Caatinga is a dwarfed scrub-forest vegetation of about 6 to 20 meters above ground level growing on hydromorphic quartzy sands (Takeuchi 1961; Klinge 1978). This kind of vegetation is found chiefly in the Guianas and in portions of the Rio Negro basin and its affluents (chiefly the Vaupés and the Içana). Smaller patches occur throughout the Amazon Basin, in areas like Roraima and Serra do Cachimbo. This type of vegetation develops in areas with a humid tropical climate where there is no dry season, in areas dominated by podzolic soils or spodosols that experience waterlogging during and after heavy rains. The vegetation varies along a gradient from high caatinga to low caatinga, or bana, which is the poorest of all. Figure 16 illustrates the interrelation of hydrology, soils, and vegetation in an area of the Upper Rio Negro.

Caatingas are not restricted to the Amazon. In Sarawak this vegetation is known as "kerangas," poor soils where rice cultivation is not possible (Jacobs 1988: 188). In other areas of Asia they are known as "padangs." Areas with xeromorphic vegetation in the humid tropics have also been noted in Borneo, Sumatra, and Malacca. Richards (1952) compared "padangs" of Malaysia to "wallaba" vegetation in the Guianas. In both cases, the vegetation is associated with extremely leached, white sandy soils. When cleared

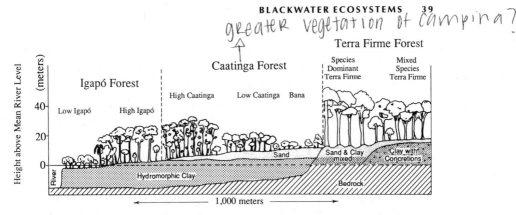

greater vegetation of campina?

Figure 16. Vegetational gradient in the Rio Negro (from Clark and Uhl 1987: 5).

of their native vegetation, the areas take an uncommonly long time to return to their original state, confirming the poverty of the environment (Uhl et al. 1982a; Uhl 1983; Jacobs 1988: 189). Comparison of the patterns of social organization, soil management, farming practices, and regional exchange between these cross-cultural areas merits the future attention of scholars.

Leaves of caatinga vegetation are hard and leathery (sclerophyllous), a feature which slows decomposition of the plant material. Leaf area index is smaller in this type of vegetation as compared with the mean in other tropical forests, probably to reduce the effects of the drought stress period. Wood volume is less and the canopy is smaller than in areas less limited (Jordan 1982a: 395). Vines are uncommon, in contrast to epiphytes. Everything suggests an oligotrophic or nutrient-poor environment. Evidence for this is apparent in the behavior of *Cecropia ficifolia*, one of the species of secondary succession common in the Rio Negro. This species grows to a lesser height in areas of white sands than it does on oxisols found on the patches of high ground covered in tropical forest. In oligotrophic areas, there is a tendency for species dominance, in contrast to the pattern more common in Amazonia, where dominance is rare in native forests. In a region near San Carlos de Río Negro in Venezuela, two species, *Micrandra spruceana* and *Eperua leucantha*, constituted 50.3 percent of the biomass (Klinge 1978: 260).

Low bana (fig. 16) reaches a height of only 3 to 7 meters with dwarfed trees and bushes ocurring mixed with grassy vegetation. In high caatinga (fig. 16) the height may reach 20 meters, approximating the structure of upland tropical forest. High bana (fig. 16) can be seen as a transitional zone between low bana and caatinga amazônica (Klinge n.d. : 20). Biomass in caatinga is twice that of bana (i.e., 28 kilograms per square meter versus 10 to 17 kilograms per square meter).

The hydrologic patterns are also implicated in the presence of this type of vegetation. Medina et al. (1978) demonstrated that even with 3,600 millimeters of annual rainfall and rains of more than 200 millimeters each month, seasonal drought can occur in these areas. By the time rainfall declines to the range of 200 to 300 millimeters a month there is a high probability of wilting due to the high evapotranspiration (5.4 to 11.5 millimeters per day), high solar reflectance (albedo), and excellent drainage of the sandy soils. The water table is near the surface, due to an impermeable B horizon, characteristic of podzolic soils or spodosols (Herrera 1979b). With every rain the water can flood an area immediately, and it drains only slowly over the next few days.

The soils are sandy and composed of near-pure quartz. These soils are known variously as spodosols, podzolic soils, and hydromorphic podzols. They have a superficial layer with a great deal of undecomposed organic matter, pH below 4.0, and a diagnostic grayish B horizon (i.e., a spodic horizon) of impermeable clays (Herrera 1979b). Further evidence for the oligotrophy of this environment is the heavy investment in root biomass. Above-ground biomass is lower in this ecosystem, but total biomass is comparable to other parts of terra firme. Roots constitute between 34 and 87 percent of total biomass, as compared with 20 percent in most areas of forested terra firme (Moran 1991: 366). Eighty-six percent of the roots are found in the A horizon of the soils, and 70 percent are considered extremely fine (Klinge and Herrera 1978). In an experiment, 99.9 percent of the calcium and potassium was absorbed by the fine roots (Stark and Jordan 1978). This is due to the mutualistic relation between mycorrhizae and the vegetation. In other areas of Amazonia the nutrient-capture mechanisms are more porous, and more nutrients escape from the immediate area of leaffall near a tree. The microorganisms in the root layer incorporate the available nitrogen, the nutrient which seems most limiting in this ecosystem. Denitrifying bacteria are almost nonexistent in this system, as compared to other areas of Amazonia. The poorer the ecosystem, the greater the development of the fine root layer and the greater the presence of toxic substances which inhibit predation of leaves. Although the number of faunal studies is very limited, herbivore populations are very low in these areas due to the lack of palatable biomass. Research in Africa and in Venezuela confirms the presence of bacteriostatic and fungistatic substances, like alkaloids and poly-phenols in oligotrophic areas (McKey et al. 1978).

Human Adaptive Strategies

The poverty of blackwater ecosystems might lead one to expect to find considerable degrees of malnutrition among human populations due to the low above-ground plant and animal biomass. Undoubtedly, the potential has been there for this to occur when local populations failed to control their fertility, spread their numbers over the landscape, or did not develop systems of exchange that could supplement local ecosystem deficiencies. Human adaptive responses to the limitations of these areas have succeeded to a remarkable degree in adjusting the population to these constraints. Nutritional status is no better and no worse than that recorded for native populations in better-endowed habitats. Population densities found in these areas are considerably lower than elsewhere in Amazonia (ca. 0.2 or much less than 1 person per square kilometer). Other adaptive responses found in this region are reliance on bitter manioc, a plant adapted to soil acidity and low nutrient levels, with its own defenses against herbivory; specialized fishing techniques to cope with low biomass and poor optical resolution of rivers; and a dispersed and low-density settlement pattern, with high de-grees of hierarchy and segmentation associated with territorial control over resources.

The populations in the Rio Negro were less affected by external forces than many others in Amazonia. Many factors are responsible for this, among them less economic interest of colonial and national authorities in these relatively poor areas (Galvão 1959: 9). Some authors have asserted that ethnic identity is much stronger in the Vaupés and Içana than in other areas of the Amazon (Jackson 1976, 1983; Chernela 1983). There are few areas of the Amazon where the population has as continous a territo-rial history as it does in the Rio Negro. The region has long served as a refuge for diverse indigenous populations fleeing into it. Therefore, it is an ideal area to study the adaptive processes of native populations to the environment.

Agriculture

Households in the Upper Rio Negro practice slash-and-burn agriculture, clearing areas of between 0.5 and 2.0 hectares between September and November. It has been observed that native populations generally avoid locating their swiddens in areas of caatinga, which through ethnoecological taxonomies are identified as inappropriate for agriculture. Clark and Uhl (1987) estimated that in the region near San Carlos de Río Negro, in Venezuela, only about 20 percent of the soils were *not* spodosols. This extremely restricted availability of soils capable of supporting crops runs counter to very old assumptions about the ease with which native populations could relocate in Amazonia and the lack of "environmental circumscription" in the basin (Carneiro 1970). The persistent tendency among anthropologists to think of terra firme as all about the same is evident in Arhem's remark (1976: 42) that the Makuna, a Tukanoan ethnic group in the Vaupés, underproduce in their horticulture, citing as evidence Carneiro's argument (1970) that shifting cultivation can produce a yearly surplus and support large settlements—evidence deriving from the Upper Xingú, one of the areas of the Amazon with unusually rich soils (Moran 1989). If the soils cultivated by the Makuna are not the oligotrophic spodosols, they are more likely than not oxisols—red or yellow soils still falling in the category of acid and nutrient poor, if less so than the spodosols. However, the degree to which oxisols are found in other parts of the Rio Negro remains an empirical question with considerable theoretical implications. Dufour (personal communication, 1989) has indicated that in the Yapú River area of the Colombian Vaupés, oxisols are more common than spodosols. In the Rio Negro, the available patches of oxisols may very well circumscribe settlement options of horticultural populations—especially when they occur near prime fishing areas (see section on fishing below).

Galvão (1959: 24) noted another factor limiting the agricultural potential of the Upper Rio Negro: the apparent avoidance of areas that required penetration into the forest and a preference for areas along riverbanks. Chernela (1983) observed just such a preference among the Uanano, a Tukanoan population in the Vaupés. Those who have studied the Bara Makú (Silverwood-Cope 1972) and the Hupdu Makú (Reid 1979) noted that the Tukanoans these Makú interacted with also limited occupation to riverbanks. This tendency to limit territorial occupation to the riverbanks may represent a compromise response to the poverty of the terrestrial ecosystem, the availability of restricted areas of fertile levees, and the importance of fisheries based on ancient territorial claims.

Similarly, flooded forests (*igapós*) are avoided for agriculture, given their importance for fisheries (Chernela 1983, 1989; Clark and Uhl 1987; Dufour 1983). Many of the fish in Amazonian river channels enter the flooded forests during the rainy season to gain weight and to spawn (Goulding 1980, 1981). When fishing gives poor results, the Arawakan Wakuenai of the Guainía River region say that the fish are spawning and locate their swiddens distant from the flooded forests. Chernela (1982, 1985, 1989) noted the same explicit avoidance of flooded forests for agriculture among the Uanano in Brazil.

The Arawakan-speaking Wakuenai, studied by Hill (1983, 1984, 1989), have ethnoecological (i.e., ethnopedological) criteria for soil selection, but they recognize the difficulty of cultivating soils under contemporary restrictions on mobility emanating from national boundaries and from exploitation by border guards when traveling with produce (Moran, field notes, 1982). In many cases, they have had to move from the preferred areas on which they had depended for a reliable agricultural yield.

The traditional criterion for soil selection among the Wakuenai was the presence of *mori* trees (unidentified species) which grow in restricted areas of yellow soils (probably an oxisol) along the Içana and Guainía rivers in Colombia. When the Wakuenai moved to Venezuela, they were unable to find the same tree and thus one crucial element of their ethnoecological taxonomy was removed. This is a general problem in Amazonia, an area where endemic species are common. Thus, while similar soils may be found in Venezuela, the indicator species may differ. Only with prolonged occupation, and trial and error, would accurate indicator species gradually emerge to replace the traditional components of the soil taxonomy (Moran 1983). This example serves to illustrate the impact of the dislocation of native peoples by colonial and national societies on their subsistence capacity. Every effort should be made to avoid future resettlement of native peoples since such movement results in a loss of precise knowledge of local habitats—not to mention the negative effects that such relocation implies for the native population in terms of nutrition, health, and other components of well-being.

The lack of a marked dry season in this region would lead us to expect that burns would be of poor quality. Generally, it is the quality of the burn that determines the yield of slash-and-burn cultivation in nonvolcanic areas of the humid tropics (Moran 1981). That is clearly the case in areas with high above-ground biomass. But in areas with lower biomass, high insolation, and high albedo resulting from reflection from the white sands, the biomass dries sufficiently to burn so well that, in fact, areas of xeromorphic vegetation tend to experience burns beyond the areas cleared. Clark and Uhl (1987) documented the problem of natural burns in this habitat, where hundreds of hectares can catch fire when as few as twenty rainless days occur. In Venezuela the anthropogenic burns occur largely in February. Planting follows, dominated by bitter manioc.

Bitter manioc cultivation solves one of the great problems of Amazonian populations: how to cultivate soils extremely poor in nutrients, extremely acid, and with toxic levels of aluminum. Manioc, a plant that appears to have evolved in just such areas of South America, can produce impressive yields in areas where nothing else will grow (Moran 1973). One of the few limitations to its cultivation is its inability to withstand waterlogging, which explains why it is cultivated on higher ground. Manioc is even adapted to drought, during which it loses its leaves and goes into dormancy, gaining its leaves again with the return of soil moisture. Fifty-four percent of Amazonia's soils experience drought severe enough to cause plants to wilt; the most susceptible of these are the white sands of blackwater basins. Beans and corn, in contrast to manioc, are unable to produce a predictable crop in these nutrient-poor areas and are unable to cope with even short-term droughts. Galvão noted that corn had been abandoned by the populations of the Içana and that it probably never had much importance in the Rio Negro Basin (1959: 24).

Dufour (1988) found more than a hundred varieties of bitter manioc among a Tukanoan population in the Colombian Vaupés, and Chernela (1986a) reported a comparable attention to bitter varieties. Very few varieties of sweet manioc were known and cultivated by them. Chernela (1986a) noted that the Uanano have regularly introduced sweet varieties of manioc into their repertoire of varieties but that these sweet varieties have inevitably failed due to insect and herbivore attack, leaving only the more bitter varieties to persist. Bitter manioc resembles the native vegetation of blackwater regions in its toxic quality, which serves to conserve nutrients for the plant through reduction of herbivory. Montagnini and Jordan (1983) found that insects consumed less than 3 percent of the tissue of bitter manioc plants due to the cyanogenetic glucosides present.

Bitter manioc produces the bulk of the calories for blackwater basin populations. Dufour (1983) showed that among the Tukanoans she studied in Colombia, 70 percent of the energy came in the form of manioc flour and manioc bread (cazabe or beijú), tapioca, manioc beer, and other forms of prepared manioc. The energetic efficiency of manioc is impressive: it yielded 15.2 calories for every calorie spent on its production. Seventy percent of the production costs occur during processing. Several authors have argued that labor is the fundamental constraint in lowland South America because of the effort devoted to manioc processing. However, the lower yields possible in this region, even under the best management, further limit the size of population aggregates. Yields vary between 3 and 8 tons per hectare, with a mean of 4.7 (Clark and Uhl 1987). By comparison, the world mean is 8.4 tons per hectare, reaching 12.7 tons in Brazil. The relatively low mean harvests confirm the nutrient-poor conditions of the environment.

The toxicity of the bitter manioc in the Rio Negro is the highest so far recorded in the world (Dufour 1988: 264). Nowhere else do we find conscious selection favoring the more toxic varieties over sweeter ones.[3] In addition, even processing seems to prefer to deal with toxicity if it will lead to greater total calories produced: the Tukanoans studied by Dufour do not remove the starchy layer below the skin as do many other Amazonian populations. This layer has a very high proportion of the cyanogenetic glucoside and also contains linarmarase, a hydrolitic enzyme that facilitates detoxification. The result is a 14 percent higher edible portion than when the layer is removed (ibid., 263).

Following a year or two of cultivation, land must be left fallow before it becomes too poor even for forest to reoccupy it. One of the ways in which native peoples help accelerate the recolonization of cleared areas is by planting fruit trees in the swiddens. Not only does this extend the length of time the land is useful, but it serves to attract birds and bats, which are the principal agents of primary forest seed dispersal in the humid tropics. In a controlled experiment, areas planted in this manner had nine times as many seeds of native trees as an area which was not planted in fruit trees at the end of the cultivation cycle. The shade of the fruit trees also serves to provide the needed shade to primary tree species of slow growth and reduces leaching of nutrients.

The length of the cultivation period and the size of clearings are of special significance in these oligotrophic habitats. The smaller the area cleared, the easier it will be for seeds from the native vegetation to recolonize the area. The length of the cultivation period affects the levels of nutrients available to the incoming seeds and the growth rate of secondary vegetation. In blackwater ecosystems, the return of the original vegetation may take over a hundred years (Uhl et al. 1982a; Uhl 1983). Uhl et al. (1982a: 319) found 271 seeds per square meter in an area studied at the end of the cultivation cycle, 90 percent of them secondary successional species. *Cecropia ficifolia* was the dominant species in San Carlos de Río Negro for the first four years, subsequently being replaced by others. It is quite likely that secondary successional species are better adapted to low levels of nutrients and can thrive where domesticated plants cannot. Succession is much slower in blackwater ecosystems: above-ground biomass after three years was only 870 grams per square meter compared to 2,000 grams per square meter in areas of oxisols on upland forest (Uhl et al. 1982a: 320). It appears that oligotrophy, as well as flooding, is responsible for this lower level of above-ground biomass production. Of course, it should be noted that the vegetation is developing its considerable below-ground root biomass component at this time, which will permit it to entrap nutrients and recycle them. After sixty years the above-ground biomass is only 40 percent that of the original vegetation (Jordan and Uhl 1978; Clark and Uhl 1987: 12).

Hunting, Fishing, Collecting, and Entomophagy

A diet based on manioc must be supplemented with foods rich in animal protein because manioc contains less than 2 percent vegetal protein. Native peoples achieve this balance through hunting, fishing, and the consumption of insects (entomophagy). Hunting is depended upon less than fishing in blackwater basins. Arhem (1976: 31) noted that hunting is a more important activity than fishing among lower-ranked Tukanoan sibs living in the headwater region where fisheries are less productive. Hunting is practiced by all populations, but we find a curious specialization in the Upper Rio Negro. Just as the dominant Tukanoan and Arawakan horticulturalists emphasize occupation of riverbanks, the Makú Indians inhabit areas deep in the forest, away from the rivers, and exploit a vast territory in their hunting (Ramos et al. 1980). Specialized trade relations between the river Indians (Tukanoans and Arawakans) and the forest Indians (Makú) have evolved to their mutual benefit and are said to be inherited. Although this is rarely the case today, usually a Makú has more or less permanent relations with a particular river Indian (Silverwood-Cope 1972: 97). The Makú trade smoked game meat and some forest wild fruits in exchange for agricultural products and fish from the river Indians. Silverwood-Cope (1972: 96) noted that 1,192 kilograms or 40.1 percent of the game meat hunted during his period of observation was traded to the river Indians by the Bara Makú. The Makú receive, in exchange, manioc bread, peppers, and tobacco. While the river Indians do some hunting and the Makú practice horticulture and some fishing, relations of interdependence that seem to be of long standing characterize the subsistence systems of these populations.

The Bara Makú recognize seventy-four species of edible animals, which are grouped into categories such as flying game, swinging-by-the-arm game, ground game, underground game, and river game. Further, they differentiate between diurnal and nocturnal species. Both the Hupdu and Bara Makú cope with the patchy and species-rich forests by focusing not so much on tree species as indicators but, rather, on forest levels. Such an emphasis represents a reasonable solution that simplifies the problems posed by endemism, patchiness, and species diversity while at the same time providing a taxonomy that focuses on the habitat of the game. Regardless of vegetation, the game tend to make their home at a certain vertical level of the forest, and hunting techniques appropriate to that level have been developed. Flying and swinging-by-the-arm game are preferentially hunted with the blowgun; these comprise 60 percent of the kills among the Bara Makú (Silverwood-Cope 1972: 69). In the northwest Amazon ground animals are scarcer, shyer, and faster-moving than the arboreal canopy species. The shotgun has largely replaced the bow and arrow for hunting other game (Arhem 1976: 34).

The Hupdu Makú studied by Reid (1979) identify at least forty species of edible forest fruits and nuts, although only about a quarter may be harvested in any significant quantity. Among the most important, some can yield up to 30 kilograms of fruit per tree. The Bara Makú recognize fifty-four different kinds of edible forest fruit, and many more that are consumed by game animals. Most hunting/gathering camps contain only about two families, with the men usually being related as affines. The informal shelters are built to stand in the shade of the trees overhead. Especially valued in forest gathering is honey. In the Bara Makú area Silverwood-Cope (1972: 67) noted the presence of eight honey-making bee species, commonly stingless bees.

The importance of fishing to the subsistence of regional populations is all the more significant given the low productivity of terrestrial fauna and the riverine fauna. Clark and Uhl (1987: 19) estimated the productivity of the Rio Negro–Casiquiare—Guainía rivers to be between 6.6 and 13.2 kilograms per hectare per year—one of the lowest values for any tropical basin. In Africa and Asia the mean values are 40 to 60 kilograms per hectare per year, and Goulding (1979) estimated the productivity of the Madeira River in Brazil at 52 kilograms per hectare per year.

The lower means result, in part, from the absence of some particularly large species like *pirarucú* or *paiche* (*Arapaima gigas*), *aruanã* (*Osteoglos-*

sum bicirrhosum), several large species of the genus *Colossoma*, and several large catfishes or pimeloids (Goulding 1979: 15). The absence of aquatic grasses in blackwater rivers, an important food source for many of the larger fishes, influences the species composition of these rivers. This is not to say that blackwater rivers are species-poor. Goulding et al. (1988) have shown that the Lower Rio Negro is among the most species-rich rivers in the world, with approximately seven hundred species, but fishers capture fewer individuals per species. Fish species in the Rio Negro are dominated by smaller species with a mean length of 40 millimeters and over one hundred species of less than 30 millimeters in length (Goulding et al. 1988: 109).

Even though the Makú are forest, rather than riverine, Indians and do not regularly use canoes, they are familiar with forty-two kinds of edible fish (Silverwood-Cope 1972). In contrast to many other Amazonian populations, which use them as the major form of subsistence fishing, the Bara Makú only rarely kill fish with bows and arrows. This may be due in part to the lower optical clarity of the blackwater rivers and streams in the region. Like the riverine Indians, the Bara Makú find fishing with nets and fish traps more profitable in these rivers. Fish poisons are commonly used when streams are very low. Arhem (1976: 34) noted that Tukanoans in the headwaters use a broader spectrum of fishing methods and equipment than lower stream Indians and obtain a lower total yield for their efforts but a larger number of small species.

Success in fishing in blackwater ecosystems depends mostly on territorial control over areas downriver, especially cataracts and flooded forest, where the fish volume is greater (see fig. 17). The most successful method of fishing is use of large fixed traps which require considerable investment in their construction and maintenance. The importance of control over the best fishing spots is evident in such a situation and reaches a considerable level of sophistication in the Rio Negro. The Upper Rio Negro, unlike the rest of the Amazon, has two dry and two wet seasons during the year (Chernela 1983: 89; Hill 1983: 71). These fluctuations, together with the migratory cycles of certain fish species, permit very precise scheduling of fishing activities. In the Upper Rio Negro fish availability may be variable, but it is predictable during the annual cycle, and the native populations are aware of this. The Uanano methods of fish capture "take into account the feeding, reproductive, and migratory cycles of fish that result from the pronounced seasonal fluctuations in the ecology of the river system" (Chernela 1983: 102). Fish was found to be a part of meals in 78 to 88 percent of cases

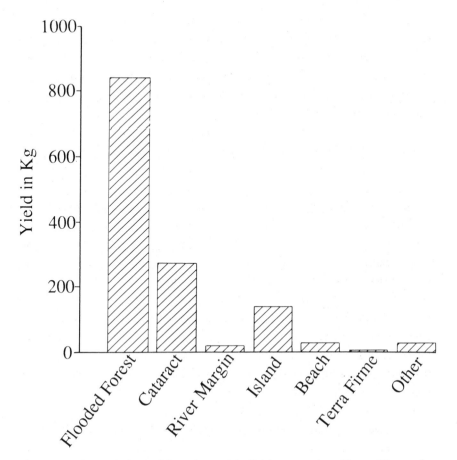

Figure 17. Association of location with fishing success (from Chernela 1983: 104).

sampled by Dufour (1987: 389). In second place was not game meat but insects.

Dufour (1987) observed that a Tukanoan population of Colombia obtained 12 to 26 percent of their animal protein during part of the year from twenty different species of insects. Such a period coincided with a time when neither fishing nor hunting was productive. Entomophagy has been noted among a number of Amazonian populations, among them the Yukpa (Ruddle 1973), the Makú (Silverwood-Cope 1972; Milton 1984b), and the Yanomamo (Smole 1976; Lizot 1977). Whether entomophagy is more frequent or makes a greater contribution to the diet in blackwater regions or not is an empirical question awaiting more detailed quantitative research.

The quantities obtainable in some seasons are impressive: up to 26 to 29 kilograms per month (Dufour 1987). Insects are also one of the few sources of protein whose consumption is not restricted by dietary taboos associated with illness and rituals (ibid., 394). Insects contribute significantly by adding variety to a manioc-based diet and seasonally provide considerable amounts of protein that supplement fishing and hunting.

Health and Nutritional Status

The effectiveness of subsistence strategies is evident in nutritional assessments of Rio Negro populations. Holmes (1985) found that the weight-for-height for people in villages in the Venezuelan Rio Negro was close to 100 percent of the international standards. The Tukanoans studied by Dufour were also close to 99 percent of the international standards of weight-for-height (1983: 330). Weight-for-height compares favorably with the nutritional status of the Suruí of Rondônia, for example, occupying a nutrient-rich area (Coimbra 1989; Moran 1991). In the case of the Suruí, their growth trajectory may have been negatively affected by recent epidemic disease and the collapse of their subsistence agriculture with depopulation. However, it should be noted that serious questions have been raised about the adequacy of weight-for-height as a measure of health (Martorell 1989; Coimbra 1989). When age-dependent measures, such as height-for-age, are used, we find that the Rio Negro populations are nutritionally stunted, although well-proportioned. Both the Rio Negro and the Rondônia populations seem nutritionally stunted, as measured by height-for-age (fig. 18).

Research among Amazonian Indians suggests that there is an absence of clinical signs of malnutrition among relatively isolated groups. With contact this situation changes and tends to deteriorate. The nutritional status can take any number of directions, depending on the degree of dislocation and transformation of the population's food production system. Signs of undernutrition increase with the intensification of contact. During periods of high mortality there is a near-total abandonment of farm work because of the loss of organization for production brought about by high adult mortality. This results in at least nutritional stunting. In general, a chronic deficiency of adequate nutrition will be reflected in lower height-for-age (i.e., stunting). Acute deficiencies are reflected in below-normal weight-for-age, but sometimes it may be hard to separate this from the effects of chronic undernutrition.[4]

Birth weight, another indicator used to assess the adequacy of maternal nutrition, was also adequate: of 175 children observed, the mean was 3.26

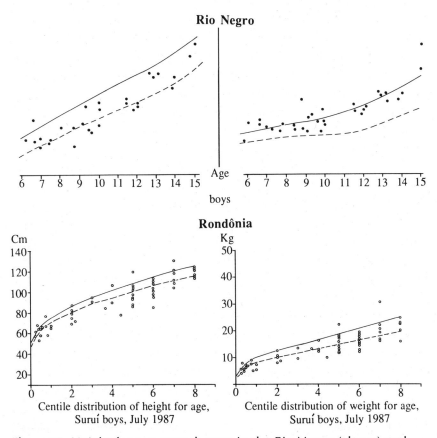

Figure 18. Height-for-age growth rates in the Rio Negro (above) and Rondônia (below) (from Holmes 1985: 242 and Coimbra 1989: 280, 281).

kilograms, well above the 2.5 to 3.0 kilogram threshold of adequacy. However, this favorable initial weight gives way to stunting by the end of the first year of life. Whether this is a result of nutritional inadequacy or of episodes of disease is not clear from the published literature. Most native Amazonians have been experiencing severe epidemic infectious diseases, and high mortality, as they come into contact with introduced diseases. The lack of timely medical services has exacerbated the stress felt by these populations.

Settlement Patterns and Social Organization

The traditional pattern in blackwater rivers of the northwest Amazon was a settlement commonly made up of one longhouse, containing four to eight nuclear families, and rarely exceeding 30 persons whether the population was riverine or forest-based (Reid 1979: 18; Reichel-Dolmatoff 1971; Arhem 1976; Jackson 1976). Makú groups of the northwest Amazon have settlements of similar size to the Tukanoans and Arawakans, living in settlements of 6 to 50, with a mean size of about 25 (Reid 1979: 18). In earlier periods in the Içana Tukanoan and Arawakan settlements could reach 50 to 100 persons and up to 200 in the Brazilian Vaupés (Köch-Grünberg 1909–1910; Galvão 1959: 38). It is not clear whether the larger settlements are a result of colonial and missionary concentration or whether such larger size reflects the greater carrying capacity of the Lower Rio Negro and the Lower Vaupés (Chernela 1983: 23).

Distance between villages varies between two and ten hours by canoe in the Colombian Vaupés (Jackson 1976: 68). Instead of being an obstacle to ethnic identity, distances between villages have encouraged the development of systematic rounds of exchange and frequent visiting. Economic exchanges between villages serve to circulate resources within the region, marked by seasonal and area scarcity. The regularity of visitation has encouraged the evolution of a pan-Vaupés culture (S. Hugh-Jones 1979). The Vaupés has greater cultural integration than many other parts of Amazonia, supported by patterns of exogamous marriage, multilingualism, exchange, and military alliances.

The societies in the northwest Amazon are characterized by complex forms of segmentation into units such as sibs and phratries which are organized into complex hierarchies. Sibs are named, ranked, exogamous, localized patrilineal descent groups (Jackson 1983: 71). The sib is the fundamental unit of Tukanoan and Arawakan society, and creation myths state that each sib has a distinct place along the river based upon when it came out of the mouth of the anaconda (Chernela 1983: 55). Thus, the local group, which is made up of one or more sibs, has ownership control over particular portions of the river. Sibs situated in the lower parts of the Vaupés and Içana are hierarchically superior to the sibs in the upper courses.

The system of marriage in the Vaupés coexists with remarkable linguistic diversity. Tukanoan marriage follows a pattern of language exogamy that serves to articulate the dispersed populations of the Vaupés (Jackson 1983). Three marriage strategies seem to occur in the Vaupés among riverine peoples (Jackson 1983; Arhem 1987): marriage with cross cousins (which serves to create dyads of closely related pairs of language groups), marriage with distant mates (which is associated with ritual capture of the woman), and marriage with strangers/enemies (which was associated with warfare in the past). Among the Cubeo, the Wakuenai, and the Uanano marriage is prescribed according to rank or hierarchical position—a pattern that may be quite ancient and may be more effective in the control of resources than other patterns found in the region (J. Hill, personal communication, 1989).

In structural terms, the Tukanoan pattern of social organization is similar, but not equivalent to, the pattern of other dispersed populations such as those in the Great Basin, the Kalahari San, and the Australian Aborigines. All these populations are inserted in regional systems characterized by interdependence, fluctuation in local group membership, and territorial fluidity. While they can function at the regional level, their hierarchy is not centralized; this would reduce the flexibility needed to adjust to regions characterized by dispersed resources and low biomass productivity. Access to resources not available locally is obtained through exchange and through exogamous marriage between individuals from distant settlements. One should expect that in these cases most marriages would take place between individuals whose areas of origin are complementary and only rarely bring together individuals whose resource base is equivalent.

In an area of the Rio Negro studied by Hill (1983), Wakuenai phratries had political control over clearly defined portions of the river. The phratric name identified individuals and marked them as to whether they were potential mates. Wright (1981) found that the territorial rights required asking for formal authorization by one phratry in order to hunt or fish in the territory of another phratry. Usually, in granting permission to fish in one's territory, a phratry gains tacit permission to use resources in the territory of the other. Hunting, fishing, and farmland are included among the goods exchanged between phratries. In practice, neighboring phratries held regular exchanges that effectively circulated goods within the region.

It is quite probable that territorial rights of sibs are pre-Columbian and fell into disuse with depopulation and missionization of the region (Goldman 1963; Köch-Grünberg 1909–1910). They persist among some groups of the region. Among the Uanano, the most prestigious sibs are downriver, in the most productive fishing areas. Downriver the settlements are larger, and the fishery is more productive. Control over the best fishing areas attracts small population aggregates who hope to share in the bounty of such areas by placing themselves at the service of the hierarchically more prestigious sibs (Chernela 1983: 24). In the Vaupés various fish species migrate to spawn. Among them are *Leporinus* sp., *Auchenipterid* sp., *Moenkhausia* sp., and *Brycon* sp. The most prestigious sib in the region had territorial rights over the largest area of flooded forest and control over three cataracts—the most productive areas for fishing (Chernela 1983: 98, 108).

The dominant sibs seem to have focused upon riverine resources and manioc cultivation. Although they hunt on occasion, they have maintained mutualistic relations with hunting/gathering groups like the Makú. The same sort of relations between asymmetrical groups found between riverine sibs can be found in the relations between the river and the forest Indians (Ramos et al. 1980). Whereas the riverine Indians exploit fixed resources—fish in flooded forest and cataracts and farmland—the forest Indians or Makú exploit the dispersed resources of the forest. This results in the circulation of production between these two areas (Milton 1984b: 20). Among the Makú nothing that can be considered a right of usufruct to specified areas has been found, as among the Tukanoans and Arawakans (Reid 1979: 122).

Stratification is also evident in patterns of exchange. Egalitarian patterns predominate in exchanges between sibs of the same status belonging to different language groups, whereas asymmetric patterns of exchange predominate between sibs of different status within the same language group or between riverine and forest populations. Exchange in the Rio Negro involves the flow of consumable goods, such as food, between mutualistic populations, in contrast to exchange among other Amazonian populations, where exchange more often than not involves the flow of ceremonial items (Neves 1989: 24). Exchange highlights the importance of prestige and hierarchy for the Tukanoans and the significance of unequal access in their worldview (Reid 1979: 200). Specialized manufactured items, cooked animal and fish foods, and raw fruits and vegetables are the main categories traded (Chernela 1983: 127). Although the exchanges are asymmetrical and favor the higher-status sibs, there is effective circulation of goods to groups with lesser access to some of the regional resources. The consequences of unequal access to resources, although not negated, are at least mollified by regular forms of exchange. Because the resources are predictable, the pattern is sustainable over time and highly regular in its regional consequences. It is precisely under these circumstances that Dyson-Hudson and Smith (1978: 25) suggested that a territorial system is most likely to develop.

Conclusions

Blackwater ecosystems, such as those found in the Rio Negro, Vaupés, and Içana, in the northwest Amazon represent the poorest and most limited areas of Amazonia. Above-ground biomass is lower, litterfall is poor in nutrients, decomposition is slow due to the acidity of the soils and the water, and the drainage limitations resulting from the podzolic soils contribute to making this area a true challenge to human populations.

Complex forms of segmentary hierarchization, often found in arid and semiarid zones, evolved in these areas to facilitate the flexible control of resources, their circulation, the maintenance of dispersed settlement, and the persistence of specialized knowledge and control. Territorial control in the Upper Rio Negro is inherited, hierarchical, and very specifically defined and legitimated in mythology.

Selection of particularly toxic varieties of bitter manioc, a greater degree of entomophagy, and hierarchical control over fishing spots further contributed to the adjustment of native peoples to these poor regions of Amazonia. This area more than any other should be protected from large-scale development activities. These are important ethnic refuge regions, of low potential for intensification but high potential for specialized exploitation of the rich species diversity found therein. While total biomass is less than elsewhere in Amazonia, species diversity is as high as, if not higher than, in other phytogeographic areas of the Amazon Basin. The native populations of this area are particularly attuned to the limitations of this ecosystem, and their expertise should guide land use and ecological research in the years ahead.

Upon close examination we find that these are not "rivers of hunger," except to outsiders who are unfamiliar with the ebbs and flows of these ecosystems. Poor in net yield they surely are—but they are also rich in species diversity and in local populations expert at making do with less.

3

Upland
Forests

Amazonian upland forests constitute one of the richest terrestrial ecosystems in the biosphere, with the greatest accumulations of species and plant biomass on the planet. This is the area that has been experiencing the most devastating rates of deforestation ever recorded in human history—already amounting to over 500,000 square kilometers (Mahar 1988). While in 1975 less than 0.6 percent of these forests had been cut down, that percentage is now believed to be close to 12 percent in the Brazilian Amazon. This is not the result of population pressure, as has been often thought, but, rather, is a product of government policies which provided tax exemptions to individuals and firms to "develop the Amazon."

This type of development has involved the conversion of a "free good" (the forest) into one given economic value through deforestation. According to long-standing legislation, deforestation constitutes an "improvement" that demonstrates that the wild landscape has now been occupied and can enter economic relations of production and exchange. Thus, a frenzy of deforestation began in the early 1970s to capture the fiscal transfers and to speculate on the development of a land market. If such land occupation had led to significant employment of the rural poor one might find some consolation in these events, but the reality is that most of the land deforested was converted to pasture land, grazed by few cattle per unit of land and tended by barely one cowhand per 300 hectares. The economic return to the people of Latin American countries has been very low—except to a handful of already wealthy individuals and firms who received capital transfers. In areas like Rondônia, Brazil, where good roads were put in, up to 26 percent of the forests have already been felled.

No less important has been the devastating impact that these processes of deforestation have had on native Amazonians. Many areas of the upland forests had served until these last two decades as refuge areas for native peoples from the incursions of European colonial and contemporary Latin American societies who sought to enslave and occupy the land of native populations. In this process the most effective agent of colonization has been epidemic disease, often spread in advance of major direct contact between Amazonians and outsiders. As recently as the late 1960s, for example, the Suruí Indians of Rondônia suffered mortality of 75 percent in the first decade of contact. The process is being repeated before the eyes of the media today in the case of the Yanomami, whose lands have been invaded by over 50,000 gold miners. Miners, often in poor health due to poverty, carry more than their share of the diseases against which native Amazonians have little resistance (Cleary 1990).

Often blamed for causing much of the deforestation of the upland forests of Amazonia have been the colonists who came to settle the land along the roads that were built in the early 1970s in Brazil and earlier in the "Andean" countries with Amazon territories (cf. Myers 1991). By and large, this blame is undeserved.[1] By the end of the 1970s colonists were responsible for less than 4 percent of the deforestation in the Brazilian Amazon (Browder 1986). While government plans aimed to move hundreds of thousands of families to the "highways of national integration" (the Transamazon Highway, the Cuiabá–Santarém highway, the North Perimeter Road, and the Carretera Marginal de la Selva), the number of families who dared to confront this exotic and often feared habitat was far more modest. Moreover, figures of immigration often fail to mention that many colonists return to their areas of origin once they see the lack of infrastructure for productive activity in much of interfluvial Amazonia. Dropout rates from colonization projects have been as high as 95 percent and more often than not over 65 percent in the first ten years of settlement. Sometimes the departing colonists are replaced by others, but in some cases whole colonization projects have been abandoned because of poor soils, steepness, malaria, or lack of access to markets.[2] Small-scale colonists generally temper their initial enthusiasm and grand plans within a couple of years and retreat to a more traditional intensive mode of production that emphasizes subsistence and modest surplus production (Moran 1981; Smith 1982b). The impact of colonists has been greater in the Andean countries and in Rondônia—although in the latter cattle ranchers have begun to take over failed colonist areas and have transformed the landscape from one like the small mixed farms of southern Brazil to one more typical of the Brazilian landscape with a predominance of large ranches.

One difficulty in studying and designing policy for upland forests lies in their very heterogeneity. In the previous chapter I have already disaggregated one type of upland forest from the rest in order to begin to bring some semblance of order to discussions of this vast ecosystem. This chapter makes several differentiations that with more research will allow other kinds of forests to be treated as distinctly as those found in blackwater river basins. While the botany of some of these areas has reached considerable degrees of sophistication, the differential way in which humans use the types of forest remains to be studied due to the persistent tendency to treat all upland forests as sufficiently alike to be lumped together for most purposes.

The upland forests' biological richness is not a function of the richness of the soils but results from sophisticated forms of nutrient recycling, complex adaptations of plants to local conditions, and management approaches practiced by local populations in the past and present (Posey and Balée 1989). Seventy percent of the nutrients in the ecosystem are tied up in the plant biomass. The soils under the lush upland tropical forests are of variable quality but are dominated by acid, nutrient-poor ones. The upland lowland forests differ from the upland premontane forests of the western Amazon. This is largely due to the biological consequences of the difference in altitude. Lowland forests are said to be found in altitudes below 600 meters above sea level, with most of the lowland forests occurring well below 300 meters. The average monthly temperatures fluctuate between 24 and 27 degrees C, a fact that unfortunately gives a very poor idea of the true variance in temperature that can occur from day to day and within a single day. Rainfall is highly variable within the basin, with a tendency to be in the 1,800-to-2,000-millimeter range in the eastern Amazon, and as high as 4,000 to 5,000 millimeters in the western Amazon and the northern periphery (fig. 6 and Eden 1978: 445). Plant and animal biomass are considerably higher in the lowland area when compared with the forests occurring at altitudes above 600 meters, creating very different conditions for the populations living in each altitudinal zone.

The biotic diversity of terra firme forests is impressive. Although collection is far from complete, it has been estimated that 550 species of birds and 20,000 species of insects live in the Amazonian upland forests. The greatest proportion of the animal biomass occurs, in fact, in the detritivore component—organisms which play the all-important function of facilitating the recycling of nutrients in rapidly decomposing organic matter following leaffall (Fittkau and Klinge 1973). Although the species richness of mammals is considerable, they constitute a much smaller proportion of total biomass, as the laws of energy would suggest. Fittkau and Klinge (1973) estimated that the animal biomass made up barely 0.2 percent of the plant biomass; but as we saw in chapter 1, more data will be necessary to be sure that these findings are generally applicable. The distribution of animal biomass is highly variable, as a function of the history of the species, the edaphic conditions, the rainfall and hydrology, and the human population densities.

Denevan (1976: 225) directed attention to the extremely low estimates of population density made by Julian Steward (1948), who suggested densities of barely 0.2 persons per square kilometer for lowland South America—a figure that would result in a pre-Columbian population of barely 1,260,000 people scattered over 6 million square kilometers. Densities no doubt varied depending on numerous factors, such as the productivity of fisheries, soils, and available crops. In general, it has been suggested that the upland inter-fluvial forests had lower population densities than savannas and floodplains in lowland South America. Prehistoric populations over the centuries seem to have brought about significant environmental modification that has enhanced the net returns to human populations and ensured that familiar environments are present from one generation to the next. For a long time after the initial arrival of the Europeans, the upland forests offered refuge to native populations fleeing from the incursions of colonial and national societies.

The indigenous populations of Amazonia have adjusted to the physical conditions of the upland forests and developed systems of management that have proven to this day superior to those brought into the area by outsiders. Many of the recent advances made in the management of upland forested regions are but scientific tests of long-proven native practices (e.g., showing the superiority of manual clearing to bulldozer clearing in terms of agricultural output and soil conditions; see Seubert et al. 1977). We have learned that the soils of many areas cannot sustain cultivation for more than three years, requiring their abandonment so that, through the accumulation of plant biomass, the area can regain its crop production potential—something well known to native peoples who practiced swidden agriculture (Meggers 1971). In contrast, in more fertile areas, land must be abandoned to forest successional forces not due to declining fertility but due to weed invasion (Carneiro 1957; Sánchez 1981). The full cycle of secondary succession can take anywhere from ten to seventy-five years,[3] depending on the microecological conditions, the way the land was used during the agricultural cycle, and the initial conditions of the soil.[4] The energetic efficiency of swidden cultivation has proven superior to any system introduced to date. More calories can be produced per unit of calorie invested than by any other system, but this efficiency depends on the availability of great expanses of forest, low demographic densities, and the use of plants with adaptations to the local habitat.

The most important environmental pressures experienced by human populations in upland forests are the great diversity of species and their distribution, the rainfall regime, the probability of locating swiddens on acid, nutrient-poor soils, and the complexity of the biotic relations. These environmental pressures are deliberately general in nature, given the widely divergent habitats currently lumped together in the category of terra firme or upland forests.

Characterization of the Environment

The productivity of the primary forest is very great because of the abundance of moisture, high solar radiation, and high levels of carbon dioxide. Most specialists do not think that the increase in global carbon dioxide will lead to significant increments in plant productivity in the lowland tropics (Woodwell 1984). The productivity of upland rain forests worldwide has been estimated to average 8 tons per hectare per year (Lieth and Whittaker 1975)—a value that approximates the annual production of leaves in the forests of the central Amazon (Luizão and Schubart 1987; Franken et al. 1979; Klinge and Rodrigues 1968). There appears to be a clear relationship between rainfall and the volume of monthly leaffall. Leaffall is two-thirds greater in the dry season, from June to October (733 kilograms per hectare per month), compared to leaffall in the wet season, from March to June (383 kilograms per hectare per month) (Klinge and Rodrigues 1968: 294; Luizão and Schubart 1987: 260). Above-ground biomass is smaller in the Central Amazon and in the blackwater basin of the Rio Negro, where the means are between 300 and 400 tons per hectare. A greater portion of the biomass in the caatingas amazônicas found in blackwater areas goes to the root-component (between 34 and 87 percent of total biomass), as compared with the upland forests, where the proportion is 20 to 26 percent (Fittkau and Klinge 1973: 5). Above-ground biomass in the uplands of San Carlos de Río Negro approximates the biomass of secondary forests and of primary montane forests, although total biomass is within the mean for Amazonian forests (Jordan and Uhl 1978: 398).

Upland forests are usually characterized as having efficient nutrient cycling. The relative efficiencies found vary from the near-perfect recycling found in the oligotrophic areas of the Rio Negro and the central Amazon to the much less efficient ones in richer areas of the Amazon where greater losses may occur from the local ecosystems. Upland forests have been measured as having a mean index of nutrient cycling of 0.7—an index developed to compare the amount of nutrients recycled as compared to the total stock of nutrients. An index of 1.0 would indicate perfect recycling of nutrients. The recycling and conservation of nitrogen in upland forests is less critical than it is in the caatingas of the Rio Negro. In upland forests, the flows of nitrogen are considerable. The reason may be that nitrogen depends on the capacity of the soil to hold it or release it. The high frequency of leguminous trees in upland forests of Amazonia, with their innate capacity to fix nitrogen, and the considerable amounts of nitrogen coming into the ecosystem with rainfall are sufficient to maintain an undegraded forest (Jordan et al. n.d.). Changes in the composition of upland forests, especially those that might lead to a lesser frequency of leguminous species or that reduce the mechanisms of forest absorption of nitrogen from rainfall, could eventually lead to forest degradation through lack of an adequate stock of nitrogen.

The most significant energy flows in the upland forests occur in the detritivore component. Went and Stark (1968) were able to demonstrate that soil fungi were the principal elements in organic matter decomposition in upland forests. The nutrients liberated through decomposition are mobilized not into the mineral soil but directly back into the plants through the interaction between the fungi and the mycorrhizae which live on the aboveground root layer that occurs in the more nutrient-poor parts of the Amazon (Fittkau and Klinge 1973: 10; Herrera et al. 1978; Jordan 1989).

The upland forests are characterized by their high diversity of species. Klinge and Rodrigues (1968: 289) found that 102 tree species per hectare could be found in a forest sampled near Manaus. Means are generally more modest, with about 83 tree species per hectare with more than 10 cm diameter above basal height (dbh) (Uhl and Murphy 1981; Black et al. 1950; Takeuchi 1961). In the Uhl and Murphy study in the Rio Negro, 67 percent of the tree species were represented by less than 4 individuals per hectare. With each increment in the area sampled, the number of species increased significantly, a situation that creates a serious problem in sampling and makes generalizations about the average number of species and the distributions of species, families, and so forth very shaky. In the uplands one does not find the kind of dominance that seems to occur in the impoverished caatingas of the blackwater basins (Uhl and Murphy 1981: 225); when it occurs, one should consider examining the history of the patch in order to understand the peculiar distributions that may explain the presence of dominance (e.g., human modification, major tree falls). On a patch of upland forest near San Carlos de Río Negro in Venezuela, Uhl and Jordan (1984) found that 18 species were responsible for 79.3 percent of the plants present, with one of them (*Licania* sp.) responsible for 19.1 percent of the total. But in other patches the distribution of *Licania* was less frequent and the indices of species diversity much different (cf. Prance et al. 1976). In a study using a larger plot size of 3.5 hectares, Pires et al. (1953) recorded 179 species with dbh above 10 centimeters (cf. also Dantas 1988: 18–24, who found an average of 200 species per hectare in four terra firme plots sampled). Much more research is still needed before firm assertions can be made

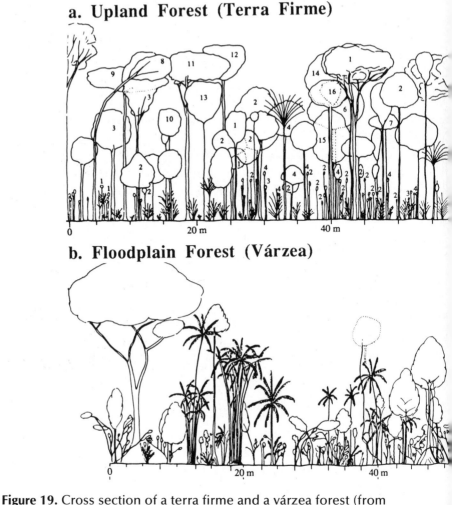

a. Upland Forest (Terra Firme)

b. Floodplain Forest (Várzea)

Figure 19. Cross section of a terra firme and a várzea forest (from Jacobs 1988).

about population distributions in Amazonia as a whole, and even within particular parts of it.

Upland forests are characterized as having a large number of individuals of small diameters and a smaller number of "giants." The height of the canopy can average 40 meters in some areas and seems to bear some relation to the age of the patch and the depth of the A horizon. The larger trees have very broad canopies that can reach up to 40 meters in diameter (Klinge and Rodrigues 1968: 289), often have the form of an umbrella, and have trunks with diameters rarely above 150 centimeters. Figure 19 provides a cross

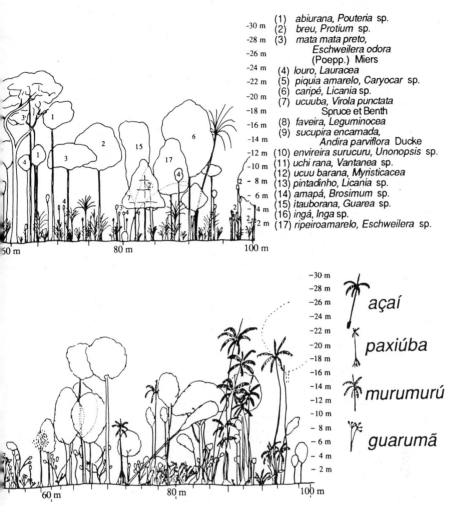

(1) abiurana, Pouteria sp.
(2) breu, Protium sp.
(3) mata mata preto,
       Eschweilera odora
       (Poepp.) Miers
(4) louro, Lauracea
(5) piquia amarelo, Caryocar sp.
(6) caripé, Licania sp.
(7) ucuuba, Virola punctata
       Spruce et Benth
(8) faveira, Leguminocea
(9) sucupira encarnada,
       Andira parviflora Ducke
(10) envireira surucuru, Unonopsis sp.
(11) uchi rana, Vantanea sp.
(12) ucuu barana, Myristicacea
(13) pintadinho, Licania sp.
(14) amapá, Brosimum sp.
(15) itauborana, Guarea sp.
(16) ingá, Inga sp.
(17) ripeiroamarelo, Eschweilera sp.

açaí

paxiúba

murumurú

guarumã

section of a typical upland forest. Of the trees measured by Klinge and Rodrigues, 92 percent had diameters between 25 and 54 centimeters. In the same study the majority of trees and palms had heights of less than 1.5 meters; these smaller trees constituted 86 percent of the total number of individuals but accounted for much less of the total biomass (Fittkau and Klinge 1973: 5).

Before the 1970s the soils of the upland forests were considered to be uniformly leached, acidic, and nutrient-poor. The red or yellow color, indicative of the presence of iron oxides, was seen as evidence that the soils of

Table 4. *Soil Types in the Amazon Basin (millions of hectares)*

	Poorly drained	Well-drained	Total	%
Acid and infertile (oxisols, ultisols)	43	318	361	75
Alluvial soils (aquepts, aquents, gleys)	56	14	70	14
Nonalluvial fertile soils (alfisols, mollisols, vertisols, tropepts, fluvents)	0	37	37	8
Extremely infertile soils (spodosols and psamments)	10	6	16	3
Total	109	375	484	100

Source: Adapted from Sánchez et al. 1982.

the Amazon would turn into an irreversible hardpan, laterite, when culti-vated for any length of time (McNeil 1964), an opinion still found among many educated persons and the public at large. Before the 1970s soil sam-pling of the uplands had been restricted to the riverbanks, wherein the probability is much higher of finding laterite (Sombroek 1966). Current es-timates are that laterite is found in 2 to 4 percent of the soils of the Amazon Basin (Sánchez et al. 1982).

Amazonian soils are among the richest and poorest in the world: 75 per-cent of the soils are poor and acid; 14 percent are poorly drained alluvial soils in floodplains and flooded forests; 7 percent are soils of medium to high fertility; and 3 percent are extremely poor soils, known as spodosols (table 4 illustrates the most recent data on the distribution of the various types of soils in the Amazon).

Relatively good soils with excellent drainage occur over about 8 percent of the basin and include alfisols, vertisols, tropepts (an inceptisol), and flu-vents (an entisol). Of smaller areal extent are the spodosols or podzolic soils found largely in blackwater river basins, found in about 3 percent of the basin. About 75 percent of the basin is dominated by acid, nutrient-poor soils classified as oxisols and ultisols.

Oxisols are deep, generally well-drained, red or yellow soils with excellent structure and little horizon differentiation. Oxisols are known in other classifications as ferralsols, as latosols, and incorrectly as "lateritic soils." They are found most often in the areas geologically affected by the Guiana and Brazilian shields. These are the oldest land surfaces in tropical America, dating from the Archean and Paleozoic periods. Parent materials are granite, gneiss, and some sandstones.

Ultisols are similar to oxisols in acidity, color, and chemical properties but, in contrast, are characterized by a notable increase in clay content with depth, absent in the oxisols. Their physical properties are less favorable than the oxisols due to the higher clay content and because they occupy steeper slopes where erosion further depletes their already low nutrients. Ultisols are also known in some classification schemes as red-yellow podzolics and as acrisols. Ultisols are the dominant soil type west of Manaus and in other well-drained areas not affected by the Guiana and Brazilian shields. They originate from alluvial materials from the Tertiary (445 to 1,200 million years ago).

These two soil orders encompass most of the reddish soils of the Amazon. Their most common constraints are their low pH, their high proportion of exchangeable aluminum, and low levels of phosphorus, potassium, calcium, magnesium, sulfur, zinc, and some micronutrients. The poor root development of many crops and native vegetation is commonly related to the high proportions of exchangeable aluminum that bring about root impedance. These soils do not turn irreversibly into laterite as some suggested earlier (McNeil 1964). The formation of laterite requires that a soil have impeded drainage and that the water table fluctuate over the long term. The substance that can turn irreversibly into hardpan, today called plinthite, occurs in 2 to 7 percent of the subsoils of Amazonia (van Wambeke 1978; Nicholaides et al. 1983). It is a threat largely near streams where a fluctuating water table brings about the creation of plinthite.

Alfisols occur in patches of variable size near areas of oxisols and ultisols. They are easily confused with the oxisols and ultisols because of their similar color and structure. However, they are not acid, have little exchangeable aluminum, and are nutrient-rich. Geologically they derive from basaltic outcrops rich in bases and less weathered than the materials around them. To distinguish between alfisols and the oxisols/ultisols requires laboratory chemical analyses, given their visual similarity. Alfisols are known as terra roxa estruturada eutrófica, luvisols, and eutric nitosols. The largest areas of alfisols occur in the Lower Xingú, Lower Tapajós, and Lower Tocantins, in the Carajás mountain region of eastern Pará, in Rondônia, in the Rio Branco area of Brazil, and in parts of the high selva of Peru.

There is also mention in the literature of an anthropogenic soil, variously known as terra preta do índio, anthrosols, and terra preta arqueológica (Smith 1980; Kern 1988). These soils drain well, are dark in color, are relatively fertile, and have an abundance of potsherds. Phosphorus concentration is very high (commonly over 180 milligrams per 100 grams) as compared with 5 milligrams per 100 grams, common in soils of Amazonia (Sombroek 1966; Smith 1980; Kern 1988). The superior quality of black earths is recognized by Amazonian populations, and they are preferred cultivation areas (Frikel 1959, 1968; Smith 1980). As we will see later in this chapter, they are often associated with types of forests that some scholars now believe are the product of long-term management by native Amazonians (Balée 1989).

Management of the Upland Forests

Some have estimated that at least 11.8 percent of the upland forests of the Brazilian Amazon are anthropogenic forests that result from the long-term management by native Amazonian populations (Balée 1989). Resource use reflects not only a population's adaptation to nature but also its efforts to overcome such limitations through environmental modification. Such management strategies offer an opportunity to learn how to overcome the limitations of the environment and benefit from the advantages it may offer.

Indigenous populations have modified the Amazonian environment, promoting diversity in some cases, while in others concentrating plants of economic interest in "islands of resources" through plant selection. In poor areas one finds evidence of drainage canals, mounding, and other practices suggestive of intensive agriculture (Denevan 1966; Zucchi and Denevan 1979). Other management practices have modified the vegetation in a permanent fashion. Many of the plant frequencies observed today "in the wild" may be the product of the conscious plant management of local populations—all the more impressive because such management has been so unintrusive and so hard for outsiders to recognize for so long.

Among the vegetations that could very well be the product of human management one can mention the forests dominated by palms, the forests dominated by bamboo, the forests with high densities of Brazil nut trees, the unusual islands of forest in the midst of the central Brazilian savannas,[5] the liana forests, and others.

Forests Dominated by Palms

Palms are excellent indicators of archaeological sites and are commonly used as proof of human occupation. *Pupunha* (*Bactris gasipaes*), *inajá* (*Maximiliana maripa*), and *buriti* (*Mauritia flexuosa*) have been used by ethnobotanists as indicative of long-term human manipulation (Balick 1984; Boer 1965; Pesce 1985; Heinen and Ruddle 1974). *Buriti* palm forests are generally found in areas of flooded forest and waterlogged on a year-round basis. *Inajá* and *pupunha* palms rarely dominate the areas where they appear, while *tucumã* (*Astrocaryum vulgare*), *Acromia, caiaui* (*Elaeis oleifera*), and *babaçú* (*Orbignya phalerata*) can become the dominant features of sizable areas of forest vegetation.

Boer (1965: 132) considered *Astrocaryum vulgare*, or *tucumã*, a species that "never" is found in virgin areas, only in areas managed by human populations. The Urubú Ka'apor of the state of Maranhão in Brazil consider the fruits of this palm attractive to tapir and other small game, a relationship that probably encouraged them to promote the growth of this palm to increase its value as a "hunting garden." This palm is also used to make hammocks, skirts, child carriers, and other articles for daily use (Balée 1989).

Andrade (1983: 23) found an association between the presence of *caiaui* (*Elaeis oleifera*) and anthropogenic black soils in areas of the Madeira River and south of Manaus. Its uses are equivalent to those of African palm oil; it seems to have come from Central America to South America before Columbus.

Best known and most intensively managed by native Amazonians is the *babaçú* palm (*Orbignya phalerata*). Forests of *babaçú* extend for over 196,370 square kilometers in the Brazilian Amazon (May et al. 1985: 115). Such dominance and areal extent are uncommon among the palms and result from the unique form of germination that characterizes this palm. When a forested area is burned, many of the seeds that are in the process of germination in the soil are protected by growing underneath the soil for a while before appearing above ground level (Anderson and Anderson 1985). These palms live approximately 184 years and serve as an indicator of human disturbance of forest areas. *Babaçú* palm forests occur in isolated areas today and in colonization areas which have further stimulated their expansion through land clearing (Anderson, May, and Balick 1991; Balée 1989).

In the areas occupied today by the Guajá, Tembé, and Urubú Ka'apor in the eastern parts of Pará and the north of Maranhão, Balée measured *babaçú* forests up to 3 hectares in total extent (Balée 1984: 94–95). The Guajá depend on the mesocarp of the *babaçú* for a substantial portion of their caloric and protein intake (Gomes, unpublished manuscript, cited in Balée 1984).

Among the Suruí Indians of the Aripuanã Reservation in Rondônia, *babaçú* forests are located on sandy soils of low fertility that are never used for agricultural production, which is based on corn rather than on manioc. The Suruí seem to know how to recognize and use the patches of alfisols in their territory, while simultaneously managing the sandy areas for *babaçú* production. They need *babaçú* products for house construction; they use only the central leaf from each palm tree for thatch, a practice that requires a large *babaçú* grove (Coimbra 1989).

Bamboo Forests

Bamboo (*Guadua glomerata*) is an important raw material used by indigenous people in the construction of flutes and arrows for hunting and fishing. In the Brazilian Amazon bamboo forests cover an area of approximately 85,000 square kilometers (Braga 1979: 55) and are indicative of past human occupation. Sombroek (1966: 188–189) was the first to suggest that these forests are anthropogenic. Balée (1989) supported this assertion based upon his research in Maranhão. The Guajá Indians today occupy bamboo forests that were previously occupied by the Guajajara of the region of the Pindaré River (Balée 1989).

Brazil Nut Forests

Forests dominated by the presence of Brazil nut trees (*Bertholletia excelsa*) occupy approximately 8,000 square kilometers in the Lower Tocantins (Kitamura and Muller 1984: 8), but sizable areas have also been noted in Amapá, the Jarí River basin, and Rondônia. It has been suggested that Brazil nut groves are associated with archaeological sites and with patches of anthropogenic black soils (Araújo-Costa 1983; Simões and Araújo-Costa 1987). Brazil nut trees prefer intense light to diffuse light in their growth and have the capacity of colonizing open areas, unlike many other mature forest species. Their dispersion seems to be aided by coatis (*Dasyprocta* sp.) (Huber 1909: 154–155), which seem to move freely between *babaçú* forests, secondary forests, and cultivated areas (Smith 1974a). The Kayapó Gorotire plant Brazil nut trees because of their importance in attracting game and for their food value to the human population (Anderson and Posey 1985; Posey 1985). Brazil nut trees are an important resource for native populations where they occur. Besides their nutritional value, they have been a major source of income for native populations since the colonial period (Laraia and da Matta 1968). Brazil nut trees are among the most long-lived species in the forest, even longer than *babaçú* palms. One of the most serious consequences of the expansion of cattle ranches in the upland forests has been their destruction of Brazil nut groves because of the ranchers' fear that the large seeds will kill cattle and the distancing of the trees from the flowering and dispersal agents that ensure their biological continuity and productivity.

Liana Forests

Liana forests are estimated to occupy 100,000 square kilometers in the Brazilian Amazon according to Pires (1973: 152) and are found chiefly in the Lower Tocantins and the Lower Xingú. Some areas have also been observed in the Lower Tapajós (Balée 1989). Liana forests have a smaller basal area than upland forests, with only 18 to 24 square meters per hectare as compared with the 40 square meters per hectare found in "virgin" upland forests, due to the high density of vines and lianas (Pires and Prance 1985: 120–122).

Liana forests are characterized by an unusual concentration of plants of economic utility for human populations: food (*babaçú*, *Theobroma*, Brazil nuts), fruits attractive to game (*Eschweilera coriacea*, *Euterpe oleracea*), materials for construction of dwellings (*Unonopsis guatterioides*, *babaçú*), materials for implements (*Cenostigma macrophyllum*, *Eschweilera coriacea*, *Sterculia pruriens*), medicines (e.g., *Alexa imperatricis* for toothache), insect repellents (*babaçú* oil), and firewood. The number of useful species is much greater, of course, and these are but a few of the ones used most often among the Assuriní and Araweté (Balée 1989).

The preference of Amazonian farmers for liana forests to prepare their swiddens has been observed several times (Sombroek 1966: 195; Moran 1977, 1981). No simple correlation can be made between liana forests and a given soil type, a particular climatic regime, or any other criteria (Falesi 1972), but they do seem to occur with greater frequency in areas with anthropogenic soil patches (Smith 1980; Heindsdijk 1957) and in alfisols (Moran 1981; Falesi 1972). Spontaneous fires do not explain the presence of liana forest, since this vegetation does not occur in areas that will catch fire, unless the forest has been cut and allowed to dry (Pires 1973: 187).

Balée (1989) studied the liana forests occupied by the Assuriní and Araweté Indians of the Lower Xingú. Among the lianas or vines that they recognized were Araceae (*Philodendron*), Bignoniaceae (*Arrabidaea*, *Memora*), Caesalpiniaceae (*Bauhinia*), Fabaceae (*Machaerium*, *Mucuna*), Mimosaceae (*Acacia, Mimosa*), and Sapindaceae (*Paullinia*). Balée suggested that, on the basis of the presence of archaeological materials dated at A.D. 1000 to 1580 and their association with liana forests, it is possible to infer that these areas were occupied by chiefdoms in the pre-Columbian era. Balée (1989) collected soil samples in the anthropogenic black soils associated with liana forests. One of those samples had a depth of the black organic horizon of 39 centimeters and 31.8 milligrams per 100 grams of phosphorus. The higher than normal concentration of phosphorus when compared to adjacent soils is indicative of prolonged human occupation. High concentrations of calcium and a pH of 5.8, together with a low aluminum saturation, confirm the optimal conditions offered by these soils for plants with high nutrient input requirements (like corn and beans). The Assuriní and Araweté, instead of adjusting to the poverty of the soils, look for and use the patches of black soils found here and there, demonstrating that human populations can overcome some of the limitations of the physical environment under the right historical, political, and economic circumstances. The use of anthropogenic black soils for agriculture requires great care, because they represent hundreds, if not thousands, of years of prehistoric organic accumulations (Smith 1980). While it has been suggested that each centimeter of anthropogenic black soil represents ten years of occupation, a recent study shows that it also depends on population densities and other edaphic factors (Kern 1988).

Agriculture and Soil Management

The populations of the upland forests have depended upon productive and efficient agriculture. Its efficiency may be a product of many influential factors, among them the impact of missionization, the Directorate introduced after the Jesuits were expelled, the impact of the rubber boom, and recent development activities. What we can observe today is but a poor reflection of the sophisticated systems that must have existed in the pre-Columbian era. Despite these negative influences, in many cases the local systems of agriculture show greater sensitivity to environmental factors than do systems introduced from outside.

The high frequency of acid, nutrient-poor soils must have had a role in the preference for manioc cultivation over so much of the Amazon Basin. Manioc is preadapted to the limitations found in the lowland tropics. The plant expanded from South America in 1540 and has become a pantropical staple because of its capacity to produce impressive yields in the worst of soils. The lack of protein in manioc requires that its cultivators find animal sources of protein to ensure an adequate diet. By and large, native Amazonians successfully achieved this balance; there are no records of any observer suggesting caloric or nutrient deficiency among Amazonian populations, except in cases when their subsistence system and health have been negatively affected by outsiders. The advantage of manioc is that its cuttings are easy to transport when villages must be moved to ensure the productivity of hunting, and the crop will produce in any soil that is not waterlogged. In this manner, two basic problems faced by native populations were resolved: how to escape from enemies (whether European or not) and how to deal with the probability of having to cultivate acid, nutrient-poor soils (Moran 1989).

In some cases the populations were able to remain somewhat isolated in areas of relatively fertile soils. Thus, the population was able to achieve a more detailed understanding of soil/crop management and to develop a greater dependence on corn than on manioc. More common, however, is a pattern where the population adjusted to needing to move and to having an agriculture largely dependent on manioc for up to 90 percent of calories, in which intensive soil management played a lesser role. But exceptions abound. The Assuriní and Araweté try to locate near anthropogenic black soils. Hecht and Posey (1989) showed how detailed the knowledge of the Kayapó is with regard to the selection and management of soils. Even the caboclos, or Amazonian peasants, who are said to have a more generalized and less detailed knowledge of the environment than Indians (Redford and Robinson 1987), have been shown to have ethnoecological criteria based on vegetational indicators for excellent soils with pH above 6.0, near-absence of aluminum saturation, and high nutrient levels (Moran 1977, 1981, and fig. 20). The soils they could identify occur in less than 8 percent of the region and suggest just how accurate their criteria could be. In contrast, the criteria used by outsiders failed to identify these rare high-quality soils (Moran 1977).

The common pattern of indigenous agriculture is to cultivate individual swiddens of less than 2 hectares per household. The pattern of slash-and-burn as traditionally practiced by native populations was able to maintain a balance in the stocks of nitrogen in the ecosystem. In one study the total stock of nitrogen in the forest was 5,354 kilograms per hectare. The burn consumed the dry leaves and volatilized the nitrogen in them (143 kilograms per hectare). This would constitute a loss of less than 3 percent of the stock of nitrogen. The majority of the tree trunks are not consumed by the fire

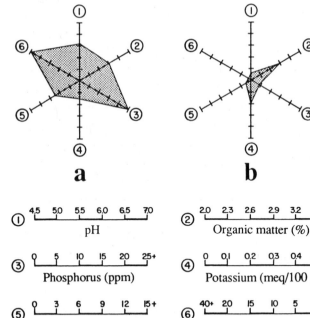

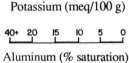

a. Forest Vegetation Indicative of Good Agricultural Soils

Local Term	Scientific Name
Pau d'arco or ipé (yellow variety)	Tabebuia serratifolia
Pau d'arco or ipé (purple variety)	Tabebuia vilaceae
Faveira	Piptadenia spp.
Mororó	Bauhinia spp.
Maxarimbé	Emmotum spp.
Pinheiro preto	(unidentified)
Babaçú	Orbignya phalerata
Açaí	Euterpe oleracea

b. Forest Vegetation Indicative of Poor Agricultural Soils

Local Term	Scientific Name
Acapú	Vouacapoua americana
Jarana	Holopyxidium jarana
Sumaúma	Ceiba pentandra
Melancieira	Alexa grandiflora
Sapucaia	Lecythis paraensis
Piquí	Caryocar microcarpum
Cajú-Açú	Anacardium giganteum
Massaranduba	Manilkara huberi (or Mimusops huberi)

Figure 20. Species of vegetation indicative of good and poor soils for agriculture identified by Amazonian caboclos (from Moran 1977).

and are gradually decomposed over a ten-year period. Of the original stock, 392 kilograms per hectare are lost as a result of the harvesting of crops, denitrification, and leaching (Jordan et al. n.d.). The very low losses due to denitrification in the area studied were the result of the high tannin content of that particular forest and may not reflect what happens elsewhere. The losses to the ecosystem were almost wholly compensated by the contribution made by rainfall and the fixing of nitrogen by leguminous plants. Losses of nitrogen were about 5 percent per year—one-third lost in the harvest, one-third through leaching, and one-third through denitrification. The nitrogen in the soil remained stable during the three years in which the area was studied, due in no small part to the contribution made by the trunks and other components that had not burned completely (which are substantial). After three years of cultivation the stock of nitrogen was 4,492 kilograms per hectare (ibid.).

The effect of burning on the upland forest deserves attention. In one area studied in the Venezuelan Amazon, the temperature on the soil surface varied between 67 and 310 degrees C, with a mean of 140 degrees. The temperature was 48 to 199 degrees C 1 centimeter below the soil surface, with a mean of 80 degrees. Burning effectively eliminated sprouting by plants that were in the forest at the time of the burn (Uhl and Clark 1983)—only one sprout out of 6.4 sprouts per square meter survived the burn. The burn also slows down the return of the successional forest: of the 752 seeds per square meter in the forest before the burn, only 157 survived the burn well enough to germinate (ibid.). The "hotter" the burn, the more complete will be the retardant effect of the burn upon sprouting by forest species and other vegetation (including weeds)—thereby enhancing the success of the cultivated plants. Mistakes in the burn result in greater weed invasion, greater pest invasion of cultivated areas, and fewer nutrients available. In general the invading plants will be better adapted to the environment than the cultivated plants and will reduce yields unless retarded by the burn. The practice of "reburning," or coivara, observed among some contemporary populations, is the result of a failed burn and rarely pays the labor invested in it. Better to sharecrop in someone else's good burn than to struggle against such odds. In the area studied by Uhl and Clark (1983), after two years of cultivation the seed stock was 1,000 per square meter—greater even than in the original forest—and was dominated by aggressive grasses.

Swiddens in upland forests are dominated by the cultivation of manioc (*Manihot esculenta*). Much smaller amounts of pineapples, cashews, sweet potatoes, bananas, peanuts, taro, cotton, tobacco, peppers, and various fruits are also found. Manioc produces enormous quantities of calories for each unit invested (nearly fifteen for each calorie spent in its production), and even per unit of land (with yields in the uplands of between 7 and 12 tons per hectare, without fertilizers). This efficiency is due in part to the plant and also to the small size of the swiddens cleared, which permits careful underclearing and cutting of the forest and effective burning. As swiddens grow larger in size, there is generally a decline in the input/output ratio and perhaps even in productivity per unit of land.

Manioc offers many advantages over other crops in those parts of Amazonia with poor soils. Those who try to change the staple crop must, inevitably, be aware of the high cost they will have to pay in soil correction through fertilization, in pesticides and herbicides, and in protection from the fungal diseases that have persistently decimated common bean production in the eastern Amazon (Corrêa 1982).

Galvão (1963), in his discussion of indigenous horticulture, presented a map in which he identified the presence of patches of corn cultivators in a sea of manioc cultivators; the patches correspond remarkably with the patches of alfisols evident in the FAO soil map, and the rest with the dominant oxisols and ultisols. Among the populations of Rondônia, like the Suruí and the Nambiquara, and in areas of the Lower Xingú and Tocantins we find an agriculture quite appropriate to the less acid and more fertile soils of those patches of upland forests.

The Suruí swiddens, for example, average 1 hectare in total area and are planted preferentially with corn. Three varieties are planted, one to cook in a number of ways and two for popcorn. Sweet potato, *Dioscorea*, and other root crops are intercropped with the corn, creating an excellent soil cover. Peanuts are also associated with sweet manioc at the edges of gardens, ensuring a supply of nitrogen at the edges where the burning may have been less complete. Nonedible plants such as cotton and tobacco are also planted near the forest.

Each day women travel to the swiddens; by ten in the morning they are ready to bring to the village an average of 20 kilos of produce to be prepared for the day's meal. The agricultural calendar (fig. 21) of the Suruí begins in June and lasts to August with the cutting and burning of new gardens. From August to October the area is planted with corn when the rains begin. By December the green corn is ready to be harvested and is associated with feasts and the preparation of fermented drink. From March to June the corn dries. Sweet manioc is used year-round, except during the green corn period.

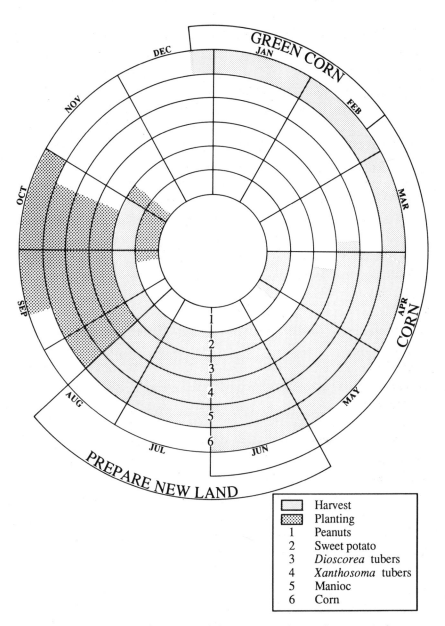

Figure 21. Agricultural calendar of the Suruí Indians (from Coimbra 1989).

In the dry season greater consumption of root crops and peanuts takes place (Coimbra 1989: 63–69).

Hunting, Fishing, and Collecting

It is not easy to generalize about the collecting done by native Amazonians, given the variation in habitats within the upland forests. One form of intervention is the modification of the habitat, as seen earlier in the chapter. Among the Suruí, the fruits and larvae of insects are articles of considerable significance. Also highly valued are Brazil nuts consumed fresh and mixed with root crops, beef, and fish. Most fresh fruits are consumed immediately, and only some are brought to the village (e.g., *Inga* sp., *muiratinga* [*Perebea mollis*], and *bacurí* [*Rheedia*]).

The larvae that grow in the *babaçú* groves, of the family Bruchidae, make a notable contribution; for example, *Pachymerus cardo* and *Cariobruchus* are consumed directly or mixed in corn soups. On the collecting trips a family may live off the larvae in a *babaçú* grove and the game that comes to the grove for over a week (Coimbra 1984). Some of the other species consumed belong to the family Curculionidae (e.g., *Rhynchophorus palmarum* and *Rhina barbirostris*), which grow in rotting wood. These larvae are managed: the Suruí cut trees with full knowledge that they attract insects and return in two or three months to collect the larvae. Consumption of ants of the genus *Atta* is also common. During swarming, enormous quantities of ants are consumed.

Honey consumption is another aspect that makes collecting such a valued activity. The honey of stingless bees (family Apidae, subfamily Meliponinae) is collected, cutting the tree where they have made their hive. Everything is consumed—the honey and the larvae—and the wax is saved for decorations and other uses (see Posey 1986a and his other articles on stingless bees).

Fishing is an important source of protein for the Suruí. In general, Amazonian populations depend far more on fishing than is commonly acknowledged. Fishing is more efficient and productive than hunting in many regions (table 5), except during the rainy season, when the increased volume of water and river turbidity make fishing less successful than hunting. For household consumption it is common to depend on the bow and arrow or the use of piscicides (*timbó*: *Derris* sp., *Caryocar glabrum*, *Clibadium sylvestre*, *Euphorbia cotinifolia*, *Lonchocarpus urucu*, *Phyllanthus brasiliensis*, and *Ryania speciosa*; see Prance 1986). The vines of these piscicides are cut in pieces and then beaten with heavy sticks, producing a

Table 5. *Mean Returns from Hunting and Fishing*

	Fishing g/work-hour	Hunting g/work-hour	Source
Pumé	405	810	Gragson 1989
Barí	350	135	Beckerman 1980
Shipibo	1140	1600	Bergman 1980
Bororo	680	200	Werner et al. 1979
Xavante	400	400	Ibid.
Mekranotí Kayapó	200	690	Ibid.
Kanela	50	110	Ibid.
Siona Secoya	675–1000	3,200	Vickers 1976

Source: Adapted from Beckerman 1989: 12, 18.

foam that brings about the asphyxiation of the fish, which float to the surface and are easy pickings. Both men and women take part in this kind of fishing. The most important fish for the Suruí are the piranhas (*Pygocentrus* sp. and *Serrasalmus* sp.), *pacús* (*Mylossema* sp. and *Myleus* sp.), *piau* (*Leporinus* sp.), *surubim* (*Pseudoplatystoma* sp.), and *mandis* (fam. Pimelodidae). Given the richness of fish species in Amazonia, the varieties on which any given population may depend will vary based upon frequency, spawning behavior, and human pressure on the resource. Fish runs in Amazonia have not received the attention they deserve and are important in regional terms, since they are associated with feasting and alliance formation.

Among the Suruí twelve mammal species and seven bird species are frequently hunted and consumed. As is the case among many other groups, hunting is an activity restricted to men. Suruí prefer to hunt alone, instead of in groups. Occasionally brothers and affines will hunt together; in those cases they may go out for as long as a week before returning to the village. The organization of hunting groups and their relation to other social units in a society deserve more attention than heretofore received. Meat not consumed immediately is smoked in order to preserve it. The preferred meats are those of the monkey *Ateles* sp. and peccaries. A dish that is highly appreciated is made with a mixture of peccary meat and Brazil nuts (*morsai*) and is used as a concentrated food during long trips.

Management of Secondary Succession

What is the impact of swidden cultivation on upland forests? After three years of cultivation the stock of nutrients in the soil is relatively stable but the loss of nutrients contributed by the burn can be fast, with as much as 70 percent of the potassium lost and almost all the phosphorus leaching within the first year. The rate of leaching will depend a great deal on the level of organic matter in the soil, the degree of infiltration of rains through the canopy of the crop, how well the soil was protected until the plants grew their canopy, the cation exchange capacity of the soil, and the demands made by the crops planted (cf. Dantas 1988; Balée and Gely 1989; Denich 1991). A great deal remains to be known about management which can reduce losses of these nutrients to ensure that at the end of cultivation the area is not so poor that the return of forest is slowed down.

The ability of secondary successional species to grow rapidly in soils too poor to support domesticated crops has always intrigued observers of the Amazon. In general, it seems that successional species have a greater proportion of their biomass in the root component, which can explore a larger area than plants with more restricted root systems: they sometimes have deeper roots because of their lower susceptibility to the limiting effects of high levels of aluminum saturation and can therefore explore a larger and deeper soil environment.

The process of secondary succession has in some cases been improved upon by native populations—not only by their promotion of succession itself but by making this return economically beneficial to the human population. A very common practice has been to intercrop fruit trees together with annual crops in a swidden. When it is time to abandon the swidden, so to speak, the fruit trees are just going into production and remain productive for several years, providing foods of considerable value. These fruit trees protect the soil as well as native trees and offer a nurturing environment for the species of the mature forest, which are reintroduced by the fruit-eating bats which visit the orchards. These practices simulate the role, for example, of *Cecropia*, a dominant in the early successional process which provides shade for slower-growing mature trees. Uhl and Clark (1983) found nine times more seeds of mature forest species in the soils around the fruit orchards than in areas where grass or no fruit trees had been planted. The principal dispersal agents in the forest are fruit-eating birds and bats, both of which visit the orchards to consume the fruits and deposit the seeds from forest areas in the orchard as they eat. The microenvironment underneath the orchard is more favorable from the point of view of temperature, light, and nutrients than that of more open areas. How densely such orchards are planted varies among populations in Amazonia and may depend on their pattern of mobility and territoriality. Recent invasions by colonists and ranchers into indigenous territories have had the indirect effect of discouraging the maintenance of long-term strategies based on the assumption of someday reaping the benefits of their planting efforts.

Social Organization, Demography, Health, and Nutrition

It is not easy to generalize about social organization, demography, health, and nutrition of the diverse populations inhabiting the upland forests of the Amazon. Some groups have begun to grow again numerically and are showing signs of vigor not only in their health but also in their political savvy. Others have been much less successful in putting aside old complaints against neighboring groups for the sake of confronting the threat posed by ranchers, colonists, and miners. Much of the difference is traceable to their different histories of interethnic contact, the trajectory of their demographic collapse and recuperation, and their ability to make linkages with external and sympathetic organizations.

Most populations of the Amazon have had to make modifications in their social organization as a result of the experience of depopulation through epidemic disease. More than 75 percent of the Suruí died in the first decade of contact, a fact still evident today in their age-sex pyramids (fig. 4). In 1974 one can see the shortening of the 0 to 4 age group as well as that of adults between the ages of 35 and 40 (fig. 2). Only 200 Suruí survived the initial impact of epidemic disease brought by interethnic contact with national society. A decade later, it was already possible to see signs of demographic catch-up (fig. 4). Between 1979 and 1988 the growth rates have been 5.4 to 5.6 percent, which permits the population to double every fourteen years. Such a demographic experience has taken place among many Amazonian populations, unfortunately not recorded with the detail available for the Suruí. While it is necessary to study the sociology of indigenous societies, this information is not sufficient to understand their social organization, subsistence, and other sociological dimensions fully. We must also study the process of organization, reorganization, and the dynamic demographic responses to changes in circumstances if we are to interpret any time-based observation.

The rapid growth of the population following the epidemics was not a product purely of biological potential but required modifications in the systems of marriage, clan affiliation, traditional forms of population control (e.g., sexual abstinence after giving birth, the couvade, which obligated the father of the child born not to have sexual relations with any woman until the child could walk). While such practices may have had value at one time, they have negative consequences under conditions of decimation and threat of biological extinction. The traditional practice ensured that the newborn could breast-feed as long as possible and that competition with a newborn would not occur too early. It is not uncommon in lowland South America as in many other populations for a child to breast-feed for several years after birth. The use of medicinal plants to control fecundity has been discontinued as families try to maximize reproductive rates rather than reduce total fertility (Coimbra 1989: 125).

The child mortality rate among the Suruí is high: 232 per 1,000 births. Thus, 23 percent of all those born die in the first year of life. In part this is due to congenital problems and in part to prevalent environmental conditions which could be eliminated if greater medical attention and better maternal nutrition were available. More than half of the child mortality among indigenous Amazonian populations could be prevented by adequate medical attention.

The rapid increase in the young population, which is a positive response to the danger of extinction, has a down side in terms of the burden it places on the small number of adults to provide adequately for a large dependent population. This has been made even more difficult by the decline in subsistence agriculture encouraged by FUNAI as it promoted coffee growing among the Suruí.

The social organization of the Suruí has changed with the demographic changes. The sexual division of labor common in Amazonian native societies leads to a high degree of complementarity. For example, a single Suruí male or a widower could not possibly prepare a swidden because he would lack a wife to collect the produce and prepare the products into a meal. Suruí social organization depends upon a system of marriage in which four exogamic patrilineal groups exchange spouses. The preference to marry cross-cousins leads to exchange of women every two generations. With depopulation a problem arises: how to obtain acceptable mates within the rules of marriage. The Suruí invented a new clan (Kaban), which, because of inherent contradictions in its origin, allowed those who claimed membership in it to marry any of the other three clans. The Kaban clan was responsible in recent years for 89.8 percent of all marriages observed (Coimbra 1989: 145).

Shapiro (1968) observed a different form of reorganization among the Tapirapé as they came out of their decimation and near extinction. By modifying the traditional structure of marriage, without negating the clan structure, they have been able to continue polygamous marriages, considered a fundamental institution in terms of maintaining patterns of social and political leadership. While they sacrificed the "purity" of one structural dimension, they guaranteed the continuity of more fundamental aspects of their organization. Even this notable invention did not entirely solve the problem of finding mates quickly enough. Some young men have responded by mixing the traditional and the modern. Several have married women of other ethnic groups and even married women belonging to Brazilian society.

None of the epidemiologic or nutritional studies has truly confronted the ecological diversity of Amazonia to date as they explain observable processes. Therefore, studies comparing the nutritional status of populations on nutrient-poor ecosystems like those of the Rio Negro with populations on alfisols cultivating corn are needed to assess the relative role of environment, history, and epidemiology of Amazonian populations (Moran 1991). Studies comparing populations living in poorly drained areas, and therefore with greater malarial potential, with populations in well-drained soils and with those where slope is important can further allow us to determine just how critical certain variables may be or how unimportant to biological or social outcomes.

Conclusions

The upland forests have great biotic diversity, a richness that will be increasingly valuable in the future, but which has sometimes been resisted by human populations because it made the search for food more complicated and uncertain. The diversity and endemism of the forests make it difficult to select swidden areas, given the lack of well-known indicators of the best areas for agriculture where endemics prevail. The effect of native Amazonians on upland forest has been to promote biotic diversity, through the creation of miniforests or groves with a high concentration of useful plants that mimic the natural gaps within rain and moist forests believed to cause the biodiversity currently present. The Amazonian populations did so in ingenious ways: creating anthropogenic forests that would make identification of favorable areas easier for future generations. This process need not have occurred in a conscious fashion. In all probability it was unintentional. But it came from careful observation of nature, from understanding the behavior of birds and bats in seed dispersal, from knowing which stingless bees were important to Brazil nut flowers for production and which palms responded well to management and fire—and how gaps created by treefalls are colonized by pioneer species. In some cases the management practices of past generations was embedded in myth, through which the origin of plants was explained. In this process each generation had the challenge and the opportunity either to balance the natural diversity of the forests with the needs of the human population or to neglect such management. In this task the native populations have been far more faithful than recent arrivals in Amazonia.

In Brazil's upland forests, the populations seem to have generally preferred liana forests because of their association with alfisols and anthropogenic black soils and their richness in useful materials. In the Upper Amazon, other types of forests with concentrations of useful plants may have also been encouraged by gradual selection. In the proximity of villages groves of palm forest, Brazil nuts, and bamboo were sometimes created as islands of resources in a sea of diversity. These areas of resource concentration were not generally created on the better soils (which were preserved for cultivation of swiddens), in contrast to recent practice by the national society that built towns, roads, and seeded with pastures some of the finest soils in Amazonia, while giving settlers land of poor quality to cultivate (Moran 1981).

The anthropogenic forests not only produce useful food and fiber but also attract wild game, thereby reducing the labor costs of hunting (Kiltie 1980; Sponsel 1986). The creation of these miniforests is equivalent to creating transitional zones wherein smaller mammals and other small animals thrive. Some of these areas are quite extensive, as in the case of *babaçú* palm forests (Anderson, May, and Balick 1991).

The general model of upland forest populations, described as hunter/collectors who moved often and subsisted on poor soils (Meggers 1971), applies, in fact, to the majority of cases—but not to all. In this chapter I have tried to show that the limiting factors of the upland forest can be managed by contemporary populations, just as they have been managed by many native Amazonians with remarkable savvy and success despite the devastating impact of colonialism and epidemic disease. Their knowledge of how to confront the diversity of the upland forest and balance human needs with the need to conserve its biotic richness must serve as a guide to future action.

4

Floodplains

Classifying an area as a floodplain can mislead us either to overestimate or to underestimate the agricultural and biological potential of these ecosystems. Any discussion about the human adaptive strategies found in Amazonian floodplains must differentiate, minimally, between three types of floodplains or várzeas: the upper floodplain, the lower floodplain, and the estuary. There are important differences in the flora, fauna, alluvium, steepness, altitude, soil acidity, and biomass production in these three types of floodplains. These differences translate into differential use and conservation of these distinct landscapes by human populations. All floodplains share some common traits—among them, the cycles of flooding—that in turn influence the flora, fauna, and strategies of human populations. Figure 22 illustrates the location of these major floodplain types in Amazonia.

Attention to these differences has been rare. Even such a fine and sophisticated analyst as Lathrap (1970) in his classic book *The Upper Amazon* seemed to lump together the characteristics of the Upper Amazon with those of the Lower Amazon and the estuary in describing the environment and cultures of the Upper Amazon. He noted that populations occupied areas of the floodplain in the Upper Amazon long ago (ca. 4000 B.P.) along the Ucayali (1970: 84–85). These dates have now been surpassed by more recent archaeological research, which suggests human occupation going back to 12,000 B.P. (Roosevelt 1991).

The growth of human populations in the floodplains of Amazonia resulted in notable migrations throughout the basin. Many of these are noted in Lathrap's book (1970) and related to competition over scarce good soils. On occasion, too, Amazonian populations seem to have modified the environment in an effort to overcome this problem. Our best evidence of this effort to date comes from the artificial farmlands created by prehistoric populations in the Llanos de Mojos (Denevan 1966). Denevan estimated that there were at least 100,000 linear raised fields covering at least 15,000 acres in the Mojos region. These raised fields follow the form of parallel point-bar formations such as may be found in the floodplains of major rivers and apparently sought to reproduce the conditions present in limited areas of riverine floodplains in upland areas (Lathrap 1970: 161). By digging ditches and mounding up the soil, it was possible to bring the more fertile soils to the surface, to retain the water longer as the floods receded, and to have year-round cultivation even during the flooding period.

Considering the magnitude of the Amazon Basin, the restricted areal extent of the floodplain is remarkable indeed, amounting to not much more than 2 percent of the whole basin (or less than 80,000 square kilometers).

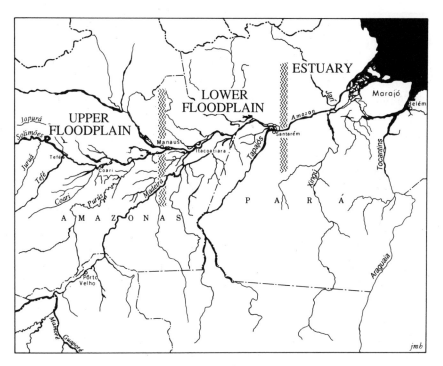

Figure 22. Map of the floodplains of the Amazon Basin.

The rivers coming down from the Andes cut through the eastern ranges of the Andes in steep-sided canyons 2,000 meters deep or more. The river commonly occupies the whole canyon and only rarely develops moderate expanses of floodplain. Only the Marañón and the Huallaga have significant areas of alluvial floodplain (Lathrap 1970: 28). Once they have gotten through the eastern escarpment, the rivers become the meandering courses that we associate with the Upper Amazon. The active floodplain of these rivers suddenly ranges from 10 to 80 kilometers in width. As the river overflows each year, it gradually changes course, and the old channel becomes a crescent-shaped expanse of open water known as an oxbow lake. The floodplain of the Upper Amazon is composed of a network of oxbow lakes, some new, some old. These processes are so powerful that they can occur in less than a generation. During flood stage, the river dumps its alluvium onto the land adjacent to the course so that natural levees are built up. The ridges of sediment formed, called point-bars, can be as regular as the ridges on a ploughed field (Lathrap 1970: 29) and are covered with increasingly mature vegetation with increases in distance from the riverbank. Levees and point-bars are the preferred sites for human populations in the Upper Amazon floodplain, according to Lathrap. Where the Ucayali and the Marañón join, the Amazon stops meandering and assumes a straighter course that grows increasingly unified as it progresses toward the mouth. As it does, the complexity of biotopes decreases and the riverbanks become more important for agriculture with more stable levees.

Because of the decimation of native Amazonians in the period of the conquest, we must rely today on caboclos and other riverine peasant populations for much of our understanding of indigenous resource use in this habitat—with the exception perhaps of the Tikuna of the upper Solimões—and on the new archaeological data being generated in recent years (Roosevelt 1980, 1989, 1991). Contemporary riverine populations are the heirs to the expertise of native Amazonians, having made their home in this zone and managing to subsist using native forms of resource use and coping with the exploitative relations of exchange with dominant external groups (Wagley 1953; Moran 1974; Parker 1985; Anderson 1990).

The most important environmental pressures felt by the populations of the floodplains have been the hydrological conditions, especially the fluctuations in river level, the seasonal variation in fish availability, and the environmental mosaics found therein. These pressures are at the same time opportunities and limiting factors. The application of appropriate techniques that effectively respond to these pressures can sustain sizable populations, whether "isolated," grouped into small villages, or found in large towns such as have been described for the time of contact with the Europeans.

Characterization of the Environment

The Upper Floodplain

The upper floodplain is a variable ecosystem, enriched by the alluvium coming from the Andes, as well as having less favorable areas from parts of the Andes with poorer parent materials—contradicting one of the common assumptions made about the pervasive high fertility of Amazonian floodplains. These highly diverse ecosystems are largely equivalent to what is sometimes called the Upper Amazon. Future studies by anthropologists, biologists, geographers, and agronomists will need to specify in much greater detail the qualities of the alluvium found in the Upper Amazon to be able to interpret the potential of each area adequately. The Upper Amazon also presents problems of steepness and altitude that have received little attention. The importance of taking these factors into account comes from the

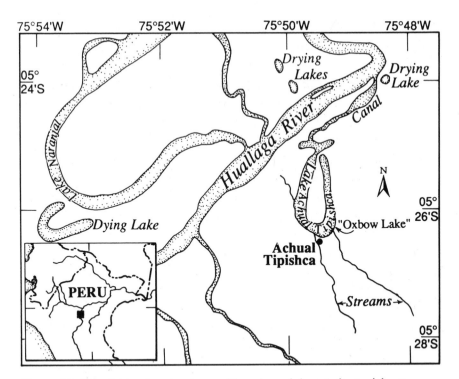

Figure 23. Dendritic river system with oxbow lakes (adapted from Stocks 1983: 249).

greater difficulty entailed in the management of soils on steep slopes and the lower biomass production that is sometimes associated with increases in altitude. Likewise, the presence of more dendritic river systems in the Upper Amazon creates much larger swampy areas, with a greater variety of biotopes than in the Lower Amazon.

Because the floodplains of the Upper Amazon are richer in biotopes than those of the Lower Amazon, as a function of the dendritic patterns of rivers like the Ucayali, the Purús, and others that have numerous meanders and oxbow lakes (fig. 23), they are rich in an infinity of microhabitats with many opportunities for resource use by human populations. The potential is greater in parts of these systems for much higher population densities, especially in the whitewater rivers, because of the high productivity of fish biomass that can easily be captured in the numerous lakes that dry up seasonally. This, however, does not apply to the floodplains in blackwater rivers, as we saw in chapter 2.

The ecological conditions of the upper floodplain vary in accordance with the geological origin of the sediments that are deposited. A recent study concluded that the soils of the Upper Amazon in Peru have physical and chemical properties very different from one another. The soils that result from the deposition of the rivers that originate in the eastern sierra of Peru (e.g., the Mayo River) have a higher pH (6.5 to 8.5) and a higher nutrient content. In contrast, the soils that derive from the calcareous deposits of the Andes of Ecuador and Peru (e.g., the Cashiboya River) are somewhat acid, with a pH between 5.0 and 6.5, but do not present any serious problems in terms of nutrient availability. Much different from either of these two drainages are those areas with alluvial soils originating from the eastern escarpments of the Peruvian Amazon (e.g., the Javarí River), which are very acid, with a pH of 4.0 to 5.0 and with aluminum saturation above 85 percent (Hoag et al. 1987: 78–79).

The Lower Floodplain

Estimates of the areal extent of the Lower Amazon vary considerably. In the Brazilian Amazon the lower floodplain has a width of between 20 and 100 kilometers, and its total area was estimated by Camargo (1958: 17) to be 64,400 square kilometers, corresponding to 1.6 percent of the total area of the drainage basin. The level of flooding varies a great deal, with a height of 10 to 20 meters being common. Most of the substantial populations live above this level of seasonal flooding, that is, on the levees which rarely flood.

The floodplain is characterized by great morphological dynamism, with rivers continually changing course, modifying the landscape, and even making whole portions of land disappear in one place and depositing the sediments elsewhere downstream. The deposition of sediments in the middle course of the river leads to the formation of levees, several meters above the average range of flooding (Sternberg 1975: 17–18). Behind these levees lakes are created, some small and others reaching very large dimensions (Junk 1970: 453). The result is the formation of microhabitats with great biotic diversity (fig. 24). The rhythm of the floods, year after year, influences everything and impresses by its sheer magnitude. The area drained by the Amazon Basin is 6,000,000 square kilometers, capturing 20 percent of the total potable water on the planet.

Rivers in the Lower Amazon have various forms. Some have few meanders but numerous islands on their courses, while rivers like the Madeira, Xingú, and Tapajós have reduced floodplains and are relatively linear (Goulding 1981: 17–21). The rivers also influence the development of the landscape by cutting canals, islands, levees, streams, and beaches. The result

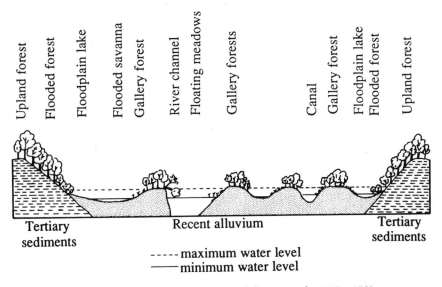

Figure 24. Floodplain biotopes (adapted from Junk 1970: 452).

of these river cycles and their movement is a constant modification of the elements of the landscape (Denevan 1984).

The variation in river levels influences the vegetation along the flood-plains. From September to January large areas become dry, while between February and July they are covered by 10 to 20 meters of water. At Manaus the mean flood level reaches 27 meters above sea level, and the river goes down to 18 meters above sea level in the dry season. Along the principal channel of the Amazon the fluctuations in river level are minimal because the north affluents have their wet season in the season opposite to the south-side affluents, thereby stabilizing the total effect of the floods along this channel. In specific rivers, by contrast, the fluctuation can be significant even in terms of particular heavy rains upriver. Some of the plants have the ca-pacity to resist flooding and to reappear in the dry period, while others invade areas beyond the flood with the help of birds, wind, and other agents of dispersal. Because of the poor transparency of whitewater rivers, few spe-cies of plants are purely aquatic.

In the Middle Amazon, where the lower floodplain clearly starts, one finds a floating vegetation associated with clear and whitewater rivers. This vegetation does not occur in blackwater areas (Sioli 1975: 483). Junk (1970) differentiated among three types of biotopes in the lower floodplain: sedimentation zones, floodplain lakes with great fluctuations in water level, and lakes with small fluctuations in water level. In the sedimentation zones of the Solimões and Amazon rivers and in lakes with great fluctuations in water level, the dominant species of floating vegetation are *Paspalum fasciculatum, Paspalum repens (canarana rasteira)*, and *Echinochloa polystachya (canarana fluvial)*. In floodplain lakes with small fluctuations in water level the dominant species are *Leersia hexandra, Scirpus cubensis*, and *Paspalum repens* (Junk 1970: 492). Figure 25 illustrates the types of vegetation associated with floodplain lakes. Of these the most biologically productive are the lakes with large fluctuations in water level, with a mean of 200,000 individuals per square meter of aquatic fauna and a biomass of 2.5 to 11.6 grams per square meter (ibid.). Some of the species of aquatic grasses formed "floating islands" up to 1 meter in depth, but here the aquatic fauna is impoverished because of the anaerobic condition of these islands (Sioli 1975: 485). *Eichhornia, Pistia*, and *Salvinia* are some of the genera found in aquatic vegetations (Fittkau et al. 1975). When the floods recede, a portion of this vegetation dries up or enters the river channels. In areas with sufficient water, the floating vegetation and the phytoplankton associated with it survive the low river levels. In between the roots of this vegetation lives a more varied and diverse aquatic fauna, in terms of taxonomic groups and number of individuals, than in any other area of the Amazon (Sioli 1975: 483). The *pirarucú (Arapaima gigas)*, one of the greatest fish in the Amazon River, is frequently found near these floating meadows, where the inhabitants of the floodplain are accustomed to fish for it (Junk 1970: 450). The presence of these floating meadows also influences the course of river travel: canoes get caught in the plants, and fishers use these areas for safe harbor when sudden storms brew up while they are away from shore (ibid.).

The floating grasses of the Amazon have considerable ecological importance (Black 1950). The genus *Paspalum* takes one form when it occurs in terrestrial ecosystems and a different form in flooded areas. With flooding, this genus develops a root system that floats in the water, reaches 80 centimeters in length without contact with the bottom, and develops very rapidly. The roots function like filters of the inorganic matter present in the waters. In floodplain lakes the system of roots also seems to capture organic matter and has a biomass of three to five times greater than when it occurs elsewhere. The productivity of *Paspalum repens (canarana rasteira)* in floodplain lakes was estimated to be in excess of 6 metric tons (dry weight) per hectare per year (Fittkau et al. 1975). *Paspalum* and other floating vegeta-

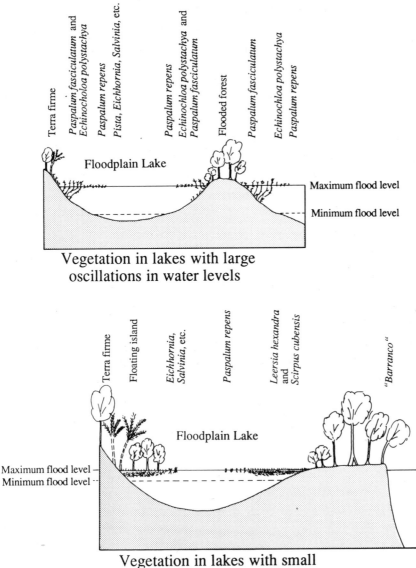

Figure 25. Vegetation in floodplain lakes with large oscillations in water levels (above) and with small oscillations in water levels (below) (adapted from Junk 1970: 457).

tion are important sources of food for cattle, as well as fish, especially in the periods of flooding when the feeding range of the cattle is restricted.

Echinochloa polystachya (*canarana fluvial* or *capim de Angola*) and *Paspalum repens* represent 80 to 90 percent of all the floating grasses along the Amazon River and in floodplain lakes (Junk 1970: 464). Generally, *Echinochloa* is rooted to the edge of the river or lake, while *Paspalum* floats freely in even the deepest water (see fig. 25). *Echinochloa* needs a dry period of rooting to the mineral soil to develop, while *Paspalum* can exist in permanent lakes where it never has direct contact with the soil.

Leersia hexandra (*ceneuaua* or *capim peripomongo*) occurs throughout the South American tropics. At Marajó Island it is associated with *Montrichardia arborescens*, *Gynerium sagittatum*, and *Cyperus giganteus* in shallow lakes (mondongos) that are nothing more than muddy depressions on the landscape (Miranda 1907). *Scirpus cubensis* occurs in association with *Leersia hexandra*, suggesting a similar ecology. The two grasses are important elements in the formation of floating islands. Floating islands also occur in the floodplain, generally associated with *Paspalum*, *Echinochloa polystachya*, *Carex*, and *Scirpus*. These islands decompose slowly and form deep shelves that are commonly referred to as floating islands when they reach 1 meter in thickness, in which sizable trees, like *Cecropia*, *Bombax munguba*, and *Cassia grandis*, can take root and grow.

Between the Xingú and Manaus and the Lower Madeira River, the typical vegetation is grasses such as *canarana*. This type of floodplain is characterized by the presence of narrow strips of forest in the levees. Behind these high areas we find floodplain grasslands dominated by *canarana*. Some of these areas are floodplain lakes in the wet season, transforming to savannas in the dry period (Pires and Prance 1985: 130). This vegetation is also of great importance for the cattle that feed on it in the period of floods and during the worst of the dry season when many of the lakes disappear.

Another vegetation of considerable significance in the floodplains is the flooded forests. The flooded forests occurring in whitewater rivers are known in Brazil as igapós (Pires and Prance 1985: 131). These are areas favored by fish for spawning and gaining weight seasonally during the high flood period (Goulding 1979, 1981). The fruits produced by the tree vegetation are an important source of food for the fisheries, especially for some of the larger fish such as *tambaqui* (*Colossoma macropomum*), a frugivore. The caboclos in the floodplain know the behavior of this species of fish and imitate the sound of the falling fruit on the water surface to attract them near their boats (Veríssimo 1895).

The lower floodplain is characterized more by opportunities than by constraints and approximates the common stereotype of the floodplain in most people's minds: soils rich in nutrients, with pH between 7.0 and 8.5, with a high biomass of fish (Junk 1984: 215). The greatest environmental pressure comes from the fluctuations in the river level, with flooding much higher than in the Upper Amazon due to increased volume of water and greater flatness in the Amazon plain. Within this environment one finds both horizontal and vertical zonation, recognized by the inhabitants of the floodplains and of great value in the exploitation of the resources of this rich habitat. Its rich potential has not been realized to this day in Amazonia in the historical period but seems to have been developed among some pre-Columbian societies and can be inferred from the experience of the Asian tropics, where the cultivation of paddy rice in the floodplain produces food for millions of people. But such a potential can only be realized by great investments in labor and/or capital in order to control the devastation of the natural floods and take advantage of harnessing the rich alluvium without losing the crops in the process. The greater interest of Latin American states in occupying their Amazonian territories has militated against an appropriate level of investment in research in the areally limited floodplain areas of the Middle and Lower Amazon. In the Peruvian Amazon the production of rice from the upper floodplains already has made that country self-sufficient in rice and provided surpluses for export and beer production.

The Estuary

The estuary goes from the mouth of the Xingú River to Marajó Island, an area estimated at 25,000 square kilometers (Anderson 1990: 66). The estuary differs from the rest of the Lower Amazon in the role played by the tides and the influence of the saline water that enters these areas daily. Archaeological studies suggest that systems of control of the water courses had been developed in pre-Columbian times, especially at Marajó Island (Roosevelt 1989). Nevertheless, a lot more research will be necessary to be certain what hydraulic systems and forms of social organization effectively harnessed the particular ebbs and flows in this region. The depopulation of the basin in the first two centuries of contact eliminated the demographic densities that were probably behind the sustainability of intensive agriculture in this habitat. Much remains to be done to reconstruct the forms of intensive use of this kind of floodplain.

This type of floodplain is formed over clayish soils that present an abundance of palms of a limited number of species adapted to waterlogged conditions. The flooding is most profoundly affected by the tides rather than by the up and down of the river. The estuary fills twice a day, instead of once a year, like most other parts of the Amazon. The plant biomass is extremely high in the estuary, and among the important species found there are: *murumurú* (*Astrocaryum murumuru*), *jupatí* (*Raphia taedigera*), *açaí* (*Euterpe oleracea*), *inajá* (*Maximiliana martiana*), *bacaba* (*Oenocarpus distichus*), *patauá* (*Jessenia bataua*), *buriti* or *miriti* (*Mauritia* sp.), and *ubim* (*Geonoma* sp.).

Research has recently shown that extractive systems in the estuary can be sustainable and quite profitable, especially in areas near towns with demand for these products (Anderson et al. 1985; Anderson and Ioris 1989; Padoch and de Jong 1987) with local populations of up to 48 persons per square kilometer. The plant extractivism practiced by the Amazonian peasants of the estuary yields income several times higher than that prevalent in the rest of the country—within an agroforestry system that shows signs of alteration of the native vegetation over less than 2 percent of the area (Anderson 1990). This is a traditional system of subsistence practiced by caboclos for more than a century (Parker 1985; Moran 1974; Wagley 1974), which has permitted use of the estuary without degrading it. Agriculture is generally less productive and more difficult than extractivism in the estuary (Lima 1956; Anderson and Ioris 1989). The estuary's low plant diversity and the presence of dominants, in comparison to the more common Amazonian pattern of high diversity and an absence of dominants (Anderson and Ioris 1989: 9), are probably due to the prevalent waterlogged conditions of the soils. Lack of soil oxygen may be one of the key limiting factors, and only a few species can thrive under these conditions. Fortunately, many of these species are of economic importance, which permits intensive use of the estuary without having a negative impact on biodiversity. The estuary vegetation is, in fact, in a constant state of secondary succession, because of the frequent treefalls provoked by the flooding, the wind, and the shallowness of the root systems due to impeded drainage. The high concentration of economic plants, regularly fertilized by alluvial deposition, and the successional nature of these forests favor the development of a productive extractive sector.

Adaptive Strategies in the Lower Floodplain

The river fluctuations influence the attitudes of the inhabitants of the floodplains. The instability of riverbanks makes fertile areas near them uncertain for agriculture from year to year and whole fields can suddenly disappear. On the beaches, the population cultivates plants of rapid growth such as corn, beans, peanuts, and rice. Jute and sugarcane are planted more often than not on the levees. In areas not affected by flooding, manioc and bananas predominate, which cannot stand waterlogging (Denevan 1984).

The most important agricultural areas are the natural levees, enriched yearly by alluvium, well-drained, and covered with high forests (Denevan 1976: 215). It has been suggested that these areas could sustain numerous populations because of the renewable fertility of the soils, the richness of the fisheries, and the ease of transportation. Their principal problems are the unpredictable occurrence of floods and the decline in fish catches during the rainy season, when the volume of water makes fishing very difficult.

The richness of the plant biomass attracts many herbivores and insectivores, which constitute an important source of protein for the human population. In these areas one can find the largest fish of the Amazon, known as *pirarucú* in Brazil and as *paiche* in Peru (*Arapaima gigas*). To date, 1,300 species of fish have been identified, and some scholars estimate that the number will surpass 2,000 species (Klinge et al. 1981: 28). The numerous species of turtles are another rich source of food used in the past but unfortunately endangered today due to excessive hunting for commercial purposes. Fishing is the most important source of protein for local populations. Its productivity depends on the nutrients coming from the Andes and from the protection of the flooded forests.

Carvajal and other chroniclers of the early years of exploration indicated that the populations along the banks of the major rivers of the floodplain were numerous and lived in villages that extended for miles (Medina 1934: 198). Denevan (1976: 217–218) estimated that the population of the lower floodplain probably had a density of 8.0 persons per square kilometer in 1651. If we correct this figure for the rate of estimated depopulation of the first century of contact, Denevan estimated a population of no less than 28 persons per square kilometer for the floodplain of the Lower Amazon in 1500.

It is quite likely that the societies of the Middle and Lower Amazon were hierarchically organized, perhaps into inherited chiefdoms, with nobles, slaves, and a lower class. These chiefdoms were in all probability expansionist in nature and capable of organizing expeditions of thousands of warriors. The best known of these are the Omagua (Myers 1989; Porro 1989). They seem to have occupied hundreds of kilometers along the main channel of the Amazon River and to have had commercial relations with distant areas. When the Europeans arrived, the Omagua appear to have been in an expansionist phase, attempting to conquer areas in the Lower Amazon—a process interrupted by the arrival of the Europeans. Roosevelt (1989: 82) suggested that the beginnings of horticulture and ceramic production go back to ca. 8,000 B.P., a date that would make the Amazonian floodplain the area with the oldest evidence for horticulture and ceramics (see also Roosevelt et al. 1992). Unfortunately, evidence is still fragmentary and based upon few sites. Current populations in the lower floodplain are characterized in most cases by extensive, rather than intensive, use of resources and give a limited view of the potential of the region.

The use of resources by local populations gives an idea of the potential present. Frecchione et al. (1989) presented an ethnoecological analysis of the knowledge of caboclos living on Lake Coari in the Middle Amazon. The vertical zonation present is recognized by the population (fig. 26)—they observe the behavior of aquatic birds to predict the changes in water level. When some of these species arrive at the beaches before the waters recede from the neighboring flooded forests, the caboclos say that heavy and continuous rains will shortly occur, thus avoiding planting rice or corn on the beaches and losing the crop to "unexpected" floods.

This zonation is the result of information gathered from one very good informant through detailed interviews. It remains to be tested whether this knowledge is widely shared or restricted—and whether *behavior* by the population locally follows this set of complex cognitive zones. It would be ideal if further research among the population of Lake Coari could be carried out to determine how these zones are variably utilized as a function of time or season, in what order of preference zonal resources are sought, and which are reliable sources versus those enjoyed only rarely due to relative scarcity.

In the lower floodplain the populations generally have greater access to substantial areas of upland forests than do populations in the upper floodplain, where the greater rainfall and river meanders limit the areal extent of nonflooded areas. In an area at a radius of 60 kilometers from Itacoatiara, studied by Smith (1979), 60 percent of the land is not flooded. Thus, agriculture is more important in the upland forests and the lower floodplain and its returns more certain than in either the estuary or the upper floodplain. The importance of a good burn is no less here than in upland forests, with the added advantage that in the floodplain river level may be an accurate indicator of the start of rains upstream and thus of the time for burning

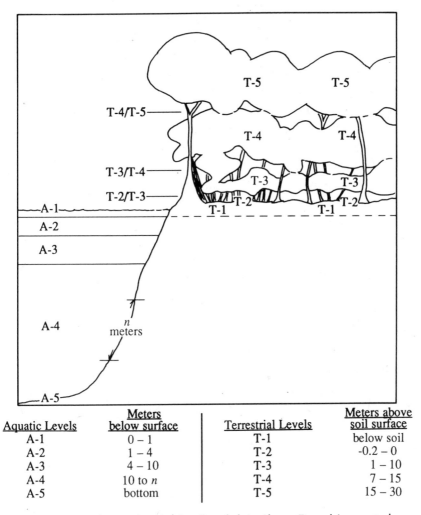

Aquatic Levels	Meters below surface	Terrestrial Levels	Meters above soil surface
A-1	0 – 1	T-1	below soil
A-2	1 – 4	T-2	-0.2 – 0
A-3	4 – 10	T-3	1 – 10
A-4	10 to n	T-4	7 – 15
A-5	bottom	T-5	15 – 30

Figure 26. Vertical zonation in the floodplain (from Frecchione et al. 1989).

swiddens. The rice, manioc, and corn plantations are replaced by fruit trees after two years, and the latter are a favorable habitat for hunting smaller game (Frecchione et al. 1989).

In the floodplain near Itacoatiara islands up to 20 kilometers across are formed. Side streams known as paranás commonly occur around islands. Many of these are ephemeral in nature, sometimes becoming clogged by aquatic vegetation. Canals connect the river or stream to the floodplain lakes (Smith 1979: 11). Floodplain lakes come into being behind the levees (fig. 31) and receive their waters from the larger rivers annually during the flood period. When interconnected, a series of lakes can form extensive complexes of up to 100 square kilometers.

The floating grasses of the floodplain lakes, with their rich microfauna, are an important food source for many of the fish, especially in the rainy season. The root zone of these plants provides shelter to the larvae of Diptera, Trichoptera, Ephemeroptera, Odonata, and crustaceans (Junk 1970 in Smith 1979: 16). The invertebrate fauna of this zone feeds fish of economic value. Some of the most important species are found in floodplain lakes and in slow-moving streams, among them the osteoglossids *pirarucú* (*Arapaima gigas*) and *aruanã* (*Osteoglossum bicirrhosum*) and the cyclids *cara roxo* (*Cichlasoma severum*) and *cara roe-roe* (*Geophagus surinamensis*).

The fish runs annually can be spectacular in parts of the Amazon; at least forty-one species participate in such runs in the four months during which they occur, involving hundreds of thousands of individuals. All the species that have fish runs are widely used in the diet of local populations (Smith 1979: 23). In the area near Itacoatiara the two species of *jaraquís* (*Semaprochilodus* sp.) constituted the most important fish caught during the runs.

Smith observed at least twelve distinct fishing methods in his study of Itacoatiara (1979: 38), some of which relied on nets, projectiles, hooks, explosives, and poisons. The relative efficiency of the various methods varied with the seasons and the species sought (see table 6). The use of nets was quite limited among Indians, becoming common only with the introduction of nylon filament. Before that, the nets made from cotton and palm fibers rotted quickly and required a lot of labor. Now they are used largely during the fish runs, in daytime fishing, and to capture some fish species like *tambaquí* (*Colossoma macropomum*), *pescada* (*Plagioscon* sp.), *caparari* (*Pseudoplatystoma tigrinum*), *surubim* (*Pseudoplatystoma fasciatum*), *peixe cachorro* (*Cynodon gibbus*), and *muela* (*Pimelodina flavipinnis*) (Smith 1979: 41). In Itacoatiara fishing with seine nets accounted for 32 percent of the total catch.

The use of gillnets was the second most productive technique in Itacoatiara at the time of the study. They seem to have relatively little importance to other indigenous populations. The Karajá of the Araguaia River, for example, made nets from parts of the secondary successional tree genus *Cecropia* particularly to capture *pirarucú* in floodplain lakes. Efforts are made to avoid netting piranhas, because they can not only destroy a lot of the fish caught but also tear up the nets. In areas near rapids or waterfalls, the castnet is employed to capture the larger fish. It is used in the fast part of the

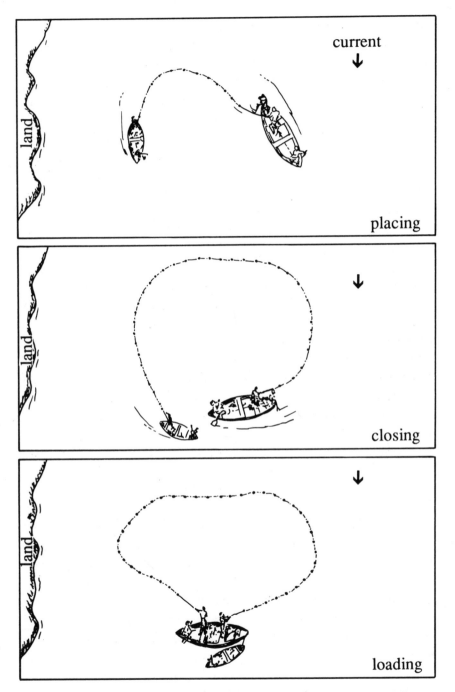

Figure 27. Fishing with seine nets: placing (above), closing (middle), loading (below) (from Smith 1979: 40).

Table 6. *Returns with Various Fishing Techniques at Itacoatiara*

Method	Hours observed	N	Kg	Kg/ work- hour	Standard deviation
Net	61.1	14	3,390.7	16.58	34.30
Gillnet	194.2	54	755.7	6.26	10.87
Harpoon	26.0	6	211.1	5.27	4.07
Deepwater gillnets	44.5	3	77.7	2.79	0.85
Hook-and-line	6.5	3	41.0	2.2	1.43
Canico	43.0	8	71.7	1.54	1.40
Castnet	6.7	1	17.1	1.27	—
Trotline	114.4	19	65.4	0.56	0.69

Source: Smith 1979: 77.

middle of rivers, whereas the gillnet is used either in the flooded forest or in waterfalls and rapids (Goulding 1979: 52–54). The ecological impact of gillnets can be negative. Goulding (1979: 112–113) showed that gillnets can capture dolphins, alligators, and *tracajá* turtles, which are often found dead due to the rapid predation by carnivore species also caught in the gillnets.

Goulding (1979) observed the use of drifting deepwater gillnets in the Madeira River. The lower part of the net has weights so that it can remain at the bottom of the river, sometimes as deep as 20 meters (fig. 28). The gillnet is most productive during the dry season when the river is 7 to 13 meters below its peak flood level.

A gig or trident is also used in fishing, especially in the flooded forests. Several important species such as *tucunaré* (*Cichla* sp), *carauaçú* (*Astronotus ocellatus*), *cara roxo* (*Cichlasoma severum*), *aruanã* (*Osteoglossum bicirrhosum*), and *traíra* (*Hoplias malabaricus*) like to rest near the surface of the water, where the fishers can harpoon them with the trident. Smith (1979: 51) calculated that the success rate in the use of the trident is greater than 50 percent. The technique is responsible for 4.5 percent of the catch measured by Smith at Itacoatiara.

The harpoon proper is rarely mentioned in the ethnographic literature, although it may have been used in pre-Columbian times. The *pirarucú* is one of the species most often fished by means of the harpoon. The weight of

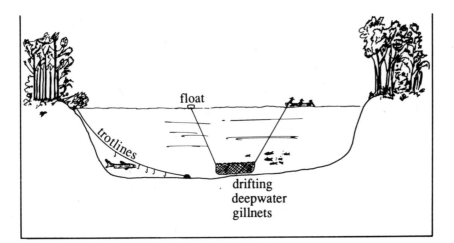

Figure 28. Fishing with baited trotlines and drifting deepwater gillnets (adapted from Goulding 1979: 53).

the *pirarucú*, which can reach 90 kilograms, makes this technique worth its costs. The *tambaquí* is also fished with harpoons but less often. This technique accounted for only 1.1 percent of the catch in Itacoatiara, which may simply reflect the decline in the populations of *pirarucú* through overfishing.

Fishing with bows and arrows has been widely diffused among Amazonian populations in the past and present. This method is most used in canals, flooded forests, and lakes. Various arrowheads with specialized purposes have been used and are often found in archaeological sites. The technique does not contribute significantly to the bulk of the commercial fish catch at Itacoatiara, accounting for only 0.4 percent of the total (Smith 1979: 58), but it can be used year-round and is the subsistence method of choice for meeting family needs. During the flood stage, the Parintintin Indians, for example, fish with bows and arrows from platforms built to hang between trees in the flooded forest. Such platforms, known as moitas, are placed near trees whose fruit is known to attract fish (W. Kracke, personal communication, 1989).

Fishing with baited trotlines is carried out by hanging many hooks from a line with fruit and sometimes animal meat as bait. The lines are tied to trees, and this technique works best in the dry season when water is low. The baited trotline has increased in importance with the arrival throughout the Amazon of refrigerator boats capable of buying the largest fish (N. Smith 1981: 63–73). *Brachyplatystoma filamentosum*, or *piraíba*, can weigh in at 110 kg, and its value when sold can be equivalent to a month's wages

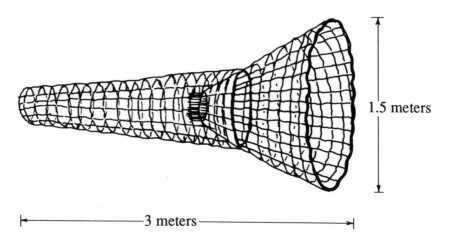

1.5 meters

|←————————3 meters————————→|

Figure 29. Conical fish trap (adapted from Goulding 1979: 59).

(Goulding 1979: 57). According to Goulding (1979: 57), the baited trot-line is the only efficient means at present by which to capture fish above 60 kilograms in weight—*pirarucú* (*Arapaima gigas*) excepted.

Conical traps have been used in the floodplain since pre-Columbian times. The traps, known in Brazil as covos or matapís, are made of a variety of plant materials. They are placed on the banks of the river, on the upstream portion of rapids and falls. The wide mouth has a diameter of up to 2 meters and faces the direction of the water. The fish enter the mouth, go through the narrow neck, and have difficulty escaping because of the sharp points aimed inward (see fig. 29) (Goulding 1979: 58–59).

A very ancient technique is the construction of large traps or weirs that fence off big parts of the river, also known as kakurís (Veríssimo 1895). Once the fish are in the large fenced area, other techniques are relied on to obtain them, whether bows and arrows, tridents, harpoons, or nets. The role of these big fish traps may have been particularly significant in main-taining large populations during high-water periods when fishing is more difficult or less productive. They can also serve as a useful storage tank for the fisheries.

Smith (1979: 83) estimated that fishing can be up to twenty-seven times more productive than hunting, in a comparison between three areas of up-land forest in the eastern Amazon. The relative productivity of these two sources of animal protein will depend a great deal on the microecological situation of each region, on the familiarity of the population with the bio-topes, and on the balance between local production and take-out rates. Much of the fish catch of the Amazon River at present is exported to the

large cities of the region, like Belém and Manaus, to the southern part of
Brazil, and to international markets.

Fishing, like hunting, is surrounded by a great number of taboos among
native Amazonians. The Kamayurá of central Brazil considered fish without
scales *remoso* (dangerous to one's health) and pregnant women were not
allowed to eat them (Oberg 1953). The Tapirapé of the Araguaia did not
permit the consumption of *pirarucú* and of *pirarara* during pregnancy (Wagley 1977: 121). The caboclos of Amazonia have maintained many of these
taboos in their cultural repertoire. In the Lower Amazon, in Itá, postpartum
women may not eat fish considered *remoso* because doing so can bring
harm to the child through the mother's milk (Wagley 1953). *Pirapitinga*
(*Colossoma bidens*) and *matrinchão* or *jatuarana* (*Brycon*) are among those
most often mentioned as being dangerous (N. Smith 1981: 87–91). Twenty-
seven other species of fish were less frequently mentioned. In general, these
avoided fish species are fatty and not appropriate for consumption when
people do not feel well.

Just as some fish are avoided when people do not feel well, Amazonian
populations consider other species particularly "healthy" and encourage
their consumption. Among these one can mention the smaller *tambaquí*,
pescada, and *traíra*. The criteria used are consistent with those applied to
hunted meats and domestic animals. The leaner it is, the safer it is to eat,
even during illness; the greater the fattiness of the flesh, the more *remoso* or
dangerous it is considered (Fleming-Moran 1974; Smith 1976, 1979, 1981;
Moran 1981). Tapir, wild pig, and domestic pig, for example, are always
considered dangerous. While these food preferences are actively practiced,
they follow the basic principle of survival. No one has observed any caboclos or Indians dying of hunger because they would not eat foods considered
culturally dangerous. In the case of the fish, the taboos do not seem to bear
any relation to the energy cost of obtaining the particular fish species or to
their dietary value. Culturally dangerous fish are relatively abundant. This
may also apply to wild game hunting taboos (but see Ross 1978 for a different assessment).

Substantial portions of animal biomass seem to be overlooked as sources
of food by local populations. Lizards and alligators are not consumed. Despite their tendency to swim near boats, Amazonian river dolphins (*Inia
geoffrensis* and *Sotalia fluviatalis*) are not fished and are, in fact, treated
with considerable respect—surrounded as they are by a rich folklore in
which dolphins transform themselves into human form, which has the effect
of protecting them from predation (Wagley 1953; Galvão 1955). Fishers

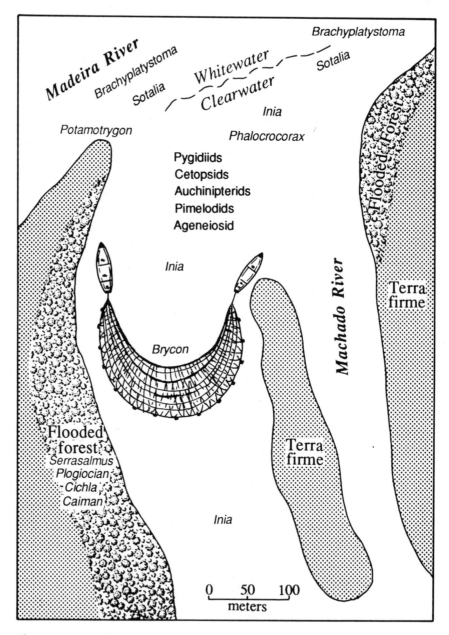

Figure 30. Dolphin/fisheries interactions (adapted from Goulding 1979: 99).

claim that in some areas the dolphins help identify schools of fish when they are going downstream (Goulding 1979: 98). Figure 30 illustrates the relations suggested by Goulding between river dolphins and other species of economic interest to the fishers of the Machado River, an affluent of the Madeira. When several dolphins chase a school of fish, the fishers go upstream, where they set their nets to capture the fish. The dolphins remain on the outside capturing whatever fish escape from the nets, benefiting from the closing in of the nets, which makes the area from which fish escape narrow. This relation is all the more curious and mutualistic when one considers that it seems that the dolphins prefer *Brycon* and that this genus accounts for 60 percent of the total catch on the Madeira (Goulding 1979: 104) and 94 percent of the catch at the mouths of rivers, which are the areas preferred by dolphins.

Numerous folk beliefs deal with the aquatic world and serve to highlight its critical importance to the population. For example, the belief in *panema* (a type of bad luck) has to do with explaining how one may be unsuccessful in hunting and fishing. This can occur when fishers or hunters do not divide their catch with relatives with whom they have obligations to share or if a menstruating woman touches their equipment (suggesting that women should not come on hunting and fishing trips). Fishers who devote particular attention to capturing the largest fish species, *pirarucú*, are said to be particularly prone to having *panema* or bad luck fishing—a notion perhaps related to taking pressure off this important and easy-to-capture species. The word *panema* comes from the *lingua geral* and seems to derive from Tupí-Guaraní. Among the Urubú Ka'apor, a Tupí-speaking indigenous group currently living in Maranhão, the term is *panem* and has the same meaning and connotations as does the Brazilian caboclo term (Balée, personal communication, 1989). The beliefs in bad luck are associated with the symbolic division of the world made by indigenous peoples between man/fish and woman/manioc, the alimentary sources upon which life is based in riverine Amazonia, which is central to all other components of social organization. These symbolic relations are also associated with the division man/wild game and woman/manioc, which applies to the distribution of duties having to do with game and agriculture.

Adaptive Strategies in the Upper Floodplain

The strategies found in the upper floodplain are of considerable sophistication, in light of the richness of biotopes found in this aquatic world.

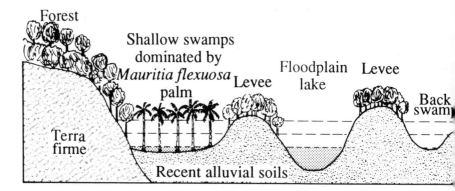

Figure 31. Biotopes in an upper floodplain region (adapted from Hiraoka 1985).

Stocks (1983) showed how the Cocamilla along the Huallaga River in Peru appear to influence the behavior of fish in a floodplain lake through the deposition of organic garbage in a particular part of the lake. Figure 23 illustrates the various biotopes found near the Cocamilla community of Achual Tipishca. The population seems to have occupied this region for at least the past 400 years and has arrived at a remarkably balanced understanding of resource use and conservation. It is quite likely that groups like the Cocamilla of the floodplain had intimate relations of mutualism very much like these and that they declined with the European arrival and depopulation. The management of giant Amazon river turtles (*Podocnemis unifilis* and *P. expansa*), for example, was universally commented upon by the early chroniclers as a remarkable strategy of resource use; they were kept in huge corrals on the river and roped through a small hole made in their shells (Smith 1974b, 1979).

The Cocamilla recognize at least five fishing biotopes in the proximity of their community (fig. 23). Streams are exploited in the dry season, between June and October, through the use of fish poisons that make the fish float to the surface, where they are easily captured in a blocked-off stream. "Dry lakes" occur at the end of the flooding period: sizable depressions where fish that got cut off from the river may be easy prey for human populations and can be captured with gillnets. "Aging lakes" are floodplain lakes that lose their connection to the river system, where fish may die gradually through lack of oxygen due to the growth of oxygen-loving aquatic plants. Fishing along the principal channel of the Huallaga River offers three biotopes: one along the banks of the river, another along the beaches, and a third along very small connecting brooks. When the fish are returning to the river, as

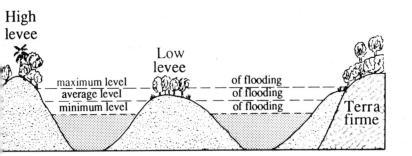

water levels begin to drop with the end of the flooding period, fishing with various types of nets is extremely rewarding in these areas. During this time of the year 94 percent of the fishing effort may be concentrated in these biotopes.

As in the lower floodplain, the population recognizes behavioral differences between species and where and when to invest fishing effort. The most common gillnet used by the Cocamilla is about 30 meters long and 3 meters wide. It is generally used between two canoes that gradually close the ends (fig. 27). The use of the harpoon, when the river levels are low, was probably more common in the past than it is today. It is appropriate for the fish of larger dimensions, such as *Hoplias malabaricus*, *Cichla ocellaris*, and *Oxydoras niger*.

Stocks (1983) observed that the Cocamilla deposit their organic garbage in the area of the lake closest to the village. This practice serves to provide a supplement to the diet of fish and to make the fish dependent upon these inputs over time—at least seasonally. It may very well be that this practice is widely diffused but has been overlooked by most ethnographers, who took it to be simply a system for garbage disposal with no subsistence returns. Fishing around this disposal area is most intensively practiced in the flooding period, when fishing is least rewarding. Fish were observed to consume the deposited garbage. Stocks (1983) estimated that 44 tons of organic garbage are deposited annually in the lake. Even though the lake is fished largely when other areas are of low production, annual fish production from the lake reaches 17.6 tons per square kilometer, an amount that exceeds by a factor of three that recorded for the Upper Xingú (Gross 1975). When the water levels begin to drop, effort switches to the brooks that drain the lake,

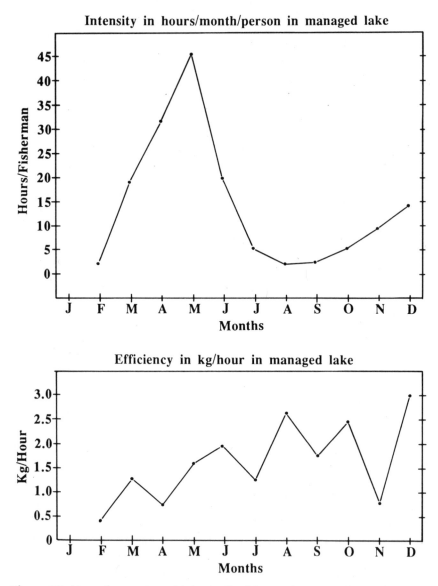

Figure 32. Use of a managed lake in the Upper Amazon: intensity (above) and efficiency (below) (from Stocks 1983: 258).

thereby capturing the fish returning to the main river channel. As the water levels continue dropping, the shallower areas along the river and the drying lakes and aging lakes are the focus of attention (fig. 32).

The populations of the upper floodplain may have had a lower density in pre-Columbian times than those of the Middle Amazon, the Lower Ama-

Table 7. *Comparison of Hunting and Fishing Efficiency*

Month	Intensity (hours/person)		Efficiency (kg/hour)	
	Fishing	Hunting	Fishing	Hunting
January	18.1	12.1	1.69	1.39
February	17.4	6.2	0.72	1.07
March	43.5	23.4	1.34	0.37
April	76.1	11.7	0.62	0.09
May	69.3	1.7	1.68	0.00
June	49.3	0.0	1.35	0.00
July	47.1	0.0	3.18	0.00
August	44.8	9.8	3.30	0.55
September	32.9	2.1	5.59	0.00
October	22.9	14.2	2.98	0.01
November	39.8	11.7	0.84	0.41
December	59.7	5.4	3.11	0.48

Source: Stocks 1983.

zon, or the estuary. The productivity of soils, hunting, fishing, and collecting vary a great deal from one place to another due to the greater mosaic quality of the Upper Amazon. However, this may be an impression resulting from the fact that in the Upper Amazon settlements were less visible from the main channel than downriver, given the greater dependence on floodplain lake fishing.

Hunting among the Cocamilla and other populations of the Upper Amazon may have been important more as a source of diversity in the diet, and to fulfill social obligations, than to add substantively to the total diet (see table 7, which compares the efficiencies of hunting and fishing). In the floodplain the productivity and rates of return from fishing are sufficiently high to relegate hunting to a lesser role than it might have in the interfluves of the uplands—even if hunting may still be more highly regarded as a status activity (W. Kracke, personal communication, 1989).

Adaptively comparable to the caboclos of the Lower Amazon are the riverine peasants, or ribereños, of the Upper Amazon. Their residential pattern still reflects the impact of the rubber boom period, which favored the dispersal of population along the rivers—their watershed was the territory exploited by single rubber tappers. In the Upper Amazon many of these populations live along the Ucayali and Marañón rivers, using resources in ways that reflect indigenous resource use (Hiraoka 1985; Bergman 1974, 1980; Lathrap 1970). In the study by Hiraoka (1985) they exploited twelve biotopes, defined through horizontal and vertical zonation and as a function of the changes in river level (fig. 31).

The agricultural activities are influenced by the pattern of drainage following the floods. The first areas to dry, the "high levee" (fig. 31), are planted in rice while the soil is still very wet, to ensure that the roots can attach well. In sandier areas bananas, manioc, and peanuts are planted. As the water level falls further, the "low levee" and the "upper levee" are planted in corn, cowpeas, squash, and rice. During the same period the biotopes on islands begin to become available: rice is planted in *gramalotal* (dominated by *Paspalum* grasses), beans on the beaches, and sugarcane in the *braval*. Vegetables and grains are planted in the *cetical*. During this period of work the population depends on the production of banana and manioc from the levees, the only areas which were not flooded and which continue to produce into the dry season. In the flooding period agriculture is restricted to these high levees, which are used continuously for two or three years before being given a rest. In the areas dominated by the palm *Mauritia flexuosa* or *burití* the fruits are valued commercially by the population (Hiraoka 1985).

The harvests possible in these biotopes can be remarkable: 4 tons of rice and 3 to 4 tons of corn per hectare, from either the *barreal* or the *gramalotal*. Manioc on the high levees has produced an average of 12 tons per hectare, as do bananas. Such productivity in an area with such a short growing period during low water suggests a remarkable knowledge of the environment and the identification of fast-growing varieties managed to take advantage of high seasonal fertility. The use of both riverine resources and small areas of upland forest provides a complementary set of resources that permits relatively high population densities to be supported. The synchrony required to manage this fluctuating aquatic system demands much more precise management than areas of upland forest to exploit the potential present.

Population density in the Upper Amazon today is about 4 persons per square kilometer. In the area studied by Hiraoka (1985), it reached 7.2 persons per square kilometer, while in the area near Iquitos it reaches 28 persons, a figure approximating the estimates made for the pre-Columbian populations at the time of European contact.

Table 8. *Use of Biotopes of the Upper Floodplain*

Biotope	Characteristics	Products
Levee top	not subject to inundation, sandy and silt-loam soils	bananas, manioc, sweet potatoes, *Vigna*, pineapples, guavas, fruit trees
High levee	infrequent flooding, sandy and silt-loam soils	manioc, plantains, peanuts, rice after floods
Upper levee	rarely flooded, clayish soils	manioc, plantains, sugarcane
Low levee	annual inundation, sandy to loamy soils	rice, corn, *Vigna*
Island Cultivation		
Cetical (*Cecropia*)	flooded most years, clay to loam soils	*Vigna*, *Phaseolus*, corn, peanuts, rice, vegetables
Cana braval (*Arundo* sp.)	flooded annually, clay to sandy soils	*Vigna* and *Phaseolus*
Gramalotal (*Paspalum* sp.)	old beaches, clay to loam soils	rice and *Vigna*
Beaches	sand to loam banks	*Vigna* on sandy, peanuts on loamy
Backswamps and Lakes		
Backswamp	shallow depressions between levees with swamp forest	construction materials
Aguajales (*Buritiçais*)	shallow swamps dominated by *Mauritia flexuosa*	*aguaje* or *burití*, palm fruit
Cocha	oxbow lake	fish and game meat

Source: Hiraoka 1985.

Conclusions

Pre-Columbian populations seem to have reached the highest population densities in the lower floodplain, the estuary, and the whitewater drainages of the Upper Amazon, along the Solimões, the Madeira, and the Huallaga. These populations learned to manage the constraints posed by seasonal flooding and to exploit the mosaiclike biotopes created by the dynamism of this wetland. All the populations studied to date seem to recognize the presence of both horizontal and vertical zonation. Such zoning is tied to the careful observation of the changes in river level and the behavior of animals.

For optimal utilization, the exploitation of the floodplains requires very detailed understanding of their internal variability and year-to-year differences. This can be achieved by relatively sedentary populations who regularly manage the same headwaters, mouths of rivers, high levees, and riverbanks. In so doing they reach a very precise understanding of the fluctuations in the biotopes present and adjust to the regularly created and destroyed islands of resources in the dynamic floodplain. They benefit from the renewable fertility of alluvial areas, at least in those areas enriched by the whitewater rivers coming from the Andes. The opportunities are not uniformly favorable, especially in areas draining rivers with more acid alluvium.

Generalizations about floodplains are difficult to make because of the constantly changing nature of these habitats. Evidently, over much of the region, the carrying capacity is relatively high. This capacity is based heavily on the productivity of the fisheries and on agriculture along the alluvial beaches and levees. The agricultural potential of the floodplain remains imperfectly developed since the arrival of Europeans, especially in the Brazilian Amazon. Such development may never be achieved if current projects in the region do not avoid destroying the basis for their productivity. The construction of hydroelectric dams to produce energy for other parts of Brazil is taking out of production some of the best areas for agriculture; mining activities are polluting the waterways and reducing their biotic potential; and the conversion of flooded forests for paddy rice should be examined carefully to determine the tradeoff between, for example, the role of a given flooded forest in sustaining the fisheries versus its contribution to agriculture.

Not all the floodplains of Amazonia are "equivalent." Each one should be examined to determine whether it is the habitat of unique and important species and whether it plays a key role in ecosystem structure or function.

The very high potential of the estuary may best be managed by agroforestry practices that maintain the integrity of that productive habitat (Anderson 1990). The estuary can produce and has produced a regular supply of products of economic value and may be managed further to increase its contribution to human populations at the same time that its role in recycling and ecosystem maintenance is preserved. Other regions may be managed with very intensive methods, especially in areas that are renewed annually. In some cases they may be exploited for electric power generation, when they do not play an important role or have unique species.

Easy formulas exist neither for Amazonia as a whole nor for the floodplains in particular. The destruction of the most fertile habitats of Amazonia is to be avoided. Figuring out how best to balance their use with their conservation and enhanced yield will depend upon our willingness to learn from those who have lived in the region for generations, coping with one of the most complex wetlands on earth.

5

Savannas

The upland savannas are characterized by two distinct and strongly marked seasons, each about six months in duration. These areas, known as cerrado in Brazil and as llanos in Colombia and Venezuela, have considerable differences in hydrologic conditions. The llanos are commonly poorly drained, whereas the cerrados are more often than not well-drained. The Brazilian cerrados occupy an area of 180 million hectares, while the llanos occupy about 120 million hectares (Sánchez 1977: 537). Figure 33 illustrates the areal distribution of the savannas in northern South America.

By the end of the Cenozoic, and principally during the Pleistocene, important climatic changes took place in South America. Temperatures seem to have declined by about 4 or 5 degrees C, the climate became drier, and the savannas extended into many areas previously and currently occupied by tropical forests (Hammen 1972; Haffer 1969: 133). Areas currently without a definite dry season may have been the few regions that were able to preserve tropical forests during the Pleistocene, such as the areas between the Juruá River and the Upper Orinoco, which are believed to have served as Pleistocene refugia (Haffer 1969: 132). These areas may be important not only in understanding the past but also in forecasting what might happen should deforestation of the tropical forests lead to increasing dryness.

The Brazilian savannas have numerous limitations to their agricultural use because of their extreme acidity, high aluminum saturation, and low nutrient and cation exchange capacity; during the dry season, plants can be stressed by the lack of moisture unless they have deep tap roots. Without irrigation and fertilization, agriculture over most of these areas is highly precarious and uncertain. The upland savannas are crisscrossed by numerous rivers, along which grow gallery forests. Native Amazonians have found in these areas a habitat that has permitted a good life based upon swidden agriculture and productive hunting and collecting. The savannas are more advantageous for hunting not necessarily because they have more animal biomass but because better visibility facilitates the work of the hunter and the patchy ecotones and strong seasonality make predicting the behavior of game easier than in upland forests.

The most important environmental pressures that influence the strategies of human populations in this habitat are the cycles of heavy rain and extreme dryness, the nutritional limitations of the soil, the presence of numerous and dispersed ecotones, and the lesser productivity of fishing.

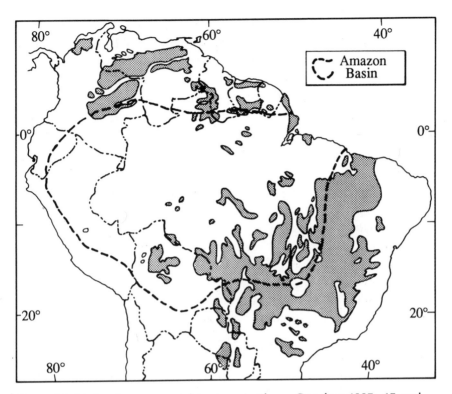

Figure 33. Upland savannas of Amazonia (from Goedert 1985: 15 and Prance 1978: 215).

Characterization of the Savannas

When we think of the Amazon we think of the lush tropical forests and rarely of the savannas. Nevertheless, large expanses of savanna can be found throughout the basin, and those habitats are no less important to native populations than the forested environments that receive the bulk of the attention. The savannas cover an area 1.8 million square kilometers in Brazil and may be found in the basins of the Middle and Upper Tocantins, Araguaia, Irirí, Xingú, and Tapajós. Others are found in the south of Rondônia and in the northern parts of Mato Grosso and Roraima.

These habitats were called "marginal" by the authors in the *Handbook of South American Indians* because of the apparent limitations of the savannas for agricultural production and the seeming lack of interest in crop nurturing by populations in the region at the time they were first ethnographically observed (Steward 1939–1946). The agricultural potential of the savannas differs significantly from that of the upland forests and the flood-plains. The practice of swidden cultivation involves problems not present in either of the two other habitats under traditional conditions.

The mean annual temperatures in the savannas vary between 20 and 27 degrees C. Generally, rainfall is in the range of 800 to 2,000 millimeters annually, with periods of dryness lasting three to seven months. The deficit in moisture in the Brazilian central plateau between May and September can be as high as 491 millimeters (Lopes and Cox 1977). Eighty percent of the rain falls in January, February, and March in the cerrados and in July, August, and September in the llanos. Brief periods of up to three weeks without rain in the rainy season, called veranicos, can have severe negative results in an area with high evapotranspiration and a low capacity for water retention in excellently drained soils (Goedert 1985). Insolation is very high in the region due to the long periods of clear skies and low humidity, resulting in 350 to 450 calories (i.e., kilocalories) per square centimeter per day of insolation (Goedert 1985: 4). If the limiting factors were corrected, the temperatures and solar radiation would be ideal for the growth of many plants of economic interest.

The soils of the savannas of central Brazil are acid, leached, and very deficient in nutrients. In over 50 percent of the cases they are oxisols with a low cation exchange capacity and high aluminum saturation (Freitas and Silveira 1977; Goodland 1971). One also finds smaller areas of entisols, inceptisols, and, more rarely, ultisols (Lopes and Cox 1977). Fifteen percent of the area is sandy in texture (Goedert 1985).

The heterogeneity of soils in areas that seem to be the same can be observed in a comparison between the eastern llanos of Colombia and the eastern llanos of Venezuela. The two savannas are dominated by oxisols and ultisols and have similar rainfall regimes. The Colombian llanos have infertile soils throughout the region, differing only in the amount of moisture, while the western portion of the llanos of Venezuela is crisscrossed by narrow valleys with superb soils (mollisols, vertisols, alfisols, and entisols). The presence of these "islands of fertility" in an ocean of poor soils has permitted the agricultural development of the savannas in the llanos of Venezuela, in contrast to the less favorable experience of people in the Colombian llanos (Sánchez 1977: 539). The outcrops of basaltic rocks that occur in these narrow valleys of Venezuela also occur in Brazil, along the gallery forests.

In a study of the soils of the savannas of Brazil, the average pH was 5.0, with a range of 4.3 to 6.2. Ninety-eight percent of the soils had a pH below

6.0. Ninety-two percent had less than 2 parts per million of phosphorus, considered the critical level for many important cereals. Ninety-six percent of the soils had less than 1.5 milliequivalents per 100 milliliters of calcium, the critical level for many crops. Although the aluminum saturation level is less severe than in many other parts of the Amazon, it is generally above 50 percent, which presents problems for many crops (Lopes and Cox 1977: 743–744). The levels of organic matter and clay are in the mid-range, although the cation exchange capacity is very low. The soils often have micronutrient deficiencies.

The soils present a problem not often mentioned: only 6 to 8 percent of the water is retained at low tensions of one bar and almost none at tensions above that. This means that the soils behave similarly to very sandy soils and retain only enough water in the top 20 centimeters to support crops for eight to ten days (Goedert 1983). When this combines with the hydraulic restrictions posed by the limited root depth attained by crops due to aluminum saturation, the harvests are in a precarious state due to the high probability of a dry spell (veranico) unless irrigation is provided. In contrast to the introduced crops, the native plants of the savannas have very deep roots and are not affected by the dry spells to the same degree (Goodland 1971; personal communication, 1989). Wolf (1975) mentioned that there is a probability of 50 percent in the Brazilian plateau of having at least fourteen continuous days without rain in the rainy season each year and a 15 percent probability that the dry spell will last twenty-one days. Corn wilts in the region after seven continuous days without rain.

The soils are deep and well-drained, with excellent structure and stability, characteristics that make them easier to manage. The area is mostly flat, with a slope of less than 3 percent, facilitating their mechanization (Goedert 1985). Oxisols have been preferred for intensive agriculture in recent years. The clay fraction is dominated by kaolinite and gibsite, and by the presence of iron oxides. Organic matter is relatively high, which can be advantageous if other limitations are dealt with. Cerradões, savannas with a frequent presence of trees, have higher organic matter levels and higher clay proportions than other areas of the savannas.

The vegetation of the region, commonly called cerrado or savanna, differs from the vegetation along the rivers (the gallery forests). There are open savannas dominated by grasses called campo sujo, areas with shrubs and small trees known as campo cerrado, and, finally, areas with thicker tree vegetation known as cerradão (Eiten 1972). Many of the species of the savanna, especially the trees and shrubs, give the appearance of vegetation from areas that experience a moisture deficit: the branches are tortuous, the trees are short, their bark is thin, and they have thick, leathery (sclerophyllous) leaves (Ferri 1977: 21). Yet one also finds vegetation with entirely different characteristics and no apparent adaptation to dry conditions. Ferri (1977: 22) demonstrated that native plants of the savanna do not behave like xerophytes, even if they manifest xeromorphy. Trees and shrubs generally have deep roots that reach down to the underground water table.

The vegetation exhibits at least five distinct types along a gradient: campo limpo is characterized by the absence of trees and shrubs and the dominance of grasses; campo sujo refers to a vegetation where trees of less than 3 meters may be found at good distances one from another; campo cerrado refers to an area with discontinuous trees and shrubs averaging 4 meters in height; cerrado, *sensu strictu*, is an area with considerable tree vegetation about 6 meters high; and cerradão is an intermediate type betwen savanna and forest with trees averaging 9 meters in height, sometimes having three distinct strata, grassland, shrubs, and trees (Ferri 1977: 37; Sánchez and Salinas 1981: 320). Eiten (1972) added a sixth category called campo úmido, such as the groves of *buriti* palm (*Mauritia flexuosa*) on poorly drained areas. Arens (1958) suggested that the presence of sclerophyllous leaves was caused by the oligotrophy of the ecosystem. Goodland confirmed this hypothesis and added that the principal factor that explained the differences between the various kinds of vegetation was the degree of aluminum saturation (in Ferri 1977: 27). Woody stems, sclerophylly, tortuous trunks that turn yellowish green when dry, and fruits that turn light blue are characteristic of plants that tolerate and even accumulate aluminum.

The variation in the types of vegetation in the savannas may also be indicative of the fertility of the soil in well-drained areas (Lopes and Cox 1977). Along the gradient from campo limpo to cerradão, the organic matter and the nutrients increase in their availability with increasing tree frequencies (Lopes 1975). This suggests that the density of tree cover results from the differences in soil fertility and their capacity to hold moisture. Table 9 aggregates the results of 510 soil samples in the savannas taken at a depth of 0 to 20 centimeters. The savannas of central Brazil have much in common with the savannas of the north such as those in Roraima. In both, for example, the dominant trees are *Curatella americana* and *Byrsonima*, and the dominant shrub is *Byrsonima verbascifolia*. In general, the Roraima savanna is less xerophytic than that of central Brazil (Takeuchi 1960: 532). Plant biomass is usually less in the llanos than in the cerrados (Goedert 1985). The mean nutrient levels of the soils bear a linear relation to the size

Table 9. *Soils and Vegetation of the Savannas*

Soil property	Campo limpo (64)	Campo cerrado (148)	Cerrado (255)	Cerradão (45)	Critical level*
Organic matter (%)	2.21	2.33	2.35	2.32	—
Potassium (meq/100 ml)	0.08	0.10	0.11	0.13	0.15
Calcium (meq/100 ml)	0.20	0.33	0.45	0.69	—
Magnesium (meq/100 ml)	0.06	0.13	0.21	0.38	0.50
Zinc (ppm)	0.58	0.61	0.66	0.67	1.00
Copper (ppm)	0.60	0.79	0.94	1.32	1.00
Iron (ppm)	35.7	33.9	33.0	27.1	—

Source: Lopes 1975. Lopes did not use the category "campo sujo" or "campo úmido" of Eiten (1972) in his study.
*Based on recommendations of the state of Minas Gerais.

of the vegetation. The basal area per hectare is intimately related to the biomass production. Figure 34 shows the productivity of the savannas. Since the density and diameter of trees follow the same direction, we must conclude that nutritional dwarfism is the result of the differences in biomass between campo sujo and cerradão (Goodland and Ferri 1979: 79).

Goodland and Ferri (1979: 74–76) characterized four types of vegetation in central Brazil, whereas six types were defined by Eiten (1972). The height of the vegetation does not seem to serve as a good criterion, nor does the total number of species present. But the height of the trees, the total basal area, the number of trees per hectare, and the number of woody species do seem to increase along the gradient proposed. The number of grasses decreases as the density of trees increases. Table 10 shows characteristics of the savannas.

Adaptive Strategies in the Savannas

The native Amazonians who live in the savannas today are, in general, less numerous that those of the lower floodplain or those living among the liana forests of the upland forests. Nevertheless, the area can support sub-

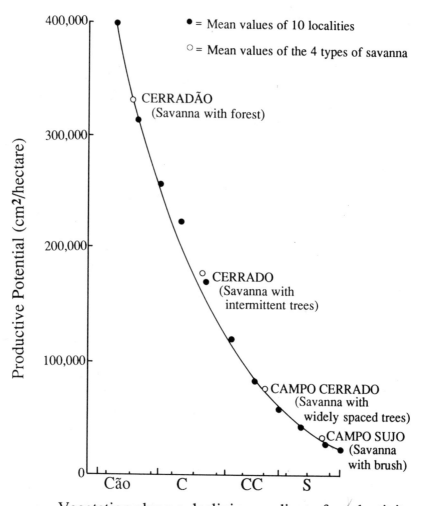

Vegetation along a declining gradient of productivity

Figure 34. Biomass productivity of savannas (adapted from Goodland and Ferri 1979).

stantial populations (Gross 1979). The chemical limitations of the soils were probably a stronger limitation in this habitat than in the upland forests because the areas that could be cultivated with the technology until recently were restricted to the gallery forests, areas more limited in total extent than the patches of alfisols and alluvial soils along floodplains in the interfluves. Balée (1984) suggested that the Gê-speakers of the savannas, during the pre-Columbian period and early periods of contact, tried systematically to drive out the larger Tupí-speaking populations well established along the Atlantic

Table 10. *Characteristics of Savannas*

	Campo sujo	Campo cerrado	Cerrado	Cerradão
Tree height (m)	1–5	3–6	4–8	6–18
No. of trees/ha	266–2070	335–2928	836–3976	1631–4925
Basal area/ha	10–60	17–142	62–253	203–513
No. of arboreal spp.	19–43	18–52	26–60	40–72
No. of shrub spp.	1–9	1–6	1–6	0–7
No. of grassy spp.	42–79	42–72	18–59	21–60
Mean no. of spp.	96	93	95	100

Source: Adapted from Goodland and Ferri 1979: 76.

coast, with the objective of occupying those more favored regions. The re-markably flexible social structure of the Gê may be a product of the necessity of these populations to mobilize for warfare (ibid.). Social structures that have the built-in capacity for fission and fusion have proven time and again to be more adapted to the impacts of colonialism and chronic warfare than those of larger but less flexible social systems.

In many cases, the populations of the central Brazilian savannas include many that fled into the upland forests to escape from the incursions of European and then national societies. This presents a unique problem in the study of human ecology: a population in the savanna may be there because it fled, either in the recent or distant past, from another region in which its social and political organization developed. Thus, its environmental practices and organization may be minimally satisfactory in the forests in which it now finds itself or may be superbly effective adaptive strategies. Another group, in contrast, may have adjusted to the upland forests and may find itself today in the savannas—but its social and cultural institutions may still reflect the constructions that came about in a forested environment rather than in a grassland. Thus, an important task for human ecological study is to attempt to distinguish between degrees of adaptation: to establish whether the observed behaviors are the result of prolonged adaptation to the current habitat. Over time, of course, any population will seek to adjust itself to its surroundings, but the strategies will reflect both the pressures of the environment and whatever previous routines and institutions it brought to the area in the first place. In cases where the previous behaviors may produce acceptable but not necessarily efficient results, it is possible that the social structures and patterns of resource use will persist with minimal modification—thereby restricting the possibilities for that population.

One of the few studies to have faced this issue was carried out by Eleonore Setz (1983) in some Nambiquara villages. She compared the subsistence ecology of a village in a savanna area with another in an upland forested area. Her study confirmed that the upland forest village depended more on agriculture than the one in the savanna, while the savanna village depended more on collecting than did the upland forest community. Fishing was more important in the upland forest village than in the savanna village. Surprisingly, hunting contributed about the same to both villages as a percentage, but the territory exploited to obtain such results was four times larger in the savanna community. The savanna population maintained two stages of settlement, a large aggregate village and a smaller band organization for hunting and collecting. The people held feasts which brought groups together to share information about scattered resources on the savanna (Setz 1983: 129). The Nambiquara on upland forests are located on excellent soils, a fact that permits them to have swiddens based on corn rather than manioc, while the savanna population living on poor soils depends on manioc in their subsistence agriculture (ibid., 148). This study is an excellent example of the correction that is needed in statements about upland forests and the fertility of gallery forests in the savannas and about the productivity of hunting in these two areas and in other conclusions based upon a very small number of studies.

The native populations of the savannas tend to locate their villages near gallery forests where they plant their swiddens. Savannas themselves are never planted because of their limitations, as noted previously. The possibility of practicing agriculture without fertilizers and irrigation is restricted to the gallery forests. For the most part, the central plateau and the llanos originated in the Cretaceous. The parent materials are sedimentary and very old, but basaltic rock outcrops are found. The basalts appear in some of the deeper valleys, giving origin to richer soils along the banks of rivers (Goodland and Ferri 1979: 138). Such fertile soils permit an agriculture with plants that are nutrient-demanding, such as corn, soybeans, and peanuts.

Native villages can be relatively large, with 500 to 1,500 inhabitants

(Flowers et al. 1982: 205). Denevan (1976: 224) estimated the densities of this habitat in 1500 at 0.5 person per square kilometer, a greater density than he assigned to the upland forests.

The Gê are the principal linguistic group in the central Brazilian area and include some of the following groups: Timbira (Kanela, Apinayé, Krahó, Gavião, do Pará [Parakaheje], and Krikatí), Akwé (Xerente and Xavante), and Kayapó (Gorotire, Txukahamai, Kubén-Kran-Degn, Kubén-Kragnotire, Diore, and Xikrín). The Bororo, Nambiquara, Parakanã, and Tapirapé also inhabit these areas but belong to linguistic groups other than the Gê (Zarur 1979: 649).

The dominant pattern of residence is one of matrilocality, with a social structure characterized by the presence of exogamous moieties, age grades, and seasonal fissioning. For at least six months each year, the populations hunt and collect in the savannas in units that are usually band size. Thus, the population has the custom of aggregating during the period of planting and harvesting and of fissioning into smaller units to exploit the dispersed resources of the savanna more fully. These seasonal fluctuations in organization reflect the cycles of the habitat, which may have influenced the emergence of the population's patterns of social structure and, in particular, its organizational flexibility (Gross 1979).

Since Nimuendajú (1946) demonstrated that the Timbira practiced a sophisticated form of agriculture the view of the *Handbook of South American Indians* that the Indians of central Brazil were "marginal" has been questioned. Archaeological research has shown that horticultural populations, installed in large villages of at least 2,000 people, were already present in the ninth century B.P. (Wust, personal communication, 1989). The archaeological data to date suggest that they depended on corn and root crops—and that manioc came to dominate only much later. It is possible that with the increase in population provoked by the arrival of refugees fleeing European contact it became necessary to occupy less fertile areas and that they turned to manioc cultivation for a solution to this problem (ibid.).

It is important to remember that the evolutionist bias of the European travelers passing through the region assigned to the category of primitive bands any group engaging to any visible extent in hunting and collecting—or whose material culture seemed to be geared to mobility rather than sedentarization. In addition, the ethnographic observations often were made in the summer, when the savanna groups were not in their large villages but in their seasonal treks. Thus, for many years it was thought that the Bororo were hunter/gatherers rather than horticulturalists—when in fact they are

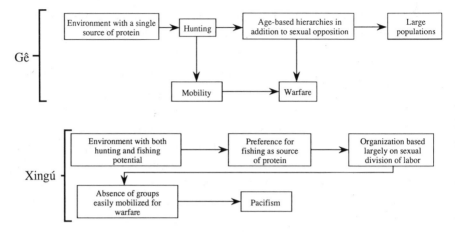

Figure 35. Gê and Xinguano ecological differences (from Zarur 1986: 279).

expert corn cultivators (Wust, personal communication, 1989). In addition, the patterns of dispersal may have been efforts on the part of these populations to avoid Europeans.

Ross (1978) and Bamberger (1967) compared the Kayapó with the populations of the Xingú in terms of their social structure and their fit with the environment. Bamberger argued that the differences in social structure between these two groups were the result of their worldview or ideology rather than the result of environmental adaptation, since both areas "were similar." Ross suggested that the environment of the Xinguanos was originally richer in fish than that of the Kayapó, which explained the greater interest of the former in fishing. The Kayapó have occupied areas of upland forests since they were first described ethnographically, but it is generally understood that they were typical populations of the savannas over a century ago. In this century the Kayapó have learned to fish in relatively effective fashion, but they still did not have canoes when Bamberger studied them, which suggests an incomplete adaptation to a riverine environment. Hunting is still more important to them than is fishing, which indicates that their ethnoecology and behavior are still geared more to the environment of a savanna than of a tropical forest (fig. 35). Obviously, there are important differences within savanna habitats and populations. The Mekranotí Kayapó fish more than they hunt because their village is located near a very productive river. Why do we find these differences in subsistence emphasis? Are some Kayapó more adapted to the environment than others? I don't think so. The diversity of sources of protein of the upland forest (e.g., the anthropogenic Brazil

nut groves) permits a broad range of alternatives due to the interplay between limitations and modification of environment possible in the forests of
Amazonia. By contrast, the dependence on hunting in the savanna limits the
number of options for the population. As one might expect, there is a
greater range of alternative forms of social organization in the upland forests than in the savannas (Zarur 1979). The Kayapó who today make their
home in the upland forests have made modifications in their forms of resource use to take advantage of the resources of the forests, maintaining
many of the elements of their social structure and ideology intact because
such elements do not represent threats to their survival in their new habitat. Their impressive demographic growth in recent years (as a result of
access to medical attention) and their traditional aggressiveness toward outsiders (as a result of their history of competition for favorable territories)
have proven adaptive under contemporary conditions of conflict with national society and the need to organize and act rapidly in response to
changes in policy.

Gê societies, in general, give less weight in their social organization to
sexual opposition than do Xinguanos (Zarur 1986). Mobility seems to be
of greater importance, as evidenced by their log races (Melatti 1976; Nimuendajú 1946). One of the functions of ceremonial moieties was the organization of teams for log races, in which both sexes participated. When
an individual started to lose speed, another member would come to take his
or her place and keep up the race. Melatti (1976: 40) argued that these races
are essential to the maintenance of the value of running and keeping physi-
cally fit, an important consideration with survival value in a population that
feels threatened by attacks from enemies. The relation of the races to other
aspects of their lives begins to emerge when one notes that racing teams are
made up of individuals who hunt together and share game kills. The stamina built up by these activities impressed observers, who noted that the Gê
can carry a log 30 kilometers in less than two and a half hours (Maybury-
Lewis 1967; Melatti 1976; Zarur 1979: 651).

The importance of mobility among the Gê in the historic period may also
be noted in the traditional absence of ceramics among them. Their material
culture seems less elaborate than that of other groups: featherwork is less
complex with the exception of the Kayapó and Bororo, and they depend on
straw for 65 percent of their inventory. In contrast to the Xinguanos of the
upland forests, with sophisticated ceramics, artistic work with wood, and
complex featherwork, the Gê assign importance to utilitarian and trans-
portable items (Zarur 1979: 651). The absence of ceramics in the ethno-

graphic accounts is curious, given that this absence does not apply to the archaeological record (Wust 1989). There is an abundance of ceramics in that record until the contact with Europeans, when the Gê stopped making them. They report breaking their pots intentionally in protest of their new situation, according to Xavante informants at Pimentel Barbosa (Wust, personal communication, 1989).

The importance of mobility may also be related to the relative importance of hunting as compared to fishing. In the savannas the existing rivers are not generally as rich in fish as rivers in the central basin. In contrast, hunting is more profitable in the open fields. Hunting is organized in age grades: men with families hunt more often than single men, who in turn hunt more often than older men (Zarur 1979: 651).

Seasonal spatial mobility seems to be a characteristic trait of Gê-speakers. Nevertheless, it should not be confused with nomadism in the strict sense of the term. The large villages are rarely, if ever, abandoned by everyone. When they are abandoned it is, more often than not, because an old site has become unsanitary and the effort at fixing up the houses would be greater than building new ones. New villages are usually built within a few hundred meters from the old location. There is no term for a specific village; references are to the general area within which villages may be sited (Wust, personal communication, 1989).

A society organized into age-grades and with a strong emphasis on physical stamina has a clear advantage in warfare. It is quite likely that the Gê of central Brazil were involved in regular conflict with the Tupí of the coast (Balée 1984) and with other equally aggressive groups of the region (Zarur 1979). The frequency of warfare may have intensified with the arrival of Europeans, who made alliances with some Tupí groups of the coast, intensifying a long-standing conflict.

The Xavante are a good example of the sort of adaptation to the savanna achieved by populations of this region. In contrast with other groups which were pushed into the moist forest, or vice versa, the Xavante have maintained their movements within this ecosystem. Until 1950 the Xavante still had a horticulture characterized by the cultivation of corn, beans, and squashes (Maybury-Lewis 1967: 48). They were noted to engage in regular and lengthy periods of nomadism. Maybury-Lewis (1967: 48) indicated that they spent barely a week a year in the preparation of cultivated fields and two weeks in the harvest. The rest of the time they spent hunting and gathering.

The Xavante used a great variety of hunting techniques: hunting alone, in group expeditions lasting several days, and in group hunts using fire to drive game. The most frequently practiced was the individual hunt, even though it was not the most productive. The Xavante rate "collective hunting" as more productive; Flowers (1983) was able to confirm that 77 percent of collective hunts were successful, in comparison to 21 percent of individual hunts. This advantage is even clearer when comparing meat yields: the daily mean per hunter from collective hunts was 4.7 kilograms, but it was only 1.7 kilograms per person from individual hunts (Flowers 1983: 362). The difference may lie in the important role played by peccaries (*Tayassu pecari*), which travel in groups of up to a hundred individuals and which are best hunted by a group. An individual can kill at best one or two, whereas a group working together can kill up to twenty-two at one time.

The results of hunting and collecting are distributed among the entire population. Differences that may exist in hunting skill or in the number of hunters in a given family are diluted by the division of the game according to established rules that cut across clans, moieties, and descent. The consumption of animal protein among the Xavante was 121 to 138 grams per capita per day in the families studied by Flowers (1983: 367), an amount more than adequate to meet nutritional needs, which explains their fine state of health and tall stature (see discussion below).

Fishing is not commonly as successful in savanna areas due to the smaller size of rivers that cut across the savannas. Among the Xavante, fishing seems to be a recently developed interest, driven by the introduction of the hook-and-line. Sometimes groups will travel a considerable distance to fish at a larger river, remaining at such sites for a week or more when the river levels are low and fishing is most productive. The savanna populations use piscicides like populations of the forest regions—perhaps even more so because of the frequency of smaller streams, to which this technique is particularly well adapted.

Gathering activities have suffered a great deal due to recent restrictions in the movement of the Xavante. While they formerly depended heavily upon the wild roots of savanna plants, they use them less today, relying instead on rice and manioc cultivation.

The process of "pacification" of the Xavante restricted their mobility; they have been obliged to plant more and hunt less. The soils along the gallery forests are reasonably good and can support the cultivation of corn and beans, crops which do not fare well in many parts of the upland forests. None of the savanna populations has the same degree of dependence on manioc as one finds in populations of blackwater river basins, of liana forests, or of the oxisol or ultisol upland forests. The Kayapó Mekranotí who live in upland forests depend on manioc for 38 percent of their calories, while the Kanela of the cerrado obtain 42 percent of their calories from this source. This contrasts with Amazonian populations of the upland forests, who consume as much as 80 percent of their calories from this one source (Flowers et al. 1982). The impact of territorial restrictions on indigenous horticulture cannot be overemphasized. Such restrictions come from the occupation of savanna areas by cattle ranchers and overexploitation of the gallery forests. The Bororo and the Kanela have very few gallery forests left to cut in their territory. This, in turn, leads to smaller harvests despite greater effort spent on land preparation (Gross et al. 1979: 1046). In some areas of gallery forest, the origin of the soils is basalt and the problem faced by farmers is the invasion of weeds rather than declining fertility. The current crisis faced by the Bororo and the Kanela cannot be solved by traditional means. The areas given to these groups did not take into account their potential for demographic expansion following the epidemic disease period.

Another effective strategy is to live in transitional areas, or ecotones, between forest and savanna. The Kayapó Gorotire (Parker et al. 1983; Posey 1986b) today occupy an area with ten distinct biotopes (fig. 36) differentiated into scrub forest, grassland with sparse trees, grassland, gallery forest, upland forest, and other categories which lie between them. Like the Xavante, the Kayapó Gorotire maintained a seminomadic pattern, trekking for four to five months each year. During these travels, they affected local flora, purposefully creating "islands of resources" planted with as many as fifty-four different species. These areas are important sources of medicinal plants, raw materials, and food to sustain the trekking and hunting bands. These islands are, in fact, interesting experiments in replanting the savanna with woody vegetation, and more should be done to study and understand how to carry them out successfully. Figure 37 illustrates the relationship between these islands of resources and the villages.

Such a pattern contrasts with that of the Kayapó Mekranotí, who live in the interior of the Amazon forest, without access to cerrado. The Mekranotí probably derive their adaptive pattern from the savanna or as part of their macro-Gê cultural tradition. As a strategy, the pattern of seasonal mobility works well in the forested regions due to the large area of unrestricted land they can exploit. In contrast to the Kayapó of Gorotire, the Mekranotí do not seem to create "islands of resources" (Werner 1978). The Mekranotí have changed their diet from a pattern based on corn and beans to one based more on manioc and bananas. The preference to live in large vil-

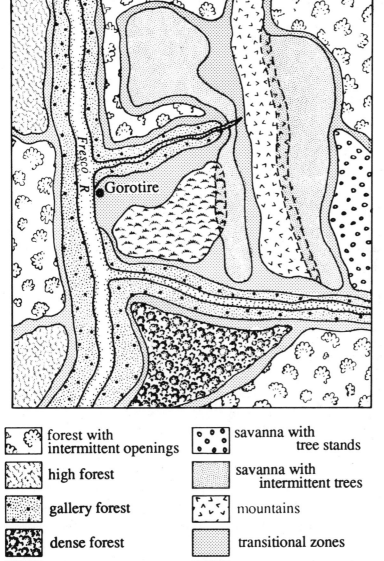

Fresco R.

Gorotire

	forest with intermittent openings		savanna with tree stands
	high forest		savanna with intermittent trees
	gallery forest		mountains
	dense forest		transitional zones
	short grassland		mixed transitional zones

Figure 36. Biotopes of the Kayapó Gorotire (adapted from Posey 1986b: 183).

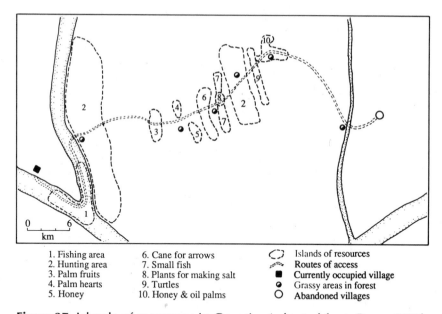

1. Fishing area
2. Hunting area
3. Palm fruits
4. Palm hearts
5. Honey

6. Cane for arrows
7. Small fish
8. Plants for making salt
9. Turtles
10. Honey & oil palms

Islands of resources
Routes of access
Currently occupied village
Grassy areas in forest
Abandoned villages

Figure 37. Islands of resources in Gorotire (adapted from Posey 1986b: 178).

lages, characterictic of the Gê, could be related to the maintenance of war potential or perhaps represents continuity with patterns of pre-Columbian settlements, as suggested by recent archaeological studies (Wust 1989). Historical studies are needed to clarify which changes have taken place in Mekranotí territories in order to establish what may have brought about changes over time.

Little attention has been paid to the horticultural activities of these populations. Evidence has been turning up with growing frequency that these populations have been cultivating for a long time. Some groups cultivate a plant (*Cissus* sp.) which is found nowhere else and seems to have been domesticated by them (Flowers et al. 1982: 214). The presence of "interlocked soft corn," an archaic form of corn, suggests that they may have domesticated this cereal independently. The Xavante cultivate a very large array of varieties of corn—white, yellow, red, and near-black. Each variety has a specific use, whether edible or ceremonial. But how are we to explain the observations made time and again about the neglect of horticultural activities?

The adaptive strategy that seemed to dominate was one of cultivating crops of rapid growth and high nutritional value in the soils of the gallery forests and scattering in the savanna for hunting and gathering. To what

Table 11. *Xavante Height and Weight Measures*

		Men			Women	
		Height	Weight		Height	Weight
	N	(cm)	(kg)	N	(cm)	(kg)
1962	24	168.1	67.2	34	154.7	54.0
1964	42	170.2	69.8	39	156.3	57.9
1977	40	168.9	66.0	48	153.1	57.7

Source: Flowers 1983: 374 (based on Neel et al. 1964: 65; Niswander et al. 1967: 492; and Flowers 1983).

degree this is a pre-Columbian pattern is only now being addressed in archaeological investigations (Wust 1988, 1989) and in the archaeological projects near the hydroelectric dam of Serra da Mesa and that of Cana Brava in the Tocantins, in the midst of traditional Akwé territory.

More recently, the Xavante have begun planting rice (Flowers 1983: 369–370). In contrast to game, which is widely distributed outside the consuming household, horticultural products' returns are kept within nuclear households. At present they invest twice as much time in agriculture as in collecting. The change reflects both the effects of demographic growth and territorial restriction (ibid., 372). When the Xavante still had considerable territorial freedom, they were visited by a team of doctors who assessed their physical condition, finding it to be excellent (Neel et al. 1964). As the Xavante became territorially restricted, Neel and Salzano (1967: 566) still found them in excellent condition, with impressive muscles, a lack of dental caries, no evidence of undernutrition among children, and low blood pressure. The Xavante are among the tallest indigenous Americans (men are 168 to 170 centimeters and women 153 to 156 centimeters) and among the heaviest (men are 66 to 69 kilograms and women 54 to 57 kilograms) (Comas 1971; see table 11). Neither their relative height nor weight has changed in the past fifteen years (Flowers 1983: 374).

Their growth trajectory and their overall health are surprising, given the great epidemiologic shocks they felt in the period between 1962 and 1977. A series of epidemics followed contact, including polio, measles, and whooping cough. The population today has a very small number of adults between the ages of fifteen and thirty as a result of the mortality experienced during that period. Neel et al. (1968) established that the Xavante were exposed to a number of pathogens: 62 percent of them had experienced malaria; 80 percent had been exposed to *Salmonella*; 58 percent to whooping cough; 71 to 95 percent to polio; 89 percent to measles; and they had antibodies against twenty-three types of arboviruses. The Xavante area is endemic of histoplasmosis and toxoplasmosis, with the highest prevalence rates found in the literature (ibid., 488). The impact of malaria is less in these areas than in wetter parts of Amazonia. No evidence of syphilis was found. The high levels of antibodies of *Bordatella pertussis* indicate the Xavante's experience with whooping cough.

One of the most serious problems of savanna populations seems to have been pneumonia and other respiratory problems. Temperatures can drop precipitously at night in the dry season, resulting in problems of the respiratory tract among the young and old. There is considerable disagreement among scientists about whether the prevalence rates are higher in this ecosystem.

It is important to continue monitoring the physical well-being of the Xavante in order to understand the ultimate impact of demographic increase and territorial restriction. In other parts of the world these changes have resulted in malnutrition and declining health. So far, the Xavante have adjusted in an impressive fashion, taking into account epidemiological and nutritional criteria. In part this can be explained in terms of their control over 205,000 hectares—a sizable territory for a population numbering 461 individuals in the 1990 census by Flowers (1992, see also the earlier census of 1977 with 249 individuals, in 1983: 359). Of course, as their numbers increase rapidly, and they have nearly doubled between 1977 and 1990, the people-to-land ratio will be radically transformed, and other adjustments will be necessary. Nevertheless, the importance of adequate territory to maintain health is made clear by the example of the Xavante.

Conclusions

The adaptive strategies of Amazonian populations in the savannas of the central plateau reflect the limitations and opportunities these areas offer under traditional levels of management. The chemical problems of the soils (acidity, nutrient poverty, poor water retention, high evapotranspiration, dry spells, and availability of gallery forests with good soils) have directed human adaptations toward a seasonal compartmentalization of resource use, emphasizing hunting and gathering on the savannas in the dry season and horticulture in the gallery forests in the wet season. The contribution of fishing varies with local habitat but does not seem to have had a marked influence on the patterns of social organization of the region's population.

The savanna populations developed sophisticated systems of social organization that represented effective responses to the fluctuations of the environment. They aggregated along the banks of the gallery forests in the rainy season to produce cereals of high nutritional value and rapid growth, followed by periods of fissioning into small bands of hunter/collectors organized according to formal criteria. Such organization favors spatial mobility and social flexibility for warfare. These mechanisms, as well as the aspects emphasizing physical stamina, gave them an important advantage during the period of contact. Some of the groups of the savanna have adjusted to areas of Amazonian upland forest. As shown in figure 33, the areas of savanna interdigitate with those of upland forest. It has not been uncommon for populations of the forest to settle on the margins of the savanna and for those on the savanna to settle on the margins of the forest—thereby gaining access to both types of habitat. It is quite probable that sizable population concentrations, and even chiefdoms, existed in this habitat in prehistory. In the case of the forest populations, decimation by disease and slavery promoted a pattern of dispersed population for self-protection. In the savannas the larger concentrations grew smaller, making it more difficult and less desirable to raid them for slave labor, but they kept their patterns of seasonal change in resource use.

The occupation and agricultural development of the savannas by the national society have been recent, but they have profoundly changed human densities in this ecosystem. The environmental responses (emphasizing mobility) that so successfully dealt with the seasonality of the environment gradually have been replaced by intensive systems of land use based on the application of fertilizers to correct the many limitations of the soils, by irrigation to deal with the dry spells, and by mechanization of the savannas to take advantage of the flatness of the terrain. The movement of population from the coasts to the center of the country and the advances in agronomic research have changed the face of the Brazilian savannas.

Intensive farming of the savannas must begin by correcting the soil acidity, adding substantial amounts of phosphorus, avoiding soil compaction, and trying to improve the subsoil so that roots can penetrate deeply and avoid wilting during the dry season (Goedert 1985). In general, farmers from the south of Brazil have preferentially expanded into the cerradão, or scrub forests, because of the higher fertility of the soils (Lopes and Cox 1977).

To correct the acidity of the soils it is necessary to apply lime. The soils seem to respond well: application of 2 tons of lime per hectare doubled the harvests of seven different crops (Goedert 1983) and the residual effect was long-lasting when the lime was applied 30 centimeters below the surface. This procedure facilitated nutrient availability, especially of calcium and magnesium (Ritchey et al. 1980). The correction of soil acidity has the immediate effect of improving the exchange of cations, facilitating the absorption of phosphorus, and increasing nitrogen fixation (Goedert 1985: 8). Fertilization is viable because of the abundance of dolomitic limestone and phosphatic rocks in the region (ibid.).

After soil acidity the other limiting factor for agriculture is the low level of phosphorus in soils, generally less than 2 parts per million. Grasses require about 3 to 5 parts per million of phosphorus and cereals about 8 to 10 parts per million (Goedert 1985: 9). Once this deficiency is corrected, crop production on these soils can be very impressive. The initial application must be very large in order to ensure deep rooting and avoid wilting.

Advances in the management of savannas for cattle ranching have been much less dramatic. Rotations, controlled burning, manipulation of the number of animals per hectare, and fertilizing with phosphorus and potassium have rarely been practiced (Sánchez 1977: 554). Mixtures of leguminous plants with grasses seem to offer some important advantages: *Melinis minutiflora* mixed with *Stylosanthes guyanensis* produced up to 250 kilograms per hectare of weight gain in the first year in the llanos of Colombia, but the legume did not survive due to pest attack (ibid.). In their natural state, the savannas support cattle herds, but the animals experience high weight losses in the dry season (Saturnino et al. 1977). Will it be worth the investment to increase the carrying capacity of the savannas for cattle, given the six-month dry season? Without irrigation it is questionable whether even cattle can give a return comparable, say, to that of soybeans. Given the advances in crop science, it is doubtful that extensive cattle ranching is justified in this environment. The savannas are capable of supporting sizable population aggregates. It is time that this ecosystem return once again to being dominated by human populations rather than being left as the domain of grazing cattle.

The future, in all likelihood, will see native populations continue to occupy parts of the savanna/forest ecotone to which they fled in the last century. The land rights of these native peoples should be assured. Their expertise in planting trees in savanna areas could offer some solutions in the restoration of previously forested areas that have been converted to pastures (cf. Posey 1985; Nepstadt et al. 1990). Their techniques for doing this, by themselves, will constitute a major contribution to the future of Amazonia and the world. Many of the areas that have been turned to pasture will need to be restored to forest, and native techniques may be far more appropriate than others that outsiders may try to introduce.

6

Human Ecology as a Critique of Development

The field of human ecology emerged, in part, in response to the growing specialization of contemporary science. Sociologists talk about environment, but they largely refer to the institutional setting within which people in organizations operate. Psychologists talk about environment, but they may refer to the household setting within which nurturing occurs. All academic disciplines talk about environment, but their conception of it tends to be very specialized and rarely refers to the total physical environment which ultimately provides the conditions for all life. People and society exist in a physical and material context that bears upon behavior, ideology, and social organization. Human ecology represents an effort to think in more integral terms. The amelioration of the state of planet earth as a setting for human life may very well depend on our capacity to begin to think in integral rather than sectoral terms.

A society's ecological ideology has great bearing on what it does or does not do. The view that the Amazon is a poor environment, a "green hell" or a "counterfeit paradise" as some have called it, led to explanations that affirmed that what we saw there—isolated, small settlements practicing swidden cultivation—was all that could be supported by that environment (Meggers 1954, 1971). Such a view tried to explain away the evidence for chiefdoms present in the accounts of the early chroniclers and even the archaeological evidence by positing that those chiefdoms came from elsewhere. A contrasting view, one that has seen the greenness of the forests as certain evidence of the richness of the habitat, has gone to the opposite extreme—calling the area "paradise," a "breadbasket for the future," "El Dorado," "the lungs of the world." This view has served to justify efforts at occupying the Amazon with outsiders, who were believed to be more capable than local inhabitants of using the presumed wealth therein—and in the process expropriated Indian lands, polluted the environment, and imposed external control on the region. Thus, an ecological ideology is not simply a process of intellectualizing. It represents a guide to action, which reflects the aspirations of those people who try to have their view prevail by any means at their disposal. In small-scale societies such an ideology may be largely consensual, while in nation-states such an ideology more often than not reflects the distribution of power and influence.

These academic questions have gained a renewed importance in the last decades of this century. It is possible to see evidence daily of a growing incoherence in our relations with nature: in the great cities pollution hurts our eyes, crime makes us modify our customary behavior, the prevalence of chronic diseases increases, and the gap between rich and poor grows. Poor people in rural areas work all day to produce food for the cities while their children go to bed hungry and lack access to medical care and education.

Brazil is a perfect example of this kind of situation: a country rich in resources, yet full of poor people. The gap grows each day. In Brazil 70 percent of the total population lives in cities. These largely poor people live alienated from the means of production, while national culture through its media tries to promote levels of consumption that only a few can ever hope to achieve. The consumerism promoted through advertising affects everyone, but hardly anyone relates it to the levels of pollution in cities, to the increase in chronic illness, to the alienation of youth, and to urban crime.

The urban-industrial system imposes its values over areas still unexplored, such as the Amazon frontier, and offers unfavorable terms of trade to the inhabitants of such areas. Thus, the value of products from rural areas is lowered in order to benefit the urban populations. This is literally an income transfer from the rural to the urban areas that ensures the impoverishment of rural people.

A number of factors underlie these processes, some of an ideological nature, others of a structural nature. The ideological basis of a capitalist economy, in which an individual seeks to maximize his or her utility, leads to a worldview that leaves it to "the invisible hand of the market" to determine the appropriate allocation of resources. Under perfect conditions of competition distribution might take place in textbook fashion. However, every capitalist economy has had the experience of individual capitalists who influence resource allocation and policy in ways that favor their particular industries (and put others in a less advantageous position). Very few industries and economic sectors can be said to operate for long under the ideal model of perfect competition. By and large, efforts are made to reduce competition by reducing the number of competitors who control the major production activities and access to the resources. Without a doubt capitalist economies have been responsible for achieving impressive levels of production and resource consumption in many nations. It must be acknowledged, too, that such economies are also responsible for the high levels of fossil fuel use which currently threaten to warm the planet, destroy the ozone layer, and pollute many of the rivers. Capitalism has a sound understanding of how to create incentives to produce more, but it has not always managed to create effective mechanisms to distribute those goods produced in socially just ways.

Socialist systems, on their part, emerged to correct these deficiencies. With time, unfortunately, these systems failed in other respects. They created mechanisms for distribution, but they forgot how to create incentives to increase production. The very structures of distribution became bureaucratized and corrupt, as recent events in Eastern Europe have made plain. Socialist economies failed to incorporate feedback mechanisms that would ensure citizen participation in the correction of the system.

Contemporary societies, whether socialist or capitalist, need a systematic way in which to think about *whole* systems that will question the assumptions of political leaders when they forget the larger context within which human populations exist and will offer alternatives to currently dominant forms of "rationality." Since the industrial revolution, many of our leaders have accepted economic criteria as the ultimate measure of how to allocate resources. This ideology has spread all over the globe—especially since World War II. Economic criteria are no doubt responsible for promoting economic growth in many nations, and few people suggest that they be replaced altogether. Nevertheless, it is important to be critical of them, too. Rationality, defined as the use of economic criteria (cost/benefit) in resource allocation, is responsible for the growing inequality between nations, between regions within nations, and between groups within nations. It is also responsible for many of the current environmental crises that we face: carbon dioxide accumulation, ozone depletion, global warming, tropical deforestation, estuarine pollution, and air pollution. It is responsible for these evils because it considers many components of the environment to be "externalities"—not easily quantifiable in economic terms and therefore not included in the calculus of supply, demand, and prices.

The value of human ecology as a form of critique and its usefulness for designing and executing environmentally appropriate activities make it an increasingly attractive field of study. The examination of the interaction between human behavior and environment permits assessment of the impacts of people on environment and vice versa. The value of human ecology as an instrument of environmental management comes from the fact that its ideas arise from the observation of people within their political, economic, social, historical, and physical context. Thus, this field of study gives full accountability of the day-to-day interactions of human populations, with particular attention to the consequences of decisions made and the identification of more or less successful outcomes. Human ecology does not promote an environmentalist morality that overlooks the needs and aspirations of particular human populations. Rather, it builds on their expertise, on their aspirations, and on the need to account for "externalities," no matter how difficult such a procedure may be. This is being recognized by some economists, for example, who have started a field called ecological economics in which they try to account for economic and biological processes in ways that most neo-classical economists could not even dream of a few years ago (Constanza 1991).

Learning from Native Amazonians

One of the fundamental problems facing the Amazon region has been the persistent ignorance of its human and ecological characteristics on the part of colonial and national societies. In the colonial period the native populations of the region were enslaved, massacred, and resettled without regard and respect for their intimate knowledge of local ecosystems. The people and the environment were disrupted in a permanent and radical fashion. Nevertheless, this impact was not the same everywhere. The populations which fled the floodplains in the first century of colonial occupation, and which survived in the upland forests, experienced highly variable degrees of interethnic contact in the following centuries. Some died out soon after, while others survived into the present. None of them survived in the same fashion in which they lived in the precolonial period. The religious missions, the Directory under Pombal, and the rubber era had a different impact on each subregion and each ethnic group of Amazonia (Oliveira 1988).

Fortunately, hundreds of ethnic groups have survived the impact of epidemics, economic exploitation, and resettlement (Gomes 1988). These populations constitute an irreplaceable source of knowledge about Amazonian ecosystems. The field of human ecology seeks to discover the day-to-day behavioral repertoires of local populations in their use and conservation of nature that may provide the basis to maintain the biotic diversity and productivity of Amazonia. Throughout this book I have presented some of the strategies of native Amazonians within particular ecosystems with the goal of learning from them how to use Amazonian biotic diversity without destroying it.

In chapter 2 we examined the complex forms of social organization, stratification, and control over resource areas that were necessary in blackwater ecosystems—areas with great environmental diversity but poor in biomass productivity. The need to protect these areas from the destructive tendencies of development-oriented national societies becomes evident upon examining the low productivity of these regions—but also their considerable potential for the extraction of substances of pharmacological value and as a "bank" of biotic diversity. These areas may have low biomass, agricultural, ranching, and logging potential, but they are among the richest in species. Therein lies their value and the importance of managing this diversity in the standing vegetation (cf. Schultes and Raffauf 1990).

In the upland forests, as we saw in chapter 3, we discover a cornucopia of management practices suggestive of the variation found there. On the better soils we find anthropogenic forests which result from the concentration of species of economic interest without excessive simplification of the area—so subtle, in fact, that until recently these forests were thought to be "natural" and "virgin" rather than the product of indigenous agroforestry management. The contemporary forestry engineer can learn a great deal from the long-term management approaches of native populations. In these soils one also finds a preference for the cultivation of corn in contrast to the dominance of manioc in the largely poor soils of the basin (Galvão 1963). The wisdom of these native preferences becomes obvious when we contrast these indigenous patterns with the imposition by the Brazilian Ministry of Agriculture of the cultivation of rice, corn, and beans along the Transamazon Highway in 1972—without regard to the differential potential of soils along a 3,000-kilometer trajectory (Moran 1977, 1981). Amazonian environmental management needs to begin to take into account the significant differences from place to place in soils, climate, flooding, distance from markets, and the higher value that some standing forests may have over alternative uses. In this regard, many of the indigenous populations are expert indeed.

In chapter 4 we examined the Indians' and caboclos' knowledge of the floodplain and the estuary. The systems of management practiced by local populations suggest that the region must be managed with considerable care if the rich fisheries of these aquatic systems are to be sustainable. Local populations, for example, avoid clearing the flooded forest and understand its function as a hatchery for the fisheries and a place where the fish gain much of their weight. We also learn from them the importance of intensively cultivating the alluvial beaches, levees, and other areas which are enriched by sedimentation during floods. This potential can only be achieved by maintenance of the local criterion for predicting the rise and fall of rivers— which relies on observation of the behavior of local fauna. Local populations also demonstrate the possibility of having ecologically advantageous mutualistic relations with native species, as in the case of the relations between river dolphins and fishers on the Madeira River (Goulding 1979).

The adaptations to the transitional areas of forest and savanna offer other interesting possibilities, as we saw in chapter 5. Those regions have been

Table 12. *Appropriate Management Strategies*

Estuary
  fast-growing fruit-producing palms; other extractive products;
  limited agriculture, usually on raised fields; intensive garden
  production near urban centers

Lower Floodplain
  fast-growing annual crops, irrigation management; fisheries
  and hatcheries development; truck farming; ecotourism

Upper Floodplain
  lake fisheries development; rice production; palm
  management

Blackwater Uplands
  agroforestry, focused on medicinal plants; bitter manioc
  agriculture; fisheries along cataracts

Nonblackwater Uplands
  agroforestry development: palm forests, bamboo forests,
  Brazil nut groves, *babaçú* palms; oil-producing trees;
  agriculture on better soils; organic matter management for
  sustained agriculture

Savannas
  cereal production on flatter land with intensive fertilization;
  restoration of ecotonal areas back to forest and agroforestry
  utilization

---

profoundly affected by the transformation of the landscape in recent years
and by their refuge status for indigenous peoples fleeing from other areas in
the past. Attention must also be drawn to the need for careful management
of the gallery forests because of their frequent association with rich, basaltic
intrusions that permit intensive forms of cultivation. The degree to which
these strategies may or may not be compatible with the growing mechanization of the savannas for soybean production remains a challenge for researchers in all fields.

   In short, attention to the ways in which indigenous peoples use Amazonian resources suggests that there is a great deal that must be learned by
anyone who pretends to enter the region and use its resources intelligently.
Table 12 summarizes some of these strategies for managing regional ecosys-

tems. An examination of the attempts to colonize the Brazilian Amazon over the past thirty years shows how easy it is to overlook the expertise of Amazonian peoples.

Colonization in the Amazon

The lack of attention to the indigenous peoples of Amazonia in recent efforts at settlement of the region, evident in the refrain from the Médici administration (1970–1974) "to give people without land to a land without people," has had devastating consequences for both local populations and the forests. The processes of deforestation began with the construction of the Belém–Brasília Highway and escalated with the construction of other north–south (Cuiabá–Santarém and BR-364 through Rondônia) and east–west (Transamazônica) highways. However, it would be a mistake to see this process as beginning only in 1964 or even in 1955. The dream of Getúlio Vargas of a nationalistic "westward march," akin to the North American assumption of a manifest destiny to reach the Pacific, influenced many civil and military leaders in Brazil during the Estado Novo. Particularly in the War College, these nationalistic goals of expanding the effective economic and political frontiers of Brazil found a home and a purpose. With the Belém–Brasília Highway that march into Amazonia began in earnest.

Settlement along the Belém–Brasília Highway brought over 2 million people and over 5 million head of cattle in the first twenty years of occupation. Along a feeder road, the PA-150, the rates of deforestation have been exponential: the area deforested has gone from 300 square kilometers in 1972 to 1,700 square kilometers in 1977 to 8,200 square kilometers by 1985 (in a total area of 47,000 square kilometers)—a rate of deforestation approximating that of Rondônia (Mahar 1988: 13–14).

The Transamazônica settlement scheme had even more pharaonic proportions, aiming to resettle 100,000 families within the first five years, providing roads, basic services, and an urban support structure. Basic research on the soils along the settlement area followed, rather than preceded, occupation of the area (Falesi 1972; IPEAN 1974; Moran 1977, 1981; Fleming-Moran and Moran 1978; Smith 1982b). The implementation of the scheme failed in many respects: the seeds distributed were inappropriate to the climate, credit was disbursed in untimely fashion, credit schemes obligated farmers to plant crops inappropriate for the soil and climatic conditions, and there was a lack of attention to the medical needs of the population.

Even the infrastructure failed. With the first oil shock in 1973, the government cut back on the feeder roads to the farms and completed only the main trunk, leaving the farmers unable to take their crops to market (Moran 1981). Fortunately, the human misery was less than it could have been. Not 100,000 but only 6,000 families migrated to this region, and the impact of all colonization at the end of the 1970s was less than 4 percent of the total (Browder 1988).

The colonization of the Belém–Brasília and the Transamazon highways overlooked basic concerns that are important to the discipline that has come to be known as human ecology. One of the first steps in human ecological analysis is to model the system in question and to determine what is known and what needs to be known before actions are taken. In 1970 there was very little information on the physical environments that would be traversed by the proposed roads and on the soil variability that settlers would encounter, and little idea of just how variable the landscape was. Thus, colonists were settled on poor soils incapable of producing even in the first year and whole villages were built on steep slopes too dangerous for the kinds of houses being built for the colonists (Smith 1976, 1982a). Entire communities were constructed, but farmers refused to move into them.

A basic problem has been the lack of inclusion of feedback processes that would permit correction of errors in the system originally designed (e.g., to locate the above community a couple of miles down the road on flatter terrain). The centralized nature of Brazilian bureaucracy (and its inflexibility) constitutes one of the greatest obstacles to the well-being of the Brazilian people—especially those furthest from the centers of power. Authoritarian bureaucratic structures are a long-standing tradition that will require considerable mobilization to change.

Research with a human ecological perspective was available on the Transamazon Highway from the inception of the project, but the agencies acting in the area showed little interest (Moran 1975, 1976, 1977, 1981; Smith 1976, 1982a; Fearnside 1979). What the colonists thought were their biggest problems differed from what the government agents thought the people needed. Settlers thought that medical assistance, roads to their farm lots, exploitation by others, and low prices for produce were their biggest obstacles to achieving a satisfactory performance. Technical personnel, in contrast, thought that the poor quality of the main trunk, plant pests, lack of seed, and weed invasion were the real problems. These differences in what each group perceived to be the constraints played a not insignificant role in the difficulties that resulted. An ecological approach with a human bias begins with how people view the environment and how they interact with it, then assesses the consequences of their decisions and suggests what readjustments may be necessary to achieve the goals desired. By contrast, the Transamazon settlement scheme imposed technical criteria developed far from the reality and experience of the settlers and failed to create forms of feedback to correct for errors discovered in the process of project implementation. A human ecological perspective is needed to begin to connect people and environment in a manner which better fits people to the complexity of the process (fig. 38).

How this works out in practice can be illustrated with events that took place in 1971 and 1972 in the Altamira area of the Transamazon scheme. While the technical personnel located arriving colonists using a first approximation of the soils of the area, the Amazonian peasants in the region used vegetational criteria to choose the better soils for agriculture (fig. 20). The former erred in the majority of cases, given the preliminary nature of the data and the scale at which they were elaborated (Moran 1984). The latter, by contrast, chose soils which were of superior quality and obtained a higher return per unit of land and per unit of labor than outsiders (Moran 1977, 1981). Despite the evidence throughout the period of intense occupation (1971–1974) in this region, the Amazon peasants were dismissed as poor farmers and were not relied upon to guide land occupation and farm selection of arriving colonists, a role they were willing to play at the outset (Moran 1975, 1976). While the agronomists who developed the soil maps were fully cognizant of the maps' limitations, the colonization personnel in charge of locating farmers on the land took the maps as precise indicators of soil quality even though the scale of the map was inappropriate for farm-level decision making.

There was very little evidence that agricultural frontiers are effective means of absorbing excess demographic growth (cf. Wood and Wilson 1984; Wagley 1974). By and large, agricultural frontiers are opened according to political goals of territorial expansion rather than for agroeconomic reasons. To attract the reluctant settlers, governments worldwide have had to provide costly incentives ranging from "160 acres of free land" in North America to promises of ready-built homes, cleared land, and below-market rates for bank credit in Brazil and Indonesia. Very little consideration is ever given to indigenous ethnic groups already living in the area being "occupied." In some cases, like the Brazilian and Venezuelan Amazon, the result is rural depopulation—rather than increments in population—because of high mortality or outmigration by indigenous people and a largely urban pattern of occupation due to more favorable economic opportunities in urban centers.

The government's promises rarely mention the problems of large-scale land clearing. The deforestation of large tracts leads to the movement of sylvatic forms of arboviruses to human hosts. Deaths from these rare arboviruses were kept from the media in the early stages of road building. Leishmaniasis continues to plague many new settlers in the region. Brazil has today the doubtful "honor" of having the largest number of new cases of malaria worldwide. One out of every five new cases occurs in Brazil, resulting to a large extent from the uncontrolled activities of miners in Amazonia and from roads built without proper bridges and drainage culverts.

The "roads of development" built in the past twenty years often blocked existing seasonal streams which drained large volumes of precipitation from the land. Behind these roads were created artificial dams which provided an ideal breeding area for mosquitoes and the spread of malaria. The problem repeats itself in the mining areas, where the land is filled with deep cavities and left in that form—thereby bringing ill to all. Until the authorities can ensure that land is restored to its original condition and that such costs are borne by those who benefit from resource exploitation, there will be little reason *not* to abuse the physical environment. In colonization areas, it is preferable to have fewer, but well-drained, roads. What is the sense of having more roads if the people are too sick to work? Despite all these problems, many of the colonists have persisted—some have even thrived. Others have migrated to urban centers and joined the mass of wage-earning urban dwellers who crowd the cities.

Planting Pastures as an Option

Although colonists and colonization have often been blamed for Amazonian deforestation, the high rates of deforestation are traceable to cattle ranching activities, especially in the south of Pará and the north of the states of Goiás and Mato Grosso. In Brazil it is estimated that the area deforested and put into pasture is at least 10 million hectares. Since 1966 the Amazon Development Agency (SUDAM) has been offering fiscal incentives and tax incentives that permit individuals and firms to apply 50 percent of their federal income tax liability to investments in approved Amazon development projects. For each cruzeiro of tax liability contributed, the federal gov-

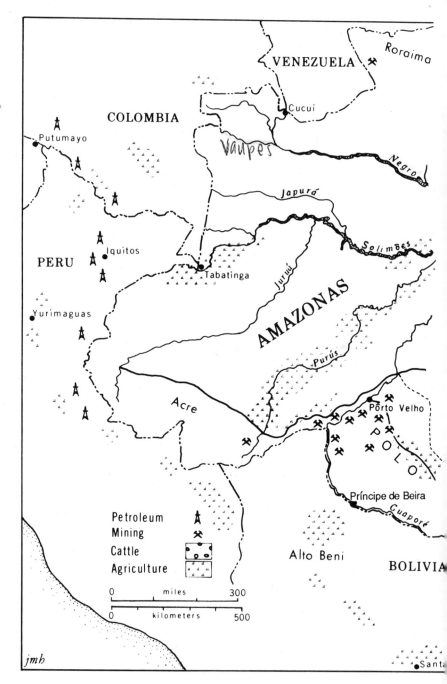

Figure 38. Development activities in the Amazon Basin.

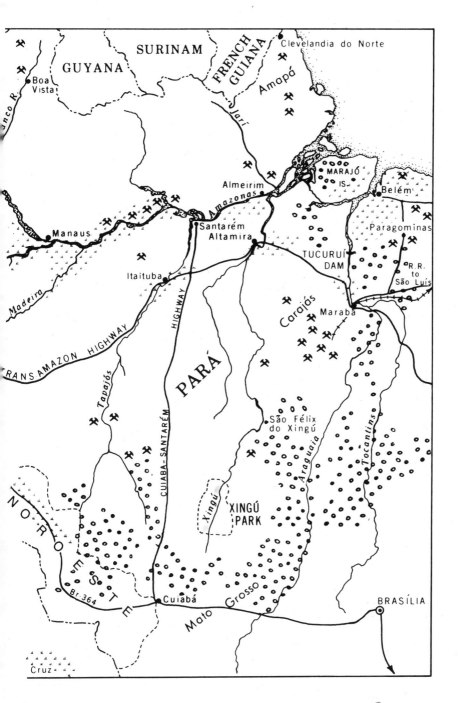

TRombetas? Napo?

ernment contributed three more and gave the project a totally tax-exempt status for ten years, and the capital gains from the four cruzeiros' investment was kept tax-free by each investor. This policy was responsible for promoting uncontrolled deforestation and was a form of income transfer from the many to the pockets of a few (Hecht 1980; Fearnside 1984, 1985, 1987b, 1988, 1989a, 1989b; Mahar 1988; Moran 1990). There has been an apparent halt to this practice since 1989, with a dramatic decline in rates of deforestation accompanying the ending of tax incentives. Whether this is a permanent change or only a pause remains to be seen.

The majority of projects approved by the Amazon Development Agency have been cattle ranches, with a mean size of 24,000 hectares, and some with more than 100,000 hectares. Of the 950 projects approved as of 1985, 631 were clearly cattle ranches (García Vásquez and Yokomizo 1986: 51, in Mahar 1988: 15). Cattle ranches have a very low labor absorption capacity, using less than one person for every 300 hectares. Even though more than 700 million dollars were transferred to cattle ranchers in the 1970s, they have produced insignificant amounts of milk and beef. Only ninety-two of the ranches were thought to have achieved some of their goals as of 1988. Recent studies have shown that unless these ranches receive the entire panoply of tax incentives, they have negative rates of return and constitute an income transfer from the majority of the Brazilian people to the wealthier components of the nation (Hecht et al. 1988).

Few researchers have undertaken studies on cattle ranching with a human ecological perspective (S. Hecht is one exception). But ecological and political economic studies permit a preliminary assessment of this form of land use. It cannot be said that cattle ranching employs people, since it is the economic activity with the lowest demand for labor. Nor can it be said that this is an effective strategy for occupying lands too poor to farm, since the ranches compete with farms for the best soils (Fearnside 1987a). In other parts of the world these are the reasons that have been given to justify the presence of cattle in human ecosystems. In reality, cattle ranching is an economic activity commonly located on marginal lands and sufficiently distant from farming areas to avoid destruction of crops by the cattle (as in the sertão of northeast Brazil).

In contrast, throughout much of Latin America and definitely in Brazil, cattle ranching has been a form of frontier land occupation under conditions of low supplies of labor. In the absence of numerous settlers, cattle served as occupiers of the frontier and a tool in the transformation of free land into land imbued with economic value. Unfortunately, when cattle are allowed to roam freely near farms they can also set back agricultural development. In several parts of the Brazilian Amazon farmers commented that cultivation was not profitable, given the destruction brought about by loose cattle. As Brazil's population grows and approximates 200 million, the day must also approach when the role of cattle in land use is reassessed.

Observation of rural populations on a worldwide basis suggests that they benefit from intensive management of animals in combination with intensive crop cultivation (Stone et al. 1990). In that manner it is possible to use the organic fertilizer provided by the animals on crops, and they can gain weight faster by consuming remains of crops and provide milk, cheese, and beef. The linkage of these intensive farms to human populations requiring high-quality horticultural crops and animal products can lead to a rise in standards of living rarely experienced by contemporary rural populations of Brazil. Intensive land use also permits balancing agricultural areas with the management of areas for conservation and leisure.

The colonization of Rondônia has resulted in greater devastation than in any other area of contemporary Amazonia. In this region, the process is more related to colonization and land speculation (Fearnside 1985, 1987a). However, even here the efforts to introduce perennial crops, especially co-coa, among the colonists have given way to the expansion of cattle ranches because of the favorable tax incentives. Today 25.6 percent of the deforested area is covered in pasture, in contrast to a mere 3.5 percent in perennial crops (Mahar 1988).

Preference for this form of land occupation could be reversed, beginning with the collection of property taxes. These taxes exist but are rarely, if ever, collected. If taxes on these enormous properties were collected, it would be possible not only to pay for the costs of collecting them but to encourage landholders to dispose of many properties, selling portions of the total areas—to the general social benefit of the Brazilian people. The elimination of fiscal incentives and tax exemptions would be a very positive policy intervention. Until now these activities have had a minimal, and sometimes negative, impact on regional development and income distribution. The rural populations of the Amazon need to be assured that the well-being of the people as a whole is being considered—and that the law of the strongest no longer applies. In rural Amazonia the large-scale landowners have relied on the use of guns and violence to ensure that their control over resources is protected from "invaders." These same gunmen can terrify the tax collectors unless the government ensures that these agents of the state act in its behalf—even in the wild frontiers of Amazonia.

Will There Always Be Amazonian Forests?

The same pressures that have destroyed the great tropical forests of the Ivory Coast, Indonesia, Malaysia, and so many other countries of Africa and Asia have begun to make their presence felt in Amazonia. Most countries of Africa and Asia entered the last decade of the twentieth century with scarcely 2 to 15 percent of their tropical forests still standing. These areas were allegedly cleared to help feed the rapidly growing populations of the world—but today these same areas are less capable of producing food and feeding themselves than they were before deforestation started.

The process began to be felt in the Americas in the small countries, as in the cases of Haiti and Costa Rica. Haiti today has barely 2 percent of its forests intact; instead of a growing agricultural capacity, it experienced a 15 percent drop in agricultural production in the past decade. Costa Rica, thanks to a militant conservation movement, has been able to stop the rapid destruction of its forests, but not before 40 percent of its forests had been felled—in areas inappropriate for agriculture. Will Amazonia have to go through the same devastating experience before policy makers and citizens act to prevent it?

The very immensity of Amazonia has served to protect it, as well as to support an attitude among public figures that its destruction is not in the realm of the possible. Yet recent events suggest that such destruction can be rapid. While less than 0.6 percent of the tropical moist and rain forests of Amazonia had been felled by 1975, that figure had risen to at least 5 percent by 1988—and some estimates put it as high as 12 percent (Mahar 1988). In either case, the areas felled and burned represent an area the size of France, probably the loss of some rare species whose value we will never come to know, release of more than 1 billion tons of carbon into the atmosphere, and a reduction in precipitation at the edges of the Amazon Basin which can reduce crop yields. The deforested areas are equivalent in extent to the total area planted in soybeans, corn, and wheat in Brazil—and have added little in the way of value to Brazil's economy or food for its people.

The forests are part of the national patrimony and a source of wealth for future generations. The deforestation permitted for the past two decades has contributed very little to the national treasury. On the contrary, a good part of the current external and internal debt of Brazil can be traced to the efforts to "develop the Amazon" in the past two decades. More than 15 billion dollars were spent by the government in a range of projects which have largely failed to produce any noticeable economic returns to repay their costs. In fact, the deforestation of Amazonia was made possible by a transfer of wealth from the poor and middle classes to the pockets of a small number of local and foreign entrepreneurs.

In Brazil national and international interests find an environment favorable to the destruction of forests (Browder 1988, 1989). At the First International Exposition of Amazonian Products in Belém in 1989, one out of every two companies present represented a logging company exporting hardwoods. In Rondônia and Roraima wood exports constitute 60 percent of the industrial value of each of these two regions. The value of wood exports has increased from 14.3 percent a decade ago to 43.6 percent by 1984 and is quickly accelerating (Browder 1988: 249).

The destruction brought about by logging is much greater than those concerns like to admit. A recent study demonstrated that the removal of a few mahogany trees affects up to 40 percent of the surrounding vegetation (Uhl and Vieira 1989). A great deal of research in human ecology is needed to derive knowledge of how to exploit forest resources with minimum impact, how to use more species in a given area, and how to manage forests so as to permit greater concentration of species of economic value—as was done by prehistoric populations in portions of Amazonia (Balée 1989)—and as documented in the Peruvian Amazon by Denevan and Padoch (1988).

There are some lessons to be learned from Asian use of forest resources. In that part of the world there are regions with great population densities that have managed to combine intensive cultivation of crops with conservation of large areas of forests. Systems of interplanting pastures with tree crops—such as rubber, cacao, bananas, and African oil palms—and annual crops have worked well in providing high income and sustainable production. The management of species with high amounts of leaffall can also help in promoting recycling (cf. Anderson 1990 for numerous instances of sustainable use of forest products).

The uses of the standing forest also need to be recovered by close study of the strategies of local peoples. The extraction of natural rubber and the use of various nuts produced by species like the Brazil nut, numerous palm fruits (*açaí, babaçú, burití, bacaba,* etc.), native oils, coloring agents, alkaloids for pharmacology, and substances with fungistatic and bacteriostatic qualities promise ways in which it may be possible to balance use and conservation in the years ahead. The economic returns from cattle ranching in Amazonia are so low that almost any extractivism will have returns at least equal to those of ranching, without requiring the biological loss of species that clear-cutting requires (Anderson 1990).

The protection of the Amazonian forests will depend on policies that will support the sustainable use of these areas. Those policies will need the knowledge of the native Amazonians for their successful implementation. The place of conservation in native ideology varies from native group to native group. Seeger (1982) suggested that among the Gê-speakers of central Brazil he found little that could be construed as a "conservationist" attitude, in contrast to the populations of the Upper Rio Negro, which have been shown to pay considerable attention to the nurturing of species within their territories. It is important to note that the populations of the Upper Rio Negro have had long-term residence in these nutrient-poor but species-rich areas, whereas the Gê have experienced considerable residential mobility. The relationship between sedentarization and a conservationist attitude may be a close one and deserves further study by human ecologists. Between these two extremes of a conservation ideology are the rest of the Amazonian populations. In the majority of cases, native Amazonians show considerable respect for nature, but their attitude is practical, directed toward using nature and ensuring its long-term productivity—without environmental romanticism. For them the forest is a source of life, which must be used but also conserved for their children. Native Amazonians do not all agree about how much to conserve. The degree of conservation practiced is very closely tied to their political, economic, demographic, and social situation (Johnson 1989).

The attitude that the forest will always be there comes from a lack of understanding of how exponential processes work. The current rates of deforestation are among the highest ever recorded. The destruction of the Asian and African rain forests should serve to alert Brazil and other countries of Amazonia that such destruction proceeds ineluctably unless contrary policies are implemented in time. The lush Atlantic forests have been reduced to less than 8 percent of their original extent, and efforts to preserve half of this area have proven both expensive and still uncertain in their success.

Specialists in biological diversity agree that the biotic inheritance of the planet will be conserved, or lost, in the 1990s. The rates of Amazonian deforestation, which exceed more than 15 hectares per minute, will undoubtedly result in the extinction of thousands of species. The pace of species loss in Amazonia at present is 500 times the rate of natural species appearance. One can hope that the rates of deforestation will be slowed in the near future. But even if this occurs, it will be necessary to have a more enlightened policy that values the standing forest and does not require cutting before it becomes valuable.

One example of a forestry policy uninformed by human ecology is the recent development of pig-iron smelters along the Carajás railroad in eastern Pará. From a human vantage point, as shown in a series of studies, the thousands of people cutting forests and turning it into charcoal to feed the smelters have both poor health and low incomes—and they know that in cutting the forests they are destroying the patrimony of their children and ensuring their impoverishment. The destruction is taking place not on the small-holders' plots but on the large cattle ranches which—now that they have exhausted the income transfers provided by the earlier policies of SUDAM—have convinced the same agency to give them authority (and funds, again) to make pig iron and to be exempt from the past conservationist rule that no one may cut more than 50 percent of the forests on his or her property. These influential individuals have succeeded in gaining another form of income transfer while creating an industry which can only last as long as the forests are within easy reach, producing a low-quality product in a world market already saturated with higher-quality output. This is what happens when "development" overlooks the fact that its true objective is improving the quality of human life—something that requires a sense of social responsibility rather than a mere concern with apparent gains in aggregate output.

Human Ecology and Social Justice

What could justify the deforestation of Amazonia? Despite the clearing of over 10 percent of the region, there have not been any notable improvements in the human condition. On the contrary, after twenty years of dramatic "development activities," and more than 15 billion dollars of investment, the benefits are not palpable. Most projects approved by SUDAM are still unable to turn a profit without continuous subsidies. This suggests that these are simply not economical operations even when they destroy resources which are not priced at their true value. Even capital-rich multinationals have had problems turning a profit. The famous Jarí Project, owned earlier by Daniel Ludwig, absorbed over 1 billion dollars in investment and was sold in the mid-1980s for barely 280 million dollars.

Economic development ought to lead to improvements in health and well-being. But, in contrast, the past twenty years of land clearing have led to

exponential growth in malaria cases, endemism of schistosomiasis in Ford-
landia, and a high prevalence of trauma. Children in Amazonia are more
undernourished today, and the rates of infant mortality are higher, than
twenty years ago. Indians are still experiencing rates of mortality that medical assistance could remedy. Amazonia today reflects the same patterns of
land and income concentration, and extreme forms of stratification, found
in the rest of Brazil. The 15 billion spent in the past twenty years on pharaonic projects in Amazonia could have been better spent on schools, health
care, and social services.

Human ecology is not a cure-all for all the problems experienced by Brazil
and other countries of Amazonia. The history of bureaucratic patrimonial-
ism (Uricoechea 1980; Faoro 1958; Roett 1973) cannot be undone over-
night. These problems cannot be resolved without a sharpened moral con-
science that explicitly addresses issues of social justice and the need to give
priority to people rather than to aggregate measures of "development" such
as gross national product and per capita income. The construction of a road
is not simply a matter for engineers to address. A road entering an "unoccupied" area attracts people with and without land. How that land is used
will depend on the current legislation, the banking system, the distance to
other centers of economic activity, the information available about the land
being settled, the agrarian traditions of the people, and the guarantee of
land tenure. There is no such thing as "unoccupied land." To offer land to
one group in society means to limit access to it by other groups. The sooner
this reality is confronted, the sooner we can work toward just agrarian
policies.

Human ecology as a critique of currently dominant models of development is not purely negative but is concerned with introducing criteria that
are more humanistic than purely economic. It is not necessary to destroy
the forests of Amazonia to use them. The Amazon is extremely variable and
offers a cornucopia of resources to human societies. The 10 percent of high-
quality soils in the region are widely known today, and these areas should
be dedicated to the intensive cultivation of crops. The caatingas of the Rio
Negro have little agricultural potential but are rich in pharmacologically
active plants that could become a source of wealth if sustainably extracted.
The Indian and the indigenous peasant working alongside the forester can
help identify and manage these species. The recent symposium volume edited by Anderson (1990) provides many alternatives to deforestation. Many
areas of low natural fertility that should not have been deforested can be
restored in ways that might permit alley cropping or agroforestry with pref-

erence for native plants and diversified plantations to reduce the impact of disease in the vegetation. Mining concerns should be required to restore areas already damaged and to guarantee restoration of any newly exploited areas.

A country that is rapidly approaching 200 million people cannot act as it did when it had a mere 20 or 30 million. Brazil is rich in resources, but they are not inexhaustible, nor is the capital required to develop megaprojects. The result of the past and current model of economic development in Latin America has been external and internal indebtedness, the neglect and break-down of basic national infrastructure, declining levels of education, rising infant mortality rates, and the impoverishment of the majority of the people.

More people are worse off today than twenty years ago. Development needs to care for this majority: it needs to empower it through better edu-cation, better health and nutrition, and a clearer idea of the relationship of natural resources to national wealth and well-being. People need jobs, but they also need green areas to relax and to dream of tomorrow.

The forces responsible for the disorderly destruction of Amazonia for the past twenty years can be expected to continue to exert pressure to maintain their privileges. They will try to maintain the tax exemptions which transfer income from the pockets of the many to the pockets of the few. They will try to avoid paying federal income taxes as well as the capital gains taxes on the sale of rural properties mandated by law.

Ameliorating the current disorders we see all around Amazonia will de-pend on the will of both those in political power and those who elect them. Both will need to resist the attractive terms offered by multinationals seeking resources without consideration for long-term value. Tax structures will have to be changed so that each citizen pays according to his or her ability and is taxed in a more progressive fashion. Members of each nation must act to control the behavior of those responsible for the destruction of forests through the use of harsh penalties to ensure compliance with the law. That destruction has not helped the people but has served merely to enrich those receiving tax exemptions.

A great deal must change for this to occur, beginning with making locally elected officials more accountable to local populations. This will also re-quire that a greater proportion of taxes remain with local government to meet needs for schools, hospitals, and road-building. This is a radical re-structuring because it implies a simultaneous dismantling of structures of power at the local and the federal level, requires changing the tax-collecting structures, and empowers local people, should they choose to mobilize in their own behalf. It is quite likely that if they knew that taxes on resale of properties would remain to be used in improving local conditions they would ensure that large-scale landowners did not escape the tax collector as they do today. If resources were closer to the locality, there might be more incentive to improve education and a faster rate of response in repairing needed roads and other essential services. Dependence on the federal government generally has a pernicious effect on local political participation. These people are perfectly capable of acting without the help of outsiders. However, the nature of the global environmental crisis cries for people everywhere to join one another as they seek more effective ways to bring local control of the use of resources through participatory procedures. Access to the technology of immediate communication was a major tool in the hands of many people in helping bring about the transformations in the former Soviet Union.

The science of human ecology is not a political platform, but it does not overlook the importance of political processes in human existence. The "rationality" of human ecosystems is a process influenced by the interest groups who control institutions and in so doing define what will be considered rational. When the dominant groups represent the will of the majority of the population through the democratic process, it may very well be that rationality reflects consensus. Unfortunately, in the majority of stratified societies, what is defined as rational favors the interests of powerful groups who dominate the political process to ensure themselves control and wealth.

A human ecological approach permits the assessment of how human ecosystems function and of the consequence of particular structures and functions. With such an approach it may be possible to correct disorders in the system when and if the political will is there. It may even suggest how the structure and function might be changed to reorder the flow of goods and the pattern of authority and control. The people of Amazonia aspire to a future with social justice, with an appreciation of indigenous populations, and with forms of management that will ensure that Amazonia is used and conserved as an essential patrimony of the people still to be born.

Environmental groups in Brazil and the other countries with Amazonian territories have joined with associations of indigenous peoples in a common struggle: to protect the forests of Amazonia from those who would destroy them. Environmental preservation is valuable and worth fighting for. The native Amazonians provide us with many ideas about how to balance use and conservation and how to be rich without necessarily always having to consume more.

Notes

1. Amazonia: People and Environment

1. The concept of an ecological system emphasizes the web of relationships that bind everything to everything else. It brings out the importance of studying populations rather than relying on ethnic group, culture, or other units of analysis divorced from the physical setting within which they exist.

An ecosystem is defined as the species that live in a given abiotic environment and the web of interrelations that unite them into a structural and functional whole. In other words, the ecosystem is the total context in which adaptation takes place (Moran 1982b). Because human beings can be found all over the planet, this context can be highly variable. A human population in a given ecosystem will be characterized by strategic behaviors that reflect both present and past environmental pressures. In general, the longer a population has been in a given environment, the greater its degree of adaptation to those environmental pressures. Similarly, a recently resettled population in an area dissimilar from its home region will manifest behavioral adaptations to the area of origin, rather than to the new, and still largely unknown, pressures of the environment. Over time, through trial and error the population will test past knowledge in the new setting, giving up only what proves to be a serious threat to well-being and adopting what enhances it. Such a process of cultural and behavioral change will proceed at a faster rate if there are people in the area with effective adaptations from whom to learn than if all behaviors and ideas have to be invented through trial and error alone.

2. Given how complex studying climatic variables could be, it is necessary to select a small number of indices that can be used productively to generate a varied array of analyses. The most basic information for human ecological studies is to know the daily precipitation and maximum and minimum daily temperatures in the area of interest (Wilken 1988). With these data it is possible to estimate other indices such as number of days of continuous rain, evapotranspiration rates (Bordne and McGuinness 1973), and available soil moisture (Baier et al. 1972). Monthly or annual means are insufficient for an adequate assessment of the role of climate in local ecosystems. Wilting can occur in a few rainless days during the dry season in parts of the Amazon, a phenomenon that we could not even consider with monthly averages. These data should ideally represent a twenty-year time-series if they are to have any chance of reflecting the effects of year-to-year fluctuations.

3. Ecosystem characterization cannot go far without a description of the variation in soil types in an area studied. In the Amazon it is rare to find soil maps at a scale appropriate for management decisions at the level of the farm (i.e., 1:10,000; cf. Moran 1984). Most maps are at the FAO scale of 1:5,000,000

or at best at 1:100,000 (RADAM 1972–1979). To get around this limitation, most investigators may need to take soil samples. To integrate these data into human ecological investigation, it is ideal to begin by collecting the local population's means of classifying soils. By asking, for example, "How many kinds of soils do you name?" it is possible to begin to construct a taxonomy that reflects locally important criteria. This might be followed by collecting the indicators used by the population to locate each type of soil. To engage in soil sampling correctly, one should take note that one soil sample is composed of 10–15 cores taken randomly from a homogeneous field at a depth of 0–20 centimeters (the so-called plow layer or rooting zone for most domesticated annual crops). In some cases, it may be helpful to take deeper soil samples if the use of the land involves rooting processes at deeper levels in the soil profile or if the goal is to classify soils. The use of an auger to a depth of 1 or 2 meters is common. In some cases a "soil pit," a somewhat large square hole to about 2 meters, is dug, which permits better observation of the soil profiles for the purposes of classification.

4. The composition of a forested area is often sampled using transects, commonly of areas of 100 or 200 square meters. Another method is to sample the vegetation 5 meters to the right and left of a 1,000-meter tape placed on the forest floor, giving an area of 1 hectare. Such a long rectangular sampling area is currently believed to offer a more accurate assessment of diversity than more square transects (Balée, personal communication, 1992). The manual of Mueller-Dumbois and Ellenberg (1974) is considered the standard (cf. Cain and Castro 1959). It is also sometimes useful to sketch a vegetational transect (fig. 19 gives an example of the structure of an upland forest in contrast to a floodplain forest). Biomass production is most often estimated by randomly placing about ten 1-meter-square screens to catch leaffall in the area of forest to be studied. Leaffall must be collected every one or two weeks to avoid losing the collection to the natural process of decomposition. Most human ecologists also collect floral specimens, given the richness of the Amazonian flora and the importance of identifying new species. Leaves, flowers, and fruits are necessary for accurate identification by systematists working with major collections such as Kew Gardens in England, the New York and the Missouri Botanical Gardens in the United States, the Goeldi Museum in Belém (Brazil), and the National Institute for Amazonian Research in Manaus (Brazil).

5. Faunal data collection must begin by asking hunters about the various kinds of habitats in hunting, sampling from each, as well as those that have been abandoned. The most common method is to scan an area of 100 square meters through visual accounting of animals seen (Eberhardt 1978; Brower and Zar 1984; Seber 1986). To determine the efficiency of hunting, data should be obtained from hunters about the distance traveled, how many animals were seen, how many were killed, how much meat was consumed on the spot, and how much brought back; whenever possible, basic morphometric measurements should be taken to permit sex and age determinations of animals hunted (Redford and Robinson 1987).

6. The myths of each society also serve to sanctify the proper relations between people and environment, in some cases going as far as tying our origin to that of other species, creating antagonisms with some, and regulating interaction with others. Some scholars, for example, have seen in the Judeo-Christian tradition and the book of Genesis, which says that "God gave man dominion over all the creatures," a basis for our utilitarian attitude toward nature. This view contrasts with that of societies where myths suggest that our soul may someday inhabit the body of an animal or tie our origin as a species to an animal of the forest (a myth commonly found in Amazonia). The latter show much greater respect toward forest animals and relate to them not purely as sources of meat. We are, after all, products of our history and cultural experience.

To study the human condition we need an interdisciplinary orientation, such as that offered by human ecology, irrespective of the ideological or political priorities chosen. The relations between people and environment are mediated by culture, by the accumulated past experiences of the population through time, and by the social and political values that dominant groups impose on individuals in a social system. Human ecology constitutes, therefore, a way to confront the dilemma of Amazonia: how will we come to know it without destroying it? Will it be possible to discover ways to use it that do not compromise its long-term conservation and its services to the planet?

7. Human beings, as social animals, organize in ways that permit them to obtain needed resources effectively. Their social organization, especially among populations depending on the immediate physical environment, often reflects solutions to problems presented by those environments. The basic dimensions that need to be described are the activities associated with resource use, the calendar of activities, and the local forms of organizing labor.

The basic method of data collection is to begin by informal interviews about the goods produced, including a list of cultivated plants, domesticated animals, fish caught, and wild food sources; the seasonal division of labor in the various activities and their relation to various markers; the utilization of the various products (for subsistence, exchange, or sale and the proportions going to each kind of use); the nature of the activities (their names, the technologies used, and the relationship of the technology, the management, and the resource); and who participates in the subsistence activities: the division of labor by sex, age, and status, the units of production (household, clan, phratry, etc.), types of mutual obligation created, the role of wage labor, sharecroppers, and so forth, and the types of residential units and subsistence units. Finally, what are the problems perceived by the population: seasonal climate, crops, getting enough labor, transportation?

8. Our perception of the environment is as influential as—sometimes more influential than—the physical reality of the environment. Ethnoecological data collection leads us to pay attention to dimensions that we might have overlooked if we presumed that a population had the same perceptions we have. Of interest, too, should be the fit between those perceptions and some measurable reality of the environment. The perception of environment is influenced by other

components of a population's social experience such as demographic structure, social organization, health and nutritional status, and historical experience in a region.

In ethnoecology, the investigation begins by asking what a population names items in a given domain—for example, "fish." Thus, one would ask the informant: "How many kinds of fish are there around here?" The informant might respond by saying: "Well, there are many . . . there are *acarí, tamuatá, bacú, pirarucú, traíra, arraia, puraque, mandubi* . . ." For each type of fish, one would subsequently ask, "Are there several kinds of (e.g.) *acarí*?" For each fish named one would seek to arrive at the maximum number of distinctions made by the informant. Then the researcher would go one by one, seeking to compare each with the other, asking: "How can one tell an *acarí boi* from an *acarí nana*?" This process gradually leads to the definition of distinctive criteria used in making such judgments; for example, while they both have a roundish head, *acarí nana* has distinctively pointy scales and *acarí boi* does not (having instead a larger head than *acarí nana*). Sometimes differences in color are important criteria, which tend to suggest attention to age differences. Such explicit attention might be indicative of the importance of age discrimination to fishers in how and when they catch fish. This possibility would have to be investigated by other means such as detailed interviews and observation. From these cognitive dimensions of the environment it is possible to move to the collection of other social and environmental data that permit discussion of the ecosystem. Recent volumes have contributed important information about the biological knowledge of native peoples which can serve as a basis for contemporary studies using Western scientific methods (Berlin 1992). Biological work in Amazonia is inconceivable without relying on the expertise of local people for location of specific plants and animals. Even more could be done if we began searching for the ecosystemic relations which local populations often also know and which remain largely uninvestigated.

9. Traditional practices such as scarification and tattooing may lie behind the high levels of antibodies against hepatitis B virus found (Baruzzi et al. 1977; Black et al. 1974; Biocca 1945; Lee et al. 1978). The presence of fungal infections (i.e., micoses), such as blastomicosis of Jorge Lobo (Baruzzi et al. 1973, 1979), *Tinea imbricata* (Baruzzi et al. 1983), and black *piedra* (Fishman 1973; Coimbra and Santos 1989), are common and generally benign. Prevalence of intestinal parasites can be high, with rates of up to 100 percent for some helminths (see Salzano and Callegari-Jacques 1988: 94–96). These high prevalence rates occur simultaneously with low parasite loads (Neel et al. 1968; Lowenstein 1973; Neel 1974; Larrick et al. 1979; Lawrence et al. 1980). The role of the traditional pattern of residential mobility among many interfluvial Amazonian populations may explain the low parasite loads, until these populations become sedentary. The impact of parasitism increases with sedentarization, greater population concentration, increased likelihood of water pollution, and changes in the use of space within the home (Coimbra 1989).

2. Blackwater Ecosystems

1. Some areas which are called "blackwater" may be so largely in color but not in the fundamental geomorphological factors that I note are characteristic of these systems. It is not so much the color of the water as the soils and characteristic vegetation which distinguish these areas from other parts of the humid tropic biome (see Moran 1991 and commentary in *American Anthropologist*, September 1992).

2. In Spanish and English the commonly used spelling is Vaupés River, while in Portuguese the spelling is Uaupés.

3. While Dufour (1988) argued that selection favors varieties that are more flavorful and interesting, this criterion implicitly favors toxic varieties and thus has the positive consequence of enhancing those varieties' persistence in this region, where plants have a higher frequency of secondary toxic compounds.

4. In monitoring populations, the age-dependent indices are very sensitive to chronic deficiencies. When weight-for-height is abnormally low, we have a sensitive index of which individuals are in emergency need of supplements due to *acute* forms of malnutrition (i.e., wasting) (Martorell 1982, 1989; Coimbra 1989). These indices can be supplemented with the measurement of subcutaneous fat using calipers. Most often used are the circumference of the upper arm, the triceps skinfold and the subscapular skinfold to estimate the muscular area, and the fat-to-muscle proportion. It has been noted that many populations seem to be "small but healthy" in that they are below established standards for height-for-age and weight-for-age but within the norm for weight-for-height. These "stunted" populations live in a state of chronic undernutrition which may reflect their marginalization from more productive habitats to which they have fled from the colonial and national forces around them, the impact of epidemic diseases, and consequent disruptions in their food production system (Coimbra 1989). Stunting in children should be viewed as a condition to be corrected so that those children can achieve their full physical and mental potential.

3. Upland Forests

1. It may apply with greater accuracy in the Asian than in the American tropics.

2. An excellent survey of colonization in the Amazon frontier can be found in Schmink and Wood 1984, an edited volume with up-to-date papers on frontier expansion.

3. Recently, a few authors have suggested figures much higher than this. Fearnside (1992) has suggested as long as 500 years, without explaining the basis for this extrapolation, while Uhl (1983) has suggested a figure of 100 years for the extremely nutrient-poor watershed near San Carlos de Río Negro. It is quite possible that this range of variation may represent alternative criteria for

restoration used by various authors, as well as actual differences in regrowth between parts of the basin experiencing contrasting kinds of land use.

4. I am currently engaged in long-term research in the Amazon Basin, monitoring the rate of regrowth after deforestation at a number of sites which vary in initial soil quality, which have experienced different kinds of land use, and which vary in the size of clearing. Variability has already proven to be quite great from site to site.

5. A controversy has erupted between Posey (1985) and Parker (1992) over whether these forest islands (*apêtê*) are anthropogenic (the product of human selective manipulation) or are the product of natural processes of secondary succession following the abandonment of cropping.

Bibliography

Ab'Saber, Aziz

1980. Os domínios morfoclimáticos na América do Sul. *Vegetalia* (São José do Rio Preto) 6: 1–21.

1982. The Paleoclimate and Paleoecology of Brazilian Amazonia. In *Biological Diversification in the Tropics*, ed. G. Prance. New York: Columbia University Press.

1986. Geomorfologia da região Carajás. In *Carajás*, ed. J. M. de Almeida. São Paulo: Editôra Brasiliense/CNPq.

1987. Ambiente e culturas: Equilíbrio e ruptura no espaço geográfico ora chamado Brasil. *Revista do Patrimônio Histórico e Artístico Nacional* 22: 236–254.

Acuña, P. Cristoval de

1859. *New Discovery of the Great River of the Amazons.* Translation of the Spanish edition of 1641 by C. R. Markham. Expeditions into the Valley of the Amazons, 1539, 1540, 1639. London: Hakluyt Society.

Adams, Richard N.

1973. *Energy and Structure.* Austin: University of Texas Press.

1988. *The Eighth Day.* Austin: University of Texas Press.

Alavi, S. M. Ziauddin

1965. *Arab Geography in the Ninth and Tenth Centuries.* Aligarh, India: Aligarh Muslim University, Department of Geography.

Alegre, J. C., et al.

1986. Effect of Land Clearing on Soil Properties of an Ultisol and Subsequent Crop Production in Yurimaguas, Peru. In *Land Clearing and Development in the Tropics*, ed. R. Lal et al. Boston: A. A. Balkema.

Alho, C. J. R.

1988. Maneje com cuidado: Frágil. *Ciência Hoje* 8: 40–47.

Alland, Alexander

1970. *Adaptation in Cultural Evolution: An Approach to Medical Anthropology.* New York: Columbia University Press.

1973. *Evolution and Human Behavior.* 2d ed. Garden City, N.Y.: Doubleday-Anchor Books.

1975. Adaptation. *Annual Review of Anthropology* 4: 59–73.

Alland, Alexander, and B. McCay

1973. The Concept of Adaptation in Biological and Cultural Evolution. In *Handbook of Social and Cultural Anthropology*, ed. John Honigmann. Chicago: Rand McNally.

Alvim, P. T.

1978a. Perspectives of Agricultural Production in the Amazon Region. *Interciencia* 3: 243–251.

1978b. Floresta amazônica: Equilíbrio entre utilização e conservação. *Ciência e Cultura* 30: 9–16.

Alvim, P. T., and F. P. Cabala

1974. Um novo sistema de representação gráfica da fertilidade dos solos para Cacau. *Cacau Atualidades* 11 (1): 2–6.

Anderson, A.

1981. White-sand Vegetation of Brazilian Amazonia. *Biotropica* 13: 199–210.

Anderson, A., ed.

1990. *Alternatives to Deforestation.* New York: Columbia University Press.

Anderson, A., and E. Anderson

1985. A "Tree of Life" Grows in Brazil. *Natural History* 94 (12): 41–46.

Anderson, A., and E. M. Ioris

1989. The Logic of Extraction: Resource Management and Income Generation by Extractive Producers in the Amazon Estuary. Paper presented at the conference Traditional Resource Use in Neotropical Forests, Gainesville, Florida.

Anderson, A., P. May, and M. Balick

1991. *The Subsidy from Nature.* New York: Columbia University Press.

Anderson, A., and D. Posey

1985. Manejo de cerrado pelos indios Kayapó. *Boletim do Museu Paraense Goeldi* (Botânica) 2 (1): 77–98.

Anderson, A., et al.

1985. Um sistema agroflorestal na várzea do estuário Amazônico. *Acta Amazônica,* suppl. 15 (1–2): 195–224.

Anderson, Robin

1976. Following Curupira: Colonization and Migration in Pará (1758–1930). Ph.D. diss., Department of History, University of California, Davis.

Andrade, E. B.

1983. Relatório da expedição para coleta de germoplasma de "Caiaui," *Eleais oleifera* na Amazônia brasileira. Belém: EMBRAPA/CPATU.

Andrade, L., and L. Santos, eds.

1988. *As hidroelétricas do Xingú e os povos indígenas.* São Paulo: Comissão Pro-Índio de São Paulo.

Araújo-Costa, F.

1983. Projeto Baixo Tocantins: Salvamento arqueológico na região de Tucuruí. Master's thesis, University of São Paulo.

Araújo Lima, Maria José

1984. *Ecologia humana: Realidade e pesquisa.* Petrópolis: Vozes.

Arens, K.

1958. O cerrado como vegetação oligotrófica. *Boletim da Faculdade de Filosofia, Ciências e Letras da Universidade de São Paulo* 224 (Botânica) 15: 59–77.

Arhem, Kaj

1976. Fishing and Hunting among the Makuna. In *Annual Report of the*

Ethnographical Museum, Gothenburg, Sweden. Gothenburg, Sweden: Göteborgs Etnografiska Museum.

1987. Wives for Sisters: The Management of Marriage Exchange in the North-west Amazon. In *Natives and Neighbors in South America*, ed. H. Skar and F. Salomon. Gothenburg, Sweden: Göteborgs Etnografiska Museum.

Ávila-Pires, F. de

1983. *Princípios de ecologia humana.* Porto Alegre: Editôra da Universidade/CNPq.

Ayres, Marcio, and F. M. Salzano

1972. Health Status of Brazilian Cayapó Indians. *Tropical and Geographical Medicine* (Dordrecht) 24: 178–185.

Azevedo, João Lucio de

1930. Os Jesuítas no Grão Pará, Suas missões e colonização. 2d ed. Coimbra: Imprensa da Universidade.

Baier, W., et al.

1972. *Soil Moisture Estimator Program System.* Technical Bulletin 78. Ottawa: Agrometereology Section, Canada Department of Agriculture.

Bajema, C. J.

1971. *Natural Selection in Human Populations.* New York: John Wiley.

Baker, Herbert

1970. Evolution in the Tropics. *Biotropica* 2 (2): 101–111.

Baker, H., and P. Hurd

1968. Intrafloral Ecology. *Annual Review of Entomology* 13: 384–414.

Baker, Paul T.

1958. The Biological Adaptation of Man to Hot Deserts. *American Naturalist* 92: 237–257.

1966. Ecological and Physiological Adaptations in Indigenous South Americans. In *The Biology of Human Adaptability*, ed. Paul T. Baker and J. S. Weiner. Oxford: Clarendon Press.

1968. Human Adaptation to High Altitude. In *High Altitude Adaptation in a Peruvian Community*, ed. P. T. Baker et al. Occasional Papers in Anthropology No. 1. University Park: Pennsylvania State University.

1969. Human Adaptation to High Altitude. *Science* 163: 1149–1156.

1976a. Evolution of a Project: Theory, Method, and Sampling. In *Man in the Andes*, ed. Paul T. Baker and M. Little. Stroudsburg, Pa.: Dowden, Hutchinson and Ross.

1976b. Work Performance of Highland Natives. In *Man in the Andes*, ed. Paul T. Baker and M. Little. Stroudsburg, Pa: Dowden, Hutchinson and Ross.

Baker, Paul T., ed.

1978. *The Biology of High Altitude Populations.* Cambridge: Cambridge University Press.

Baker, Paul T., and J. S. Dutt

1972. Demographic Variables as Measures of Biological Adaptation: A

Study of High Altitude Human Populations. In *The Structure of Human Populations*, ed. G. A. Harrison and A. J. Boyce. Oxford: Clarendon Press.

Baker, Paul T., and M. Little, eds.

　1976. *Man in the Andes*. US/IBP Synthesis Series, No. 1. Stroudsburg, Pa: Dowden, Hutchinson and Ross.

Baker, Paul T., and W. T. Sanders

　1972. Demographic Studies in Anthropology. *Annual Review of Anthropology* 1: 151–178.

Baker, Paul T., and J. S. Weiner, eds.

　1966. *The Biology of Human Adaptability*. Oxford: Clarendon Press.

Baker, Paul T., et al., eds.

　1968. *High Altitude Adaptation in a Peruvian Community*. Occasional Papers in Anthropology, No. 1. University Park: Pennsylvania State University.

Baldanzi, Giampiero

　1959. Efeitos da queimada sobre a fertilidade do solo. Pelotas, Rio Grande de Sul (Brazil): Instituto Agronómico do Sul.

Baldus, Herbert

　1954. *Bibliografia crítica de etnologia brasileira*. São Paulo: Comissão IV Centenário da Cidade de São Paulo.

　1970. *Tapirapé: Tribu Tupí no Brasil central*. São Paulo: Companhia Editôra Nacional.

Balée, W.

　1984. The Ecology of Ancient Tupí Warfare. In *Warfare, Culture and Environment*, ed. R. B. Ferguson. New York: Academic Press.

　1985. Ka'apor Ritual Hunting. *Human Ecology* 13: 485–510.

　1989. The Culture of Amazonian Forests. *Advances in Economic Botany* 7: 1–21.

　1992. People of the Fallow: A Historical Ecology of Foraging in Lowland South America. In *Conservation of Neotropical Forests*, ed. K. Redford and C. Padoch. New York: Columbia University Press.

Balée, W., and A. Gely

　1989. Managed Forest Succession in Amazonia: The Ka'apor Case. *Advances in Economic Botany* 7: 129–158.

Balick, M.

　1984. Ethnobotany of Palms in the Neotropics. In *Ethnobotany in the Neotropics*, ed. G. Prance and J. Kallunki. Advances in Economic Botany, No. 1. New York: New York Botanical Garden.

Bamberger, Joan

　1967. Environment and Cultural Classification: A Study of the Northern Kayapó. Ph.D. diss., Department of Anthropology, Harvard University.

Barbira-Scazzocchio, F., ed.

　1979. *Land, People and Planning in Contemporary Amazonia*. Cambridge: Center for Latin American Studies, University of Cambridge.

Barclay, George
   1958. *Techniques of Population Analysis*. New York: John Wiley.
Barlett, Peggy
   1977. The Structure of Decision-making in Paso. *American Ethnologist* 4: 285–308.
Barry, R. G., and R. J. Chorley
   1970. *Atmosphere, Weather, and Climate*. New York: Holt, Rinehart and Winston.
Barth, Fredrik
   1956. Ecologic Relationships of Ethnic Groups in Swat, North Pakistan. *American Anthropologist* 58: 1079–1089.
   1969. *Ethnic Groups and Boundaries: The Social Organization of Cultural Differences*. Boston: Little, Brown.
   1972. Ethnic Processes on the Pathan-Baluch Boundary. In *Directions in Sociolinguistics*, ed. J. Gumperz and D. Hymes. New York: Holt, Rinehart and Winston.
Bartholomew, W., et al.
   1953. *Mineral Nutrient Immobilization under Forest and Grass Fallow in the Yangambi (Belgian Congo) Region*. Institut National pour L'Étude Agronomique du Congo Série 57: 1–27.
Baruzzi, R. G., et al.
   1973. Occurrence of Lobo's Blastomycosis among Caiabi Brazilian Indians. *International Journal of Dermatology* 12 (2): 95–98.
   1977. The Kren-Akarore: A Recently Contacted Indigenous Tribe. In *Health and Disease in Tribal Societies*. Ciba Foundation Symposium No. 49. Amsterdam: Elsevier.
   1979. História natural da doença de Jorge Lobo. *Revista do Instituto de Medicina Tropical de São Paulo* 21: 302–358.
   1983. Tinea imbricata em índios do Parque Nacional do Xingú. Resumo, IX Congresso da Sociedade Brasileira de Medicina Tropical, Rio de Janeiro.
Basso, Ellen
   1973. *The Kalapalo Indians of Central Brazil*. New York: Holt, Rinehart and Winston.
Bates, H. W.
   1892. *The Naturalist on the River Amazons*. London: Murray.
Bates, Marston
   1952. *Where Winter Never Comes*. New York: Scribner's.
   1953. Human Ecology. In *Anthropology Today*, ed. Alfred L. Kroeber. Chicago: University of Chicago Press.
Bateson, Gregory
   1963. The Role of Somatic Change in Evolution. *Evolution* 17: 529–539.
   1972. *Steps to an Ecology of Mind*. New York: Ballantine Books.

Beckerman, Steve

1979. The Abundance of Protein in Amazonia: A Reply to Gross. *American Anthropologist* 81: 533–560.

1980. Fishing and Hunting by the Barí of Colombia. In *Working Paper on South American Indians*, ed. R. Hames, vol. 2. Bennington, Vt.: Bennington College.

1983. Carpe Diem: An Optimal Foraging Approach to Barí Fishing and Hunting. In *Adaptive Responses of Native Amazonians*, ed. R. Hames and W. Vickers. New York: Academic Press.

1989. Hunting and Fishing in Amazonia: Hold the Answers; What Are the Questions? Paper presented at the Wenner-Gren conference Amazonian Synthesis, Nova Friburgo, Rio de Janeiro, June 2–10, 1989.

Behrens, Clifford

1981. Time Allocation and Meat Procurement among the Shipibo Indians of Eastern Peru. *Human Ecology* 9: 189–220.

1986. The Cultural Ecology of Dietary Change Accompanying Changing Activity Patterns among the Shipibo. *Human Ecology* 14: 367–395.

1989. The Scientific Basis for Shipibo Soil Classification and Land Use. *American Anthropologist* 91: 83–100.

1991. Applications of Satellite Image Processing to the Analysis of Amazonian Cultural Ecology. In *Applications of Space Age Technology in Anthropology*, ed. C. Behrens and T. Sever. John Stennis Space Center, Miss.: NASA.

Bell, R. R., and C. A. Heller

1978. Nutrition Studies: An Appraisal of the North Alaskan Eskimo Diet. In *The Eskimo of Northwestern Alaska: A Biological Perspective*, ed. P. L. Jamison, S. L. Zegura, and F. A. Milan. Stroudsburg, Pa.: Dowden, Hutchinson and Ross.

Beltrão, M. C.

1978. *Pre-história do Estado do Rio de Janeiro*. Rio de Janeiro: Editôra Fornese Universitária.

Benchimol, L.

1989. *Amazônia*. Manaus: Imprensa Popular.

Bennema, J.

1977. Soils. In *Ecophysiology of Tropical Crops*, ed. P. Alvin and T. Kozlowski. New York: Academic Press.

Bennett, John

1967. Social Adaptation in a Northern Plains Region: A Saskatchewan Study. In *Symposium on the Great Plains of North America*, ed. C. C. Zimmerman and S. Russel. Fargo: North Dakota Institute for Regional Studies.

1969. *Northern Plainsmen*. Chicago: Aldine.

1972. The Significance of the Concept of Adaptation for Contemporary Socio-cultural Anthropology. In *Proceedings of the Eighth Congress of Anthropological and Ethnological Sciences* S-7: 237–241.

1973. Adaptive Strategy in the Canadian Plains. *Canadian Plains Studies* 1: 181–199.

1976. *The Ecological Transition*. London: Pergamon Press.

Bergman, R. W.

1974. Shipibo Subsistence in the Upper Amazon Rain Forest. Ph.D. diss., University of Wisconsin.

1980. *Amazon Economics: The Simplicity of Shipibo Indian Wealth*. Dell Plain Latin American Studies No. 6. Syracuse: Department of Geography, Syracuse University.

Berkes, F.

1984. Competition between Commercial and Sport Fishermen: An Ecological Analysis. *Human Ecology* 12: 413–429.

Berlin, B.

1992. *Ethnobiological Classification*. Princeton, N.J.: Princeton University Press.

Berlin, Elois

1986. Nutrition Research in Amazonian South America. *Training Manual in Nutritional Anthropology*. Special Publication No. 20. Washington, D.C.: American Anthropological Association.

Berlin, E., and E. Markell

1977. An Assessment of the Nutritional and Health Status of an Aguaruna Jivaro Community, Amazonas, Peru. *Ecology of Food and Nutrition* 6: 69–81.

Bertalanffy, Ludwig von

1968. *General Systems Theory*. Rev. ed. New York: Braziller.

Bicchieri, M. G., ed.

1972. *Hunters and Gatherers Today: A Socio-economic Study of Eleven Such Cultures in the Twentieth Century.* New York: Holt, Rinehart and Winston.

Biocca, E.

1945. Estudos etno-biológicos sobre os índios da região do Alto Rio Negro-Amazonas, II: Transmissão ritual e transmissão criminosa da espiroquetose discrônica. *Arquivos de Biologia* (São Paulo) 29 (265): 7–12.

Birdsell, J. B.

1953. Some Environmental and Cultural Factors Influencing the Structure of Australian Aboriginal Populations. *American Naturalist* 87: 171–207.

1968. Population Control Factors: Infanticide, Disease, Nutrition and Food Supply. In *Man the Hunter*, ed. R. B. Lee and I. DeVore. Chicago: Aldine.

1976. Realities and Transformations: The Tribes of the Western Desert of Australia. In *Tribes and Boundaries in Australia*, ed. N. Petersen. Canberra: Australian Institute of Aboriginal Studies.

Black, F. L.

1966. Measles Endemicity in Insular Populations: Critical Community Size and Its Evolutionary Implications. *Journal of Theoretical Biology* 11: 207–211.

1975. Infectious Disease in Primitive Societies. *Science* 187: 515–518.

1980. Modern Isolated Pre-agricultural Populations as a Source of Information on Prehistoric Epidemic Patterns. In *Changing Disease Patterns and Human Behavior*, ed. N. F. Stanley and R. A. Joshe. London: Academic Press.

Black, F. L., et al.

1974. Evidence for Persistence of Infectious Agents in Isolated Human Populations. *American Journal of Epidemiology* 100: 230–250.

1977. Nutritional Status of Brazilian Kayapó Indians. *Human Biology* 49 (2): 139–153.

Black, G. A.

1950. Os capins aquáticos da Amazônia. *Boletim Técnico, Instituto Agronómico do Norte* 19: 53–94.

Black, G. A., et al.

1950. Some Attempts to Estimate Species Diversity and Population Density of Trees in Amazonian Forests. *Botanical Gazette* 3 (4): 413–425.

Boas, Franz

1896. The Limitations of the Comparative Method of Anthropology. *Science* (new series) 4: 901–908.

1911. *The Mind of Primitive Man*. New York: Macmillan.

1964. *The Central Eskimo*. Lincoln: University of Nebraska Press. Originally published in 1888 by the Smithsonian Institution Press.

Boer, J. G. W.

1965. Palmae. In *Flora of Suriname*, ed. J. Lanjouw, vol. 5, part 1. Leiden: Brill.

Bogue, Donald

1969. *Principles of Demography*. New York: John Wiley.

Boom, B.

1987. *Ethnobotany of the Chacobo Indians, Beni, Bolivia*. Advances in Economic Botany No. 4. New York: New York Botanical Garden.

Bordne, E. F., and J. L McGuinness

1973. Some Procedures for Calculating Evapotranspiration. *Professional Geographer* 25: 22–28.

Boserup, Ester

1965. *The Conditions of Agricultural Growth*. Chicago: Aldine.

Boster, James

1983. A Comparison of the Diversity of Jivaroan Gardens with That of the Tropical Forest. *Human Ecology* 11: 69–84.

1984. Inferring Decision-making from Preferences and Behavior: An Analysis of Aguaruna Jivaro Manioc Selection. *Human Ecology* 12: 343–358.

Boulding, Kenneth

1978. *Ecodynamics: A New Theory of Societal Evolution*. Beverly Hills, Cal.: SAGE.

Boyden, Stephen

1974. Modeling Energy Requirements in Human Communities. In *Energy*

Flow in Human Communities, ed. Paul L. Jamison and S. M. Friedman. University Park, Pa.: US/IBP and SSRC.

Braga, P.
1979. Subdivisão fitogeográfica, tipos de vegetação, conservação, i inventário florístico da floresta amazônica. Supp. *Acta Amazônica* 9: 53–80.

Brochado, José Proença
1977. *Alimentação na floresta tropical.* Porto Alegre: Universidade Federal do Rio Grande de Sul.

Brookfield, H. C.
1968. New Directions in the Study of Agricultural Systems in Tropical Areas. In *Evolution and Environment*, ed. E. T. Drake. New Haven, Conn.: Yale University Press.

Brookfield, H. C., and P. Brown
1963. *Struggle for Land: Agriculture and Group Territories among the Chimbu of the New Guinea Highlands.* Melbourne: Oxford University Press.

Brooks, Reuben, and D. G. Colley
1973. Which Comes First, the Snail or the Egg?: The Problem of Schistosomiasis Diffusion in Brazil. Nashville: Vanderbilt University. Mimeo.

Browder, J.
1986. Logging the Rainforest: A Political Economy of Timber Extraction and Unequal Exchange in the Brazilian Amazon, Ph.D. diss., University of Pennsylvania.

1988. Public Policy and Deforestation in the Brazilian Amazon. In *Public Policies and the Misuse of Forest Resources*, ed. R. Repetto and M. Gillis. New York: Cambridge University Press/World Resources Institute.

1992. The Limits of Extractivism. *Bioscience* 42 (3): 174–182.

Browder, J., ed.
1989. *Fragile Lands of Latin America.* Boulder, Colo.: Westview Press.

Brower, J. E., and J. H. Zar
1984. *Field and Laboratory Methods for General Ecology.* 2d ed. Dubuque, Ia.: William C. Brown.

Browman, D. L.
1974. Pastoral Nomadism in the Andes. *Current Anthropology* 15: 188–196.

Brown, G. M., and J. Page
1952. The Effect of Chronic Exposure to Cold on Temperature and Blood Flow to the Hand. *Journal of Applied Physiology* 5: 221–227.

Brown, P., and A. Podolefsky
1976. Population Density, Agricultural Intensity, Land Tenure and Group Size in the New Guinea Highlands. *Ethnology* 15: 211–238.

Brues, A. M.
1972. Models of Race and Cline. *American Journal of Physical Anthropology* 37: 389–400.

Brush, Stephen

1975. The Concept of Carrying Capacity for Systems of Shifting Cultivation. *American Anthropologist* 77: 799–811.

1976. Man's Use of an Andean Ecosystem. *Human Ecology* 4: 128–132, 147–166.

1977. *Mountain, Field and Family: The Economy and Human Ecology of an Andean Valley.* Philadelphia: University of Pennsylvania Press.

1982. The Natural and Human Environment of the Central Andes. *Mountain Research and Development* 2 (1): 19–38.

Brush, S., and D. Guillet

1985. Small-scale Pastoral Production in the Central Andes. *Mountain Research and Development* 5 (1): 19–30.

Brush, S., J. Heath, and Z. Huaman

1981. The Dynamics of Andean Potato Agriculture. *Economic Botany* 35: 70–88.

Buckley, Walter

1967. *Sociology and Modern Systems Theory.* Englewood Cliffs, N.J.: Prentice-Hall.

Buckley, Walter, ed.

1968. *Modern Systems Research for the Behavioral Scientist.* Chicago: Aldine.

Buckman, Harry, and N. Brady

1969. *The Nature and Properties of Soils.* 7th ed. New York: Macmillan.

Budyko, M. I.

1974. *Climate and Life.* New York: Academic Press.

Bunker, Stephen

1980. The Impact of Deforestation on Peasant Communities in the Medio Amazonas of Brazil. *Studies in Third World Societies* 13: 45–60.

1985. *Underdeveloping the Amazon.* Urbana: University of Illinois Press.

Burling, R.

1964. Cognition and Componential Analysis: God's Truth or Hocus-Pocus? *American Anthropologist* 66: 20–28.

Butzer, Karl

1973. *Environment and Archaeology: An Ecological Approach to Prehistory.* New York: Aldine.

1976. *Early Hydraulic Civilization in Egypt: A Study in Cultural Ecology.* Chicago: University of Chicago Press.

Cain, Stanley, and G. M. de Oliveira Castro

1959. *Manual of Vegetation Analysis.* New York: Hafner Publishing.

Camargo, F. C.

1958. Report on the Amazon Region. *Problems of Humid Tropical Regions.* Paris: UNESCO.

Cancian, Frank

1972. *Change and Uncertainty in a Peasant Economy.* Stanford, Cal.: Stanford University Press.

Cardoso de Oliveira, Roberto
 1968. Problemas e hipóteses relativas a fricção interétnica: Sugestões para uma metodologia. *América Indígena* 28: 339–388.
 1978. *A sociologia do Brasil indígena.* 2d ed. Brasília: Editôra da Universidade de Brasília.
Carneiro, Robert L.
 1957. Subsistence and Social Structure: An Ecological Study of the Kuikuru. Ph.D. diss., Department of Anthropology, University of Michigan.
 1961. Slash-and-Burn Agriculture: A Closer Look at its Implications for Settlement Patterns. In *Man and Culture*, ed. Anthony F. Wallace. Fifth International Congress of Anthropological and Ethnological Sciences.
 1970. The Transition from Hunting to Horticulture in the Amazon Basin. *Eighth Congress of Anthropological and Ethnological Sciences* 3: 243–251.
 1974. Slash-and-Burn Cultivation among the Kuikuru and Its Implications for Cultural Development in the Amazon Basin. In *Native South Americans*, ed. Patricia Lyon. Boston: Little, Brown.
Carvajal, G. de
 1934. *The Discovery of the Amazon.* Washington, D.C.: American Geographical Society. Originally published in 1542.
Carvalho, J. C. M.
 1951. *Relações entre os índios do Xingú e a fauna regional.* Rio de Janeiro: Museu Nacional, Publicações Avulsas.
Castiglioni, Arturo
 1958. *A History of Medicine.* 2d ed. New York: Alfred A. Knopf.
Cavalli-Sforza, L., and M. Feldman
 1981. *Cultural Transmission and Evolution.* Princeton, N.J.: Princeton University Press.
CEDI
 1987. *Terras indígenas no Brasil.* São Paulo: Centro Ecuménico de Documentação e Informação (CEDI)/Conselho Nacional de Geologia.
 1988. *Emprêsas de mineração e terras indígenas.* São Paulo: CEDI/CONAGE.
CEDI/CIMI
 1986. *Áreas indígenas e grandes projetos.* Mapa do CIMI.
Chagnon, Napoleon
 1968. *Yanomamo: The Fierce People.* New York: Holt, Rinehart and Winston. 2d ed. 1974.
 1973. The Culture Ecology of Shifting Cultivation among the Yanomama Indians. In *Peoples and Cultures of Native South America*, ed. D. Gross. New York: Doubleday.
Chagnon, N., and R. Hames
 1980. La "hipótesis protéica" y la adaptación indígena a la cuenca del Amazonas. *Interciencia* 5 (6): 346–358.

Chantre y Herrera, J.
  1901. *Historia de las misiones de la Compañía de Jesús en el Marañón español.* Madrid: A. Avrial.
Charnov, E. L.
  1976. Optimal Foraging: The Marginal Value Theorem. *Theoretical Population Biology* 9: 129–136.
Chase, H.C.
  1962. *Relationship of Certain Biologic and Socio-economic Factors to Fetal, Infant and Early Childhood Mortality.* Albany: New York State Department of Health.
Chaumeil, J. P.
  1981. *Historia y migraciones de los Yagua de finales del siglo XVII hasta nuestros días.* Lima: CAAP. Serie Antropol. 3.
Chernela, Janet
  1982. Indigenous Forest and Fish Management in the Vaupés Basin of Brazil. *Cultural Survival Quarterly* 6 (2): 17–18.
  1983. Hierarchy and Economy of the Uanano Speaking Peoples of the Middle Vaupés Basin. Ph.D. diss., Department of Anthropology, Columbia University.
  1985. Indigenous Fishing in the Neotropics: The Tukano Uanano of the Blackwater Uaupés River Basin in Brazil and Colombia. *Interciencia* 10 (2): 78–86.
  1986a. Os cultivares de mandioca na área do Uaupés. In *Suma etnológica brasileira*, ed. B. Ribeiro, vol. 1. Petrópolis: Vozes/FINEP.
  1986b. Pesca e hierarquização tribal no Alto Uaupés. In *Suma etnológica brasileira*, ed. B. Ribeiro, vol. 1. Petrópolis: Vozes/FINEP.
  1989. Managing Rivers of Hunger: The Tukano of Brazil. *Advances in Economic Botany* 7: 238–248.
CIMI
  1981. Levantamento das patologias que ocorrem nas áreas indígenas. *Boletim CIMI* (Goiânia) 10: 14–15.
Clark, K., and C. Uhl
  1987. Farming, Fishing and Fire in the History of the Upper Rio Negro Region of Venezuela. *Human Ecology* 15: 1–26.
Clay, Jason
  1988. *Indigenous People and Tropical Forests.* Cambridge: Cultural Survival.
Cleary, David
  1990. *Anatomy of the Amazon Gold Rush.* Iowa City: University of Iowa Press.
Cochrane, T. T., and P. Sánchez
  1982. Land Resources, Soils, and Their Management in the Amazon Region. In *Amazonia: Agriculture and Land Use Research*, ed. S. Hecht. Cali, Colombia: CIAT.

Cody, M. L.
  1974a. *Competition and Community Structure*. Princeton, N.J.: Princeton
    University Press.
  1974b. Optimization in Ecology. *Science* 183: 1156–1164.
Coimbra, Carlos E. A., Jr.
  1984. Estudos de ecologia humana entre os Suruí do parque indígena Ari-
    puanã, Rondônia. 1. O uso de larvas de coleópteros (Bruchidae e Curcu-
    lionidae) na alimentação. *Revista Brasileira de Zoologia* 2 (2): 35–47.
  1987. O sarampo entre sociedades indígenas brasileiras. *Cadernos de Sáude
    Pública* 3: 22–37.
  1988. Human Settlements, Demographic Pattern, and Epidemiology in Low-
    land Amazonia: The Case of Chagas Disease. *American Anthropologist*
    90: 82–97.
  1989. From Shifting Cultivation to Coffee Farming: The Impact of Change
    on the Health and Ecology of the Suruí Indians in the Brazilian Amazon.
    Ph.D. diss., Department of Anthropology, Indiana University.
Coimbra, Carlos E. A., Jr., and Ricardo V. Santos
  1989. Black Piedra among the Zoró Indians from Amazonia (Brazil). *Myco-
    pathologia* 107: 57–60.
Colchester, Marcus
  1981. Ecological Modelling and Indigenous Systems of Resource Use: Some
    Examples from the Amazon of S. Venezuela. *Antropológica* 55: 51–72.
Colinvaux, P. A., et al.
  1985. Discovery of Permanent Amazon Lakes and Hydraulic Disturbance in
    the Upper Amazon Basin. *Nature* 313: 42–45.
Colson, Elizabeth
  1971. *The Social Consequences of Resettlement*. Manchester: Manchester
    University Press.
Comas, J.
  1971. Anthropometric Studies in Latin American Indian Populations. In
    The Ongoing Evolution of Latin American Populations, ed. F. Salzano.
    Springfield, Ill.: C. C. Thomas.
Conklin, Harold C.
  1954. An Ethnoecological Approach to Shifting Agriculture. *Transactions of
    the New York Academy of Sciences* 17 (2): 133–142.
  1957. *Hanunóo Agriculture*. Rome: Food and Agricultural Organization.
  1961. The Study of Shifting Cultivation. *Current Anthropology* 2: 27–61.
  1963. *The Study of Shifting Cultivation*. Washington, D.C.: Pan American
    Union.
  1969. An Ethnoecological Approach to Shifting Agriculture. In *Environ-
    ment and Cultural Behavior*, ed. Andrew P. Vayda. New York: Natural
    History Press.
Connell, Joseph
  1978. Diversity in Tropical Rain Forests and Coral Reefs. *Science* 199:
    1302–1310.

Constanza, R., ed.

  1991. *Ecological Economics*. New York: Columbia University Press.

Coon, C. S., S. Garn, and J. Birdsell

  1950. *Races: A Study of the Problem of Race Formation in Man*. Springfield, Ill.: C. C. Thomas.

Correa, F., ed.

  1990. *La selva humanizada: Ecología alternativa en el trópico húmedo colombiano*. Bogotá: Instituto Colombiano de Antropología.

Corrêa, J. R. V.

  1982. Contrôle da murcha da teia micélica na Transamazônica. In *Comunicado Técnico* 2. Belém: EMBRAPA.

Cottrell, Fred

  1955. *Energy and Society: The Relation between Energy, Social Change, and Economic Development*. New York: McGraw-Hill.

Crawley, M. J.

  1973. Modeling and the Synthesis of Ecological Systems. In *Ecological Energetics of Homeotherms*, ed. J. A. Gessaman. Logan: Utah State University Press.

Crockett, C. M., and J. F. Eisenberg

  1987. Howlers: Variation in Group Size and Demography. In *Primate Societies*, ed. Hans Kummer. Chicago: University of Chicago Press.

Cruz, Laureano de la

  1885. *Nuevo descubrimiento del Marañón, 1651: Varones ilustres de la Orden Seráfica en el Ecuador*. Quito: Imprensa del Clero.

Cuevas, E., and E. Medina

  1986. Nutrient Dynamics within Amazonian Rain Forest Ecosystems. *Oecologia* 68: 466–472.

Cyert, R. M., and J. G. March

  1963. *A Behavioral Theory of the Firm*. Englewood Cliffs, N.J.: Prentice-Hall.

Dantas, Mario

  1988. Studies on Succession in Cleared Areas of Amazonian Rain Forest. Ph.D. diss., Oxford University (UK).

Denevan, William

  1966. *The Aboriginal Cultural Geography of the Llanos de Mojos, Bolivia*. Berkeley: University of California Publications.

  1970. Aboriginal Drained-Field Cultivation in the Americas. *Science* 169: 647–654.

  1971. Campa Subsistence in the Gran Pajonal, E. Peru. *Geographical Review* 61: 496–518.

  1973. Development and the Imminent Demise of the Amazon Rain Forest. *Professional Geographer* 25 (2): 130–135.

  1974. Campa Subsistence in the Gran Pajonal. In *Native South Americans*, ed. Patricia Lyon. Boston: Little, Brown.

  1976. The Aboriginal Population of Amazonia. In *The Native Population of the Americas in 1492*, ed. W. Denevan. Madison: University of Wisconsin Press.

1980. Swidden and Cattle versus Forest. *Studies in Third World Societies* 13: 25–44.

1984. Ecological Heterogeneity and Horizontal Zonation of Agriculture in the Amazon Floodplain. In *Frontier Expansion in Amazonia*, ed. M. Schmink and C. Wood. Gainesville: University of Florida Press.

1986. The Cultural Ecology, Archaeology, and History of Terracing and Terrace Abandonment in the Colca Valley of Southern Peru. Technical Report to the National Science Foundation and the National Geographic Society. Department of Geography, University of Wisconsin, Madison.

Denevan, W., and C. Padoch, eds.

1988. *Swidden-Fallow Agroforestry in the Peruvian Amazon*. Advances in Economic Botany No. 5. New York: New York Botanical Garden.

Denevan, W., and K. Schwerin, eds.

1978. Adaptive Strategies in Karinya Subsistence, Venezuelan Llanos. *Antropológica* 50: 3–91.

Denich, M.

1991. *Estudo da importância de uma vegetação secundária nova para o incremento da produtividade do sistema na Amazônia oriental*. Belém: EMBRAPA/GTZ.

Denslow, J., and C. Padoch, eds.

1988. *People of the Rain Forests*. Berkeley: University of California Press/ Smithsonian.

Deutsch, K. W.

1968. Toward a Cybernetic Model of Man and Society. In *Modern Systems Research for the Behavioral Scientist*, ed. Walter Buckley. Chicago: Aldine.

Dice, Lee

1955. *Man's Nature and Nature's Man*. Ann Arbor: University of Michigan Press.

Dickinson, Joshua

1972. Alternatives to Monoculture in the Humid Tropics of Latin America. *Professional Geographer* 24 (3): 217–222.

Dickinson, Robert

1981. Effects of Tropical Deforestation on Climate. *Studies in Third World Societies* 14: 411–441.

Dourado, M. C., ed.

1991. *Direito ambiental e a questão amazônica*. Belém: Universidade Federal do Pará. Série Cooperação Amazônica.

Dubos, René

1968a. Man and His Environment: Adaptations and Interactions. In *The Fitness of Man's Environment*. Washington, D.C.: Smithsonian Institution Press.

1968b. *So Human an Animal*. New York: Scribner's.

184   BIBLIOGRAPHY

Ducke, A., and G. Black
  1953. Phytogeographical Notes on the Brazilian Amazon. *Anais Acad. Bras. Ciências* 25 (1): 1–46.
  1954. Notas sôbre a fitogeografia da Amazônia brasileira. *Boletim Técnico Inst. Agron. do Norte* 29: 1–62.
Dufour, Darna
  1983. Nutrition in the Northwest Amazon. In *Adaptive Responses of Native Amazonians*, ed. R. Hames and W. Vickers. New York: Academic Press.
  1984. The Time and Energy Expenditure of Indigenous Women Horticulturalists in the New Amazon. *American Journal of Physical Anthropology* 65: 37–46.
  1987. Insects as Food: A Case Study from the Northwest Amazon. *American Anthropologist* 89: 383–397.
  1988. Cyanide Content of Cassava Cultivars used by Tukanoan Indians of Northwest Amazonia. *Economic Botany* 42 (2): 255–266.
  1989. Diet and Nutritional Status of Amazonian Peoples. Paper presented at the Wenner Gren conference Amazonian Synthesis, Nova Friburgo, Rio de Janeiro, June 2–10, 1989.
  1990. Use of Tropical Rain Forests by Native Amazonians. *Bioscience* 40: 652–659.
Dunn, Frederick
  1968. Epidemiological Factors: Health and Disease in Hunter-Gatherers. In *Man the Hunter*, ed. R. B. Lee and I. DeVore. Chicago: Aldine.
  1972. Intestinal Parasitism in Malayan Aborigines. *Bulletin of the World Health Organization* 46: 99–113.
Durham, William
  1976. The Adaptive Significance of Cultural Behavior. *Human Ecology* 4: 89–121.
  1991. *Coevolution: Genes, Culture and Human Diversity*. Stanford, Cal.: Stanford University Press.
Durnin, J. V. G. A.
  1975. Energy Expenditure in Humans. In *Institute of Ecology (TIE): A Manual of Energy Flow Studies*. Mimeo. Available from Institute of Ecology, Indianapolis, Ind.
Durnin, J. V. G. A., and A. Passmore
  1955. Human Energy Expenditure. *Physiological Reviews* 35: 801–839.
Dutt, J. S.
  1976. Altitude, Fertility, and Early Childhood Mortality: The Bolivian Example. *American Journal of Physical Anthropology* 44: 175.
Dyson-Hudson, R., and E. A. Smith
  1978. Human Territoriality: An Ecological Reassessment. *American Anthropologist* 80: 21–41.
Eberhardt, L. L.
  1978. Transect Methods for Population Studies. *Journal of Wildlife Management* 42: 1–31.

Eden, Michael

1978. Ecology and Land Development: The Case of Amazonian Rainforest. *Transactions of the Institute of British Geographers* (N.S.) 3: 444–463.

1982. Silvicultural and Agroforestry Developments in the Amazon Basin of Brazil. *Commonwealth Forestry Review* 61 (3): 195–202.

Eden, M., and A. Andrade

1987. Ecological Aspects of Swidden Cultivation among the Andoke and Witoto Indians of the Colombian Amazon. *Human Ecology* 15: 339–359.

Eden, M., et al.

1984. Terra Preta Soils and Their Archeological Context in the Caquetá Basin of South Eastern Colombia. *American Antiquity* 49 (1): 125–140.

Eder, James

1977. Agricultural Intensification and the Returns to Labour in the Philippine Swidden System. *Pacific Viewpoint* 19: 1–21.

Edgerton, Robert

1971. *The Individual in Cultural Adaptation*. Berkeley: University of California Press.

Ehrlich, P., and P. Raven

1964. Butterflies and Plants: A Study of Co-evolution. *Evolution* 18: 586–608.

Eidt, R. C.

1977. Detection and Examination of Anthrosols by Phosphate Analysis. *Science* 197: 1327–1333.

Eighmy, J. L., and R. Jacobsen

1980. Extension of Niche Theory in Human Ecology. *American Ethnologist* 7: 286–299.

Eisenberg, J. F., and K. Redford

1979. A Biogeographic Analysis of the Mammalian Fauna of Venezuela. In *Vertebrate Ecology in the Northern Neotropics*, ed. J. F. Eisenberg. Washington, D.C.: Smithsonian Institution Press.

Eisenberg, J. F., and R. W. Thorington

1973. A Preliminary Analysis of a Neotropical Mammal Fauna. *Biotropica* 5 (3): 150–161.

Eisenberg, J. F., et al.

1979. Density, Productivity, and Distribution of Mammals in Two Venezuelan Habitats. In *Vertebrate Ecology in the Northern Neotropics*, ed. J. F. Eisenberg. Washington, D.C.: Smithsonian Institution Press.

Eiten, G.

1972. The Cerrado Vegetation of Brazil. *Botanical Review* 38 (2): 201–341.

Elizabethsky, Elaine

1986. Etnofarmacología de algumas tribus brasileiras. In *Suma ethnológica brasileira*, ed. B. Ribeiro, vol. 1. Petrópolis: Vozes.

Ellen, Roy

1982. *Environment, Subsistence and System*. New York: Cambridge University Press.

1984. Trade, Environment and the Reproduction of Local Systems in the Moluccas. In *The Ecosystem Concept in Anthropology*, ed. E. F. Moran. Washington, D.C.: American Association for the Advancement of Science.

Ellis, James E., and Calvin Jennings

1975. A Comparison of Energy Flow among the Grazing Animals of Different Societies. In *Institute of Ecology (TIE): A Manual of Energy Flow Studies*. Mimeo. Available from Institute of Ecology, Indianapolis, Ind.

Emlen, J. M.

1966. The Role of Time and Energy in Food Preference. *American Naturalist* 100: 611–617.

Emmons, L. H.

1984. Geographic Variation in Densities and Diversities of Non-flying Mammals in Amazonia. *Biotropica* 16: 210–222.

English, Richard

1985. Himalayan State Formation and the Impact of British Rule in the Nineteenth Century. *Mountain Research and Development* 5 (1): 61–78.

Evans, Clifford

1955. New Archaeological Interpretations in Northeastern South America. In *Aboriginal Culture History*. Washington, D.C.: Anthropological Society of Washington.

Ewel, J. J.

1986. Designing Agricultural Ecosystems for the Humid Tropics. *Annual Review of Ecology and Systematics* 17: 245–271.

Fagundes-Neto, U., et al.

1981. Avaliação nutricional das crianças índias do Alto Xingú. *Jornal de Pediatria* (Rio de Janeiro) 50 (5): 179–182.

Falesi, Ítalo Cláudio

1972. *Os solos da rodovia transamazônica*. Belém: IPEAN.

1974. Soils of the Brazilian Amazon. In *Man in the Amazon*, ed. C. Wagley. Gainesville: University of Florida Press.

1976. *Ecossistema de pastagem cultivada na Amazônia brasileira*. Belém: EMBRAPA/CPATU. Boletim Técnico No. 1.

Faoro, R.

1958. *Os donos do poder*. Rio de Janeiro: Editôra Globo.

Farnworth, Edward, and Frank Golley, eds.

1974. *Fragile Ecosystems: Evaluation of Research and Applications in the Neotropics*. New York: Springer-Verlag.

Fearnside, P.

1979. *Human Carrying Capacity of the Brazilian Rainforest*. New York: Columbia University Press.

1980. A previsão de perdas de terra através de erosáo de solo sub varios usos da terra na área de colonizaçáo da rodovia transamazônica. *Acta Amazônica* 10: 505–511.

1984. A floresta vai acabar? *Ciência Hoje* 2 (10): 42–52.

1985. Rondônia: Sem florestas na próxima década? *Ciência Hoje* 4 (19): 92–94.

1986a. Alternativas de desenvolvimento na Amazônia brasileira: Uma avaliação ecológica. *Ciência e Cultura* 38 (1): 37–59.

1986b. Predição da qualidade da queimada na transamazônica para simulação do agroecossistema em estimativas de capacidade de suporte humano. *Ciência e Cultura* 38 (1): 1804–1811.

1987a. Distribuição de solos pobres na colonização de Rondônia. *Ciência Hoje* 6 (33): 74–78.

1987b. Frenesi de desmatamento no Brasil: A floresta amazônica irá sobreviver? In *Homem e Natureza na Amazônia*, ed. G. Kohlhepp and A. Schrader. Tubingen: Geographisches Institut.

1988. O carvão de Carajás. *Ciência Hoje* 8 (48): 17–21.

1989a. Extractive Reserves in Brazilian Amazonia. *Bioscience* 39: 389–393.

1989b. A Prescription for Slowing Deforestation in Amazonia. *Environment* 31: 16–20, 39–40.

1992. Greenhouse Gas Emissions from Deforestation in the Brazilian Amazon. In *Tropical Forestry and Global Climate Change*, ed. W. Makundi and J. Sathaya. Berkeley: Lawrence Berkeley Laboratory, workshop proceedings.

Federov, A.

1966. The Structure of the Tropical Rain Forest and Speciation in the Humid Tropics. *Journal of Ecology* 54: 1–11.

Feldman, J.

1977. Effects of Tuberculosis on Sexual Functioning. *Medical Aspects of Human Sexuality* 11: 29ff.

Ferdon, Edwin

1959. Agricultural Potential and the Development of Cultures. *Southwestern Journal of Anthropology* 15: 1–19.

Fernandes, Florestan

1949. *A organização social dos índios Tupinambá*. São Paulo: Ed. Progresso.

1952. *A função social da guerra na sociedade Tupinambá*. São Paulo: Editôra do Museu Paulista.

Fernandes, F. R. C., ed.

1987. *Subsolo brasileiro*. Brasília: MCT/CNPq.

Fernandes, F. R. C., et al.

1987. *A questão mineral na Amazônia: Seis ensaios críticos*. Brasília: MCT/CNPq.

Ferreira, Alexandre Rodrigues

1983. *Viagem filosófica ao Rio Negro*. Facsimile edition from the original published between 1885 and 1888 in the *Revista do Instituto Histórico e Geográfico Brasileiro*. Belém: Museu Goeldi/CNPq.

Ferreira Penna, D. S.
　1876. *Breves notícias sôbre os Sambaquís do Pará*. Archivo do Museu Nacional do Rio de Janeiro 1: 85–99.
Ferri, M. G.
　1977. Ecologia dos cerrados. In *IV simpôsio sôbre o cerrado*, ed. M. G. Ferri. São Paulo: Universidade de Sâo Paulo/Editôra Itatáia.
Ferri, M. G., ed.
　1977. *IV simpôsio sôbre o cerrado*. São Paulo: Universidade de São Paulo/ Editôra Itatáia.
Figueroa, A.
　1904. *Relación de las misiones de la Compañía de Jesús en el país de los Maynas*. Madrid: Librería G. de V. Suárez.
Fishman, Olga
　1973. Black Piedra among Brazilian Indians. *Revista do Instituto de Medicina Tropical de São Paulo* 15: 103–106.
Fittkau, E. J.
　1968. The Fauna of South America. In *Biogeography and Ecology in South America*, ed. E. J. Fittkau et al., vol. 2. The Hague: W. Junk.
Fittkau, E. J., and H. Klinge
　1973. On Biomass and Trophic Structure of the Central Amazonian Rain Forest Ecosystem. *Biotropica* 5 (1): 2–14.
Fittkau, E. J., et al.
　1975. Productivity, Biomass, and Population Dynamics in Amazonian Water Bodies. In *Tropical Ecological Systems*, ed. F. Golley and E. Medina. New York: Springer-Verlag.
Fittkau, E. J., et al., eds.
　1968. *Biogeography and Ecology in South America*. 2 vols. The Hague: W. Junk.
Fleming-Moran, M.
　1974. The Folk View of Natural Causation and Disease in Brazil and Its Relation to Traditional Curing Practices. Master's thesis, Department of Anthropology, University of Florida, Gainesville.
Fleming-Moran, M., and C. Coimbra
　1989. Blood Pressure Studies among Amazonian Native Populations: A Review from an Epidemiological Perspective. *Social Science and Medicine* 31: 593–601.
Fleming-Moran, M., and E. Moran
　1978. O surgimento de classes sociais numa comunidade planejada para ser igualitária. *Boletim do Museu Paraense Emílio Goeldi* (Antropologia) 69: 1–38.
Flowers, Nancy
　1983. Seasonal Factors in Subsistence, Nutrition, and Child Growth in a Central Brazilian Indian Community. In *Adaptive Responses of Native Amazonians*, ed. R. Hames and W. Vickers. New York: Academic Press.

1992. Demographic Crisis and Recovery: A Case Study of the Xavante of Pimentel Barbosa. Unpublished ms.

Flowers, N., et al.
1982. Variation in Swidden Practices in Four Central Brazilian Indian Societies. *Human Ecology* 10: 203–217.

Foin, T., and W. Davis
1987. Equilibrium and Disequilibrium Models in Ecological Anthropology. *American Anthropologist* 89: 9–31.

Foley, Robert
1987. *Another Unique Species: Patterns in Human Evolutionary Ecology.* New York: Longman's.

Foller, Maj-Lis
1990. *Environmental Changes and Human Health: A Study of the Shipibo-Conibo in Eastern Peru* No. 8. Göteborg, Sweden: Humanekologiska Skrifter.

Forde, C. D.
1939. *Habitat, Economy and Society.* London: Methuen.

Foresta, R. A.
1991. *Amazon Conservation in the Age of Development.* Gainesville: University of Florida Press.

Fosberg, F. R., et al.
1961. Delimitation of the Humid Tropics. *Geographical Review* 51 (3): 333–347.

Frake, Charles
1961. Cultural Ecology and Ethnography. *American Anthropologist* 64 (1), part 1: 53–59.

Franco, H. B., and M. de F. Mendes Leal, eds.
1990. *As crianças da Amazônia: Um futuro ameaçado.* Série Cooperação Amazônica. Belém: Universidade Federal do Pará.

Franken, M., et al.
1979. Litterfall in Inundation, Riverine and Terra Firme Forests of Central Amazonia. *Tropical Ecology* 20 (2): 225–235.

Frecchione, J., et al.
1989. The Perception of Ecological Zones and Natural Resources in the Brazilian Amazon: An Ethnoecology of Lake Coari. *Advances in Economic Botany* 7: 260–282.

Freitas, F. G., and C. O. Silveira
1977. Principais solos sôbre vegetação de cerrado e sua aptidão agrícola. In *IV simpôsio sôbre o cerrado*, ed. M. G. Ferri. São Paulo: Universidade de São Paulo/Editôra Itatáia.

Freitas-Filho, A. S., and N. B. Oliveira
1955. Estudo sôbre o estado nutritivo dos Xavantes. *Revista Brasileira de Medicina* 12: 565–567.

Friedman, Jonathan
1974. Marxism, Structuralism and Vulgar Materialism. *Man* 9: 444–469.

Frikel, Protasio

1959. Agricultura dos índios Mundurukú. *Boletim do Museu Paraense Emílio Goeldi* (Antropologia) n.s. 4: 1–35.

1968. *Os Xikrín*. Belém: Publicações Avulsas do Museu Goeldi.

Frisancho, A. R.

1981. New Norms of Upper Limb Fat and Muscle Areas for Assessment of Nutritional Status. *American Journal of Clinical Nutrition* 34: 2540–2545.

Frisch, Rose, and Journal McArthur

1974. Menstrual Cycles: Fatness as a Determinant of Minimum Weight Necessary for Their Maintenance or Onset. *Science* 185: 949–951.

Fritz, Samuel

1922. *Journal of the Travels and Labors of Father Samuel Fritz in the River of the Amazons between 1686 and 1723*. London: Hakluyt Society.

Fundação SOS Mata Atlântica

1988. Seminario sôbre manejo racional de florestas tropicais. Rio de Janeiro: Fundação SOS Mata Atlântica.

Furley, P.

1979. Development Planning in Rondônia. In *Land, People and Planning in Contemporary Amazonia*, ed. F. Barbira-Scazzocchio. Cambridge: Center for Latin American Studies, University of Cambridge.

Galvão, Eduardo

1949. *Apontamento sôbre os índios Kamaiuna: Observações zoológicas e antropológicas*. Museu Nacional. Publ. Avulsas No. 5.

1955. *Santos e visagens*. Rio de Janeiro: Brasiliana.

1959. Aculturação indígena no Rio Negro. *Boletim do Museu Paraense Emílio Goeldi* (Antropologia) n.s. 7: 1–60.

1963. Elementos básicos da horticultura de subsistencia indígena. *Revista do Museu Paulista* n.s. 14: 120–144.

García Vásquez, J., and C. Yokomizo

1986. Resultados de 20 anos de incentivos fiscais na agropecuária na Amazônia. *XIV Encontro Nacional de Economía* 2: 47–84.

Garlick, J. P., and R. W. J. Keay, eds.

1977. Human Ecology in the Tropics. 2d ed. London: Taylor and Francis.

Geertz, Clifford

1963. *Agricultural Involution*. Berkeley: University of California Press.

1972. The Wet and the Dry: Traditional Irrigation in Bali and Morocco. *Human Ecology* 1: 23–40.

Geisler, R., and J. Schneider

1976. The Element Matrix of Amazon Waters and Its Relationship with the Mineral Content of Fishes. *Amazoniana* 6 (1): 47–65.

Gentry, Alwyn, ed.

1992. *Four Neotropical Rainforests*. New Haven, Conn.: Yale University Press.

Glacken, Clarence
 1967. *Traces on a Rhodian Shore*. Berkeley: University of California Press.
Gliessman, S., et al.
 1983. Ancient Raised-Field Agriculture in the Maya Lowlands of Southeast-
 ern Mexico. In *Drained-Field Agriculture in Central and South America*,
 ed. J. P. Darch. BAR International Series No. 189. London: BAR.
Goedert, W.
 1983. Management of the Cerrado Soils of Brazil. *Journal of Soil Science*
 34: 405–428.
 1985. Management of Acid Tropical Soil in the Savannas of South America.
 IBSRAM Workshop, Brasília.
Goldenweiser, Alexander
 1937. *Anthropology*. New York: F. S. Crofts.
Goldman, I.
 1948. Tribes of the Vaupés-Caquetá Region. *Handbook of South American
 Indians*, vol. 3. Washington, D.C.: Bureau of American Ethnology.
 1963. *The Cubeo*. Urbana: University of Illinois Press.
Golley, F.
 1983. *Tropical Rain Forest Ecosystems*. Ecosystems of the World Series 14.
 New York: Elsevier.
Gomes, Mercio Pereira
 1988. *Os índios e o Brasil*. Petrópolis: Vozes.
Gómez-Pompa, A., et al.
 1972. The Tropical Rain Forest: A Non-Renewable Resource. *Science* 177:
 762–765.
Goodland, Robert
 1971. The Cerrado Oxisols of the Triângulo Mineiro, Central Brazil. *Anais
 da Academia Brasileira de Ciências* 43 (2): 407–414.
 1981. Environmental Ranking of Amazonian Development Projects in Brazil. *Environmental Conservation* 7: 9–26.
Goodland, R., and M. G. Ferri
 1979. *Ecologia do cerrado*. São Paulo: Editora Itatáia/USP.
Goodland, R. J., and H. S. Irwin
 1975. *Amazon Jungle: Green Hell to Red Desert?* Amsterdam: Elsevier.
Goodman, D., and A. Hall, eds.
 1990. *The Future of Amazonia: Destruction or Sustainable Development*.
 London: Macmillan.
Goulding, Michael
 1979. *Ecologia da pesca do Rio Madeira*. Manaus: INPA.
 1980. *The Fishes and the Forest*. Berkeley: University of California Press.
 1981. *Man and Fisheries on an Amazon Frontier*. The Hague: W. Junk.
 1990. *Amazon: The Flooded Forest*. New York: Sterling.
Goulding, M., et al.
 1988. *Rio Negro: Rich Life in Poor Water*. The Hague: SPB Academic
 Publishing.

Gragson, Theodore

　　1989. Time Allocation of Subsistence and Settlement in a Ciri Khonome
　　Pume Village of the Llanos of Apure. Ph.D. diss., Pennsylvania State
　　University.

Gross, Daniel

　　1975. Protein Capture and Cultural Development in the Amazon Basin.
　　American Anthropologist 77: 526–549.

　　1979. A New Approach to Central Brazilian Social Organization. In *Brazil:
　　Anthropological Perspectives*, ed. M. Margolis and W. Carter. New York:
　　Columbia University Press.

　　1983. Village Movement in Relation to Resources in Amazonia. In *Adaptive
　　Responses of Native Amazonians*, ed. R. Hames and W. Vickers. New
　　York: Academic Press.

Gross, Daniel, ed.

　　1973. *Peoples and Cultures of Aboriginal South America*. New York: Natu-
　　ral History Press.

Gross, Daniel, and Barbara Underwood

　　1970. Technological Change and Caloric Costs. *American Anthropologist*
　　73: 725–740.

Gross, D., et al.

　　1979. Ecology and Acculturation among Native Peoples of Central Brazil.
　　Science 206: 1043–1050.

Guillet, David

　　1981. Land Tenure, Ecological Zone, and Agricultural Regime in the Cen-
　　tral Andes. *American Ethnologist* 8: 139–156.

　　1987. Terracing and Irrigation in the Peruvian Highlands. *Current Anthro-
　　pology* 28: 409–430.

Haffer, J.

　　1969. Speciation in Amazonian Forest Birds. *Science* 165: 131–137.

Halbrecht, I.

　　1956. Latent Genital Tuberculosis as the Main Cause of Tubal Occlusion in
　　Primary Sterility. *International Journal of Fertility* 1: 367–374.

Halle, F., et al.

　　1978. *Tropical Trees and Forests: An Architectural Analysis*. New York:
　　Springer-Verlag.

Hames, Raymond

　　1979. A Comparison of the Efficiencies of the Shotgun and the Bow in Neo-
　　tropical Forest Hunting. *Human Ecology* 7: 219–252.

　　1982. Proteína y cultura en la Amazonía. *Amazonía Peruana* 3 (6): 127–143.

Hames, R., ed.

　　1980. *Studies on Hunting and Fishing in the Neotropics*. Working Papers on
　　South American Indians No. 2. Bennington, Vt.: Bennington College.

Hames, R., and W. Vickers

　　1982. Optimal Diet Breadth Theory as a Model to Explain Variability in
　　Amazonian Hunting. *American Ethnologist* 9: 358–378.

Hames, R., and W. Vickers, eds.
   1983. *Adaptive Responses of Native Amazonians*. New York: Academic
      Press.
Hammen, T. van der
   1972. Changes in Vegetation and Climate in the Amazon Basin and Sur-
      rounding Areas during the Pleistocene. *Geologie en Mijnbouw* 51 (6):
      641–643.
Hanna, J. M., and P. T. Baker
   1974. Comparative Heat Tolerance of Shipibo Indians and Peruvian Mesti-
      zos. *Human Biology* 46: 69–80.
Hansluwka, Harald
   1985. Measuring the Health of Populations: Indicators and Interpretations.
      Social Science and Medicine 20: 1207–1224.
Hardesty, D. L.
   1975a. The Human Ecological Niche. *American Anthropologist* 74:
      458–466.
   1975b. The Niche Concept: Suggestions for Its Uses in Human Ecology. *Hu-
      man Ecology* 3: 71–85.
   1980. The Use of General Ecological Principles in Archaeology. *Advances in
      Archaeological Method and Theory* 3: 157–187.
Harris, Larry, et al.
   1975. Modelling and Systems Studies as a Tool in Understanding Human
      Ecology. In *Institute of Ecology (TIE): A Manual of Energy Flow Studies*.
      Mimeo. Available from Institute of Ecology, Indianapolis, Ind.
Harris, Marvin
   1968. *The Rise of Anthropological Theory*. New York: Crowell.
   1974a. *Cows, Pigs, Wars and Witches*. New York: Vintage Press.
   1974b. Why a Perfect Knowledge of All the Rules One Must Know to Act
      Like a Native Cannot Lead to the Knowledge of How Natives Act. *Jour-
      nal of Anthropological Research* 30 (4): 242–251.
   1977. *Cannibals and Kings*. New York: Random House.
Harrison, G. A., and A. J. Boyce, eds.
   1972. *The Structure of Human Populations*. Oxford: Clarendon Press.
Harrison, G. A., et al.
   1977. *Human Biology*. 2d ed. Oxford: Clarendon Press.
Hartman, T.
   1984. *Bibliografia crítica da etnologia brasileira*. Vol. 3. Berlin: Dietrich Rei-
      mer Verlag.
Hartshorn, G. S.
   1978. Tree Falls and Tropical Forest Dynamics. In *Tropical Trees as Living
      Systems*, ed. P. B. Tomlinson and M. H. Zimmerman. Cambridge: Cam-
      bridge University Press.
Hartt, C.
   1885. Contribuição sôbre a etnologia do Vale do Amazonas. *Archivos do
      Museu Nacional do Rio de Janeiro* 6: 1–175.

Hawkes, K., K. Hill, and J. O'Connell

1982. Why Hunters Gather: Optimal Foraging and the Aché of Eastern Paraguay. *American Ethnologist* 9: 379–398.

Hawley, Amos

1950. *Human Ecology: A Theory of Community Structure.* New York: Ronald Press.

1973. Ecology and Population. *Science* 179: 1196–1201.

Hecht, S.

1980. Deforestation in the Amazon Basin: Magnitude, Dynamics and Soil Resource Effects. *Studies in Third World Societies* 13: 61–108.

1982. Agroforestry in the Amazon Basin. In *Amazonia: Agriculture and Land Use Research*, ed. S. Hecht. Cali, Colombia: Centro Internacional de Agricultura Tropical (CIAT).

Hecht, S., ed.

1982. *Amazonia: Agriculture and Land Use Research.* Cali, Colombia: Centro Internacional de Agricultura Tropical. (CIAT)

Hecht, S., and A. Cockburn

1989. *The Fate of the Forest.* London: Verso.

Hecht, S., and D. Posey

1989. Preliminary Results on Soil Management Techniques of the Kayapó Indians. *Advances in Economic Botany* 7: 174–188.

Hecht, S., et al.

1988. The Economics of Cattle Ranching in E. Amazonia. *Interciencia* 13 (5): 233–240.

Hegen, E. E.

1966. *Highways into the Upper Amazon.* Gainesville: University of Florida Press.

Heider, Karl

1972. Environment, Subsistence and Society. *Annual Review of Anthropology* 1: 207–226.

Heindsdijk, D.

1957. *Forest Inventory in the Amazon Valley.* Rome: Food and Agriculture Organization.

Heinen, H. D., and K. Ruddle

1974. Ecology, Ritual and Economic Organization in the Distribution of Palm Starch among the Warao. *Journal of Anthropological Research* 30: 116–138.

Helm, June

1962. The Ecological Approach in Anthropology. *American Journal of Sociology* 67: 630–639.

Hemming, John

1978. *Red Gold: The Conquest of the Brazilian Indians.* Cambridge: Harvard University Press.

1987. *Amazon Frontier: The Defeat of the Brazilian Indians.* Cambridge, Mass: Harvard University Press.

Hemming, John, ed.
    1985. *Change in the Amazon Basin.* 2 vols. Manchester: Manchester University Press.
Hern, Warren
    1976. Knowledge and Use of Herbal Contraceptives in a Peruvian Amazon Village. *Human Organization* 35: 9–19.
    1977. High Fertility in a Peruvian Amazon Indian Village. *Human Ecology* 5:355–368.
    1988. Polygyny and Fertility among the Shipibo: An Epidemiologic Test of an Ethnographic Hypothesis. Ph.D. diss., Department of Epidemiology, University of North Carolina, Chapel Hill.
Herrera, Antonio de
    1856. *The Voyage of Francisco de Orellana down the River of the Amazons, A.D. 1540–1541.* Expeditions into the Valley of the Amazons, 1539, 1540, 1639. London: Hakluyt Society.
Herrera, Rafael
    1979a. Nutrient Distribution and Cycling in Amazon Caatinga Forest. Paper presented at the International Symposium on Tropical Ecology, Kuala Lumpur.
    1979b. Nutrient Distribution and Cycling in an Amazonian Caatinga Forest on Spodosols in S. Venezuela. Ph.D. diss., University of Reading, England.
    1985. Nutrient Cycling in Amazonian Forests. In *Key Environments: Amazonia*, ed. G. Prance and T. Lovejoy. London: Pergamon.
Herrera, R., and C. Jordan
    1981. Nitrogen Cycle in a Tropical Amazon Rainforest: The Caatinga of Low Mineral Nutrient Status. In *Terrestrial Nitrogen Cycles*, ed. F. Clark and T. Rosswall. *Ecological Bulletin* (Stockholm) 33: 493–505.
Herrera, R., et al.
    1978. Amazon Ecosystems: Their Structure and Functioning with Particular Emphasis on Nutrients. *Interciencia* 3 (4): 223–231.
Hill, Jonathan
    1983. Wakuenai Society: A Processual-Structural Analysis of Indigenous Cultural Life in the Upper Rio Negro Region of Venezuela. Ph.D. diss., Department of Anthropology, Indiana University.
    1984. Social Equality and Ritual Hierarchy: The Arawakan Wakuenai of Venezuela. *American Ethnologist* 11: 528–544.
    1989. Ritual Production of Environmental History among the Arawakan Wakuenai of Venezuela. *Human Ecology* 17: 1–25.
Hill, J., and E. F. Moran
    1983. Adaptive Strategies of Wakuenai People of the Rio Negro Basin. In *Adaptive Responses of Native Amazonians*, ed. R. Hames and W. Vickers. New York: Academic Press.
Hill, Kim, and K. Hawkes
    1983. Neotropical Hunting among the Ache of Eastern Paraguay. In *Adap-*

tive Responses of Native Amazonians, ed. R. Hames and W. Vickers. New York: Academic Press.

Hill, Kim, et al.
  1984. Seasonal Variance in the Diet of Aché Hunter-Gatherers in Eastern Paraguay. *Human Ecology* 12: 101–136.

Hiraoka, Mario
  1985. Mestizo Subsistence in Riparian Amazonia. *National Geographic Research* 1: 236–246.
  1986. Zonation of Mestizo Riverine Farming Systems in Northeast Peru. *National Geographic Research* 2: 354–371.

Hoag, R., et al.
  1987. Alluvial Soils of the Amazon Basin. In *Tropsoils*, ed. N. Caudle and C. McCants. Technical Report 1985–1986. Raleigh: North Carolina State University.

Holdridge, L. R.
  1967. *Life Zone Ecology*. Rev. ed. San Jose, Costa Rica: Tropical Science Center.

Holling, C. S.
  1973. Resilience and Stability of Ecological Systems. *Annual Review of Ecology and Systematics* 4: 1–23.

Holmberg, Allan
  1969. *Nomads of the Long Bow*. New York: Natural History Press.

Holmes, Rebecca
  1981. Estado nutricional en 4 aldeas de la selva amazónica, Venezuela. M.A. thesis, Instituto Venezolano de Investigaciones Científicas (IVIC), Caracas, Venezuela.
  1984. Non-Dietary Modifiers of Nutritional Status in Tropical Forest Populations of Venezuela. *Interciencia* 9 (6): 386–391.
  1985. Nutritional Status and Cultural Change in Venezuela's Amazon Territory. In *Change in the Amazon Basin*, ed. J. Hemming, vol. 2. Manchester: Manchester University Press.

Huber, J.
  1909. Matas e madeiras amazônicas. *Boletim do Museu Paraense Emílio Goeldi* (Historia Natural e Etnografia) 6: 91–225.

Hueck, K.
  1965. *As florestas da América do Sul*. Brasília: Editôra Universidade de Brasília.

Hugh-Jones, Christine
  1979. *From the Milk River*. Cambridge: Cambridge University Press.

Hugh-Jones, Stephen
  1979. *The Palm and the Pleiades*. Cambridge: Cambridge University Press.

Humboldt, A. von
  1852. *Personal Narrative of Travels to the Equinoctial Regions of America, 1799–1804*. 3 vols. London: H. G. Bohn.

Huntington, Ellsworth
   1915. *Civilization and Climate*. New Haven, Conn.: Yale University Press.
   1927. *The Human Habitat*. New York: Van Nostrand.
   1945. *Mainsprings of Civilization*. New York: John Wiley.
Hurtado, A. M., et al.
   1985. Female Subsistence Strategies among Ache Hunter Gatherers in
      E. Paraguay. *Human Ecology* 13: 1–28.
Hutchinson, G. E.
   1978. *An Introduction to Population Ecology*. New Haven, Conn.: Yale
      University Press.
IPEAN
   1974. *Os solos da rodovía transamazônica: Trecho Itaituba–Humaitá*.
      Belém: EMBRAPA/IPEAN.
Jackson, Jean
   1972. Marriage and Linguistic Identity among the Bará Indians of the Vau-
      pés. Ph.D. diss., Department of Anthropology, Stanford University.
   1976. Vaupés Marriage: A Network System in the Northwest Amazon. In
      Regional Analysis, ed. C. Smith, vol. 2. New York: Academic Press.
   1983. *The Fish People: Linguistic Exogamy and Tukanoan Identity in N.W.
      Amazonia*. Cambridge: Cambridge University Press.
Jackson, J., and A. K. Romney
   1973. A Note on Bará Exogamy. Unpublished ms.
Jacobs, Marius
   1988. *The Tropical Rain Forest: A First Encounter*. New York: Springer-
      Verlag.
Jamison, Paul, and S. Friedman, eds.
   1974. *Energy Flow in Human Communities*. University Park, Pa.: U.S. In-
      ternational Biological Program and Social Science Research Council.
Janzen, D. H.
   1970. Herbivores and the Number of Tree Species in Tropical Forests.
      American Naturalist 104: 501–528.
   1974. Tropical Black Water Rivers. *Biotropica* 6: 69–103.
   1975. Tropical Agroecosystems. In *Food: Politics, Economics, Nutrition and
      Research*, ed. Philip Abelson. Washington, D.C.: American Association
      for the Advancement of Science.
Jelliffe, D. B.
   1966. *The Assessment of the Nutritional Status of the Community*. Mono-
      graph Series No. 53. Geneva: World Health Organization.
   1978. *La salud del niño en los trópicos*. Washington, D.C.: Organización
      Panamericana de la Salud. Publicación Científica No. 361.
Johnson, Allen
   1974. Ethnoecology and Planting Practices in a Swidden Agricultural Sys-
      tem. *American Ethnologist* 1: 87–101.
   1975. Time Allocation in a Machiguenga Community. *Ethnology* 14 (3):
      301–310.

1977. The Energy Costs of Technology in a Changing Environment: A Machiguenga Case. In *Material Culture*. Proceedings of the American Ethnological Society. St. Paul, Minn.: West Publishing.

1982. Reductionism in Cultural Ecology: The Amazon Case. *Current Anthropology* 23: 413–428.

1989. How the Machiguenga Manage Resources: Conservation or Exploitation of Nature? *Advances in Economic Botany* 7: 213–222.

Johnson, A., and C. Behrens

1982. Nutritional Criteria in Machiguenga Food Production Decisions. *Human Ecology* 10: 167–189.

Johnson, A., and T. Earle

1987. *The Evolution of Human Societies*. Stanford, Cal.: Stanford University Press.

Johnston, F. E., et al.

1971. The Anthropometric Determination of Body Composition among the Peruvian Cashinahua. *American Journal of Physical Anthropology* 34: 409–416.

Jolly, A.

1972. *The Evolution of Primate Behavior*. Chicago: University of Chicago Press.

Jordan, C. F.

1982a. Amazon Rain Forests. *American Scientist* 70: 394–401.

1982b. The Nutrient Balance of an Amazonian Rain Forest. *Ecology* 63 (3): 647–654.

1985. *Nutrient Cycling in Tropical Forest Ecosystems*. New York: John Wiley.

n.d.a. Conversion of Rain Forests: Effects of Nutrient Conserving Mechanisms. Mimeo.

n.d.b. Mycorrhizae and the Direct Nutrient Cycling Hypothesis at San Carlos. Mimeo.

n.d.c. Oligotrophic and Eutrophic Rain Forest Ecosystems. Mimeo.

Jordan, C. F., ed.

1989. *An Amazonian Rain Forest*. Man and the Biosphere Series No. 2. Park Ridge, N.J.: Parthenon.

Jordan, C., and R. Herrera

1981. Tropical Rain Forests: Are Nutrients Really Critical? *American Naturalist* 117: 167–180.

Jordan, C., and J. Heuveldop

1981. The Water Budget of an Amazonian Forest. *Acta Amazônica* 11: 87–92.

Jordan, C., and C. Uhl

1978. Biomass of a Tierra Firme Forest of the Amazon Basin. *Oecologia Plantarum* 13: 387–400.

Jordan, C., et al.
    1980. Nutrient Scavenging of Rainfall by the Canopy of an Amazonian Rain
    Forest. *Biotropica* 12: 61–66.
    n.d. The Nitrogen Cycle in a Tierra Firme Rain Forest on Oxisol in the
    Amazon Territory of Venezuela. Mimeo.
Junk, W. J.
    1970. Investigations on the Ecology and Production-Biology of the "Floating
    Meadows" on the Middle Amazon, I: Floating Vegetation and Ecology.
    Amazoniana 2 (4): 449–495.
    1975. Aquatic Wildlife of Fisheries. In *The Use of Ecological Guideliines for
    Development in the American Humid Tropics.* Morges, Switzerland: In-
    ternational Union for Conservation of Nature and Natural Resources.
    1984. Ecology of the Várzea of Amazonian Whitewater Rivers. In *The Ama-
    zon: Limnology and Landscape Ecology of a Mighty Tropical River and
    Its Basin,* ed. H. Sioli. Dordrecht: W. Junk.
Jurion, F., and J. Henry
    1969. *Can Primitive Farming Be Modernized?* London: Agra-Europe.
Kampf, N., and D. C. Kern
    in press. Efeitos de antigos assentamentos indígenas na formação de solos
    com terra preta arqueológica na região de Oriximiná. *Revista Brasileira
    de Ciência do Solo.*
Kaplan, H., and K. Hill
    1985. Food Sharing among Ache Foragers: Tests of Explanatory Hypothe-
    ses. *Current Anthropology* 26: 223–246.
Kates, R. W.
    1971. Natural Hazard in Human Ecological Perspective: Hypotheses and
    Models. *Economic Geography* 47: 438–451.
Katzer, I.
    1933. Geologia do Estado do Pará. *Boletim do Museu Paraense de História
    Natural* (Belém) 9: 1–269.
Keegan, William
    1986. The Optimal Foraging Analysis of Horticultural Production. *Ameri-
    can Anthropologist* 88: 92–107.
Keene, Arthur
    1981. Optimal Foraging in a Nonmarginal Environment. In *Hunter-
    Gatherer Foraging Strategies,* ed. B. Winterhalden and E. Smith.
    Chicago: University of Chicago Press.
Keller, W., et al.
    1976. Anthropometry in Nutritional Surveillance. *Nutrition Abstracts and
    Reviews* 46 (8): 591–609.
Kemp, William
    1971. The Flow of Energy in a Hunting Society. *Scientific American* 224 (3):
    104–115.
Kern, Dirse Clara
    1988. Caracterização pedológica de solos com terra preta arqueológica

na região de Oriximiná, Pará. Master's thesis, Faculty of the School of Agronomy, Federal University of Rio Grande do Sul, Porto Alegre.

Kiemen, M. C.

　1973. *The Indian Policy of Portugal in the Amazon Region, 1614–1693.* New York: Octagon Books.

Kiltie, R. A.

　1980. More on Amazon Cultural Ecology. *Current Anthropology* 21: 541–544.

King, J. A.

　1973. The Ecology of Aggressive Behavior. *Annual Review of Ecology and Systematics* 4: 117–138.

Kitamura, P. C., and C. C. Muller

　1984. Castanhais nativos de Marabá: Fatores de depredação e bases para a sua preservação. *Documentos* 30. Belém, Pará: EMBRAPA/CPATU.

Klinge, H.

　1967. Podzol Soils: A Source of Blackwater Rivers in Amazon. In *Atas do simpôsio sôbre a biota amazônica,* ed. H. Lent, vol. 3.

　1978. Studies on the Ecology of Amazon Caatinga Forest in Southern Venezuela. *Acta Científica Venezolana* 29: 258–262.

　n.d. Low Amazon Caatinga or Bana. Unpublished ms.

Klinge, H., and R. Herrera

　1978. Biomass Studies in Amazon Caaatinga Forest in S. Venezuela. *Tropical Ecology* 19 (1): 93–110.

Klinge, H., and W. Rodrigues

　1968. Litter Production in an Area of Amazonian Terra Firme Forest. *Amazoniana* 1: 287–302.

Klinge, H., et al.

　1975. Biomass and Structure in a Central Amazonian Rain Forest. In *Tropical Ecological Systems,* ed. Frank B. Golley and E. Medina. New York: Springer-Verlag.

　1981. Fundamental Ecological Parameters in Amazonia, in Relation to the Potential Development of the Region. In *Tropical Agricultural Hydrology,* ed. R. Lal and E. Russell. New York: John Wiley.

Kloos, P.

　1977. *The Akuriyó of Surinam.* No. 27. Copenhagen: International Working Group on Indigenous Affairs.

Köch-Grünberg, Theodor

　1909–1910. *Zwei Jahre unter den Indianern: Reisen in Nordwest-Brasilien, 1903–05.* 2 vols. Berlin: E. Wasmuth.

Kosak, V., et al.

　1979. *The Heta Indians.* New York: American Museum of Natural History, Anthropological Papers 55 (6): 351–434.

Kroeber, Alfred
1939. *Cultural and Natural Areas of Native North America*. Berkeley: University of California Press.

Kurland, J., and S. Beckerman
1985. Optimal Foraging and Hominid Evolution: Labor and Reciprocity. *American Anthropologist* 87: 73–93.

Ladell, W. S. S.
1964. Terrestrial Animals in Humid Heat: Man. In *Handbook of Physiology: Adaptation to the Environment*, ed. D. B. Dill. Washington, D.C.: American Physiological Society.

Laraia, R., and R. da Matta
1968. *Índios e castanheiros*. São Paulo: Zahar.

Larrick, J. W., et al.
1979. Patterns of Health and Disease among the Waorani Indians of E. Ecuador. *Medical Anthropology* 3: 147–189.

Lasker, Gabriel
1976. Human Biological Adaptability. In *Human Ecology*, ed. Peter Richerson and J. McEvoy. North Scituate, Mass.: Duxbury Press.

Lathrap, D.
1968. Aboriginal Occupation and Changes in River Channel on the Central Ucayali, Peru. *American Antiquity* 33 (1): 62–79.
1970. *The Upper Amazon*. New York: Praeger.

Laughlin, Charles D., Jr., and I. Brady, eds.
1978. *Extinction and Survival in Human Populations*. New York: Columbia University Press.

Lave, C., and J. March
1975. *An Introduction to Models in the Social Sciences*. New York: Harper and Row.

Lawrence, D. N., et al.
1980. Epidemiological Studies among Amerindian Populations of Amazonia, III: Intestinal Parasitoses in Newly Contacted and Acculturating Villages. *American Journal of Tropical Medicine and Hygiene* 29: 530–537.

Lechtig, A., et al.
1972. Influencia de la nutrición materna sobre el crecimiento fetal en poblaciones rurales de Guatemala. *Arquivos Latino Americanos de Nutrición* 22: 117–131.

Lee, Richard B., and I. DeVore, eds.
1968. *Man the Hunter*. Chicago: Aldine.

Lee, R. V., et al.
1978. A Novel Pattern of Treponemal Antibody Distribution in Isolated South American Indian Populations. *American Journal of Epidemiology* 107: 46–53.

Leeds, Anthony
1974. The Ideology of the Yaruro Indians in Relation to Socio-Economic

Organization. In *Native South Americans*, ed. Patricia Lyon. Boston: Little, Brown.

Lees, Susan, and D. Bates
1977. The Role of Exchange in Productive Specialization. *American Anthropologist* 79: 824–841.

Leibenstein, H.
1976. *Beyond Economic Man*. Cambridge, Mass.: Harvard University Press.

Leigh, Egbert Giles, Jr.
1975. Structure and Climate in Tropical Rain Forest. *Annual Review of Ecology and Systematics* 6: 67–86.

Levins, Richard
1966. Strategy of Model Building in Population Biology. *American Scientist* 54: 421–431.
1968. *Evolution in Changing Environments*. Princeton, N.J.: Princeton University Press.

Lewontin, R. C., ed.
1968. *Population Biology and Evolution*. Syracuse, N.Y.: Syracuse University Press.

Lieth, H., and M. J. A. Werger, eds.
1989. *Tropical Rain Forest Ecosystems: Biogeographical and Ecological Studies*. Amsterdam: Elsevier.

Lieth, H., and R. H. Whittaker, eds.
1975. *Primary Productivity of the Biosphere*. Paris: UNESCO.

Lima, R. R.
1956. A agricultura nas várzeas do estuário amazônico. *Boletim do Instituto Agronômico do Norte* (Belém) 23.

Linares, Olga
1976. Garden Hunting in the American Tropics. *Human Ecology* 4: 331–349.

Lindblom, Charles
1964. The Science of Muddling Through. In *The Making of Decisions*, ed. W. J. Gore and J. W. Dyson. New York: Free Press.

Lindeman, R. L.
1942. The Trophic-Dynamic Aspect of Ecology. *Ecology* 23: 399–418.

Little, Michael
1982. The Development of Ideas on Human Ecology and Adaptation. In *A History of American Physical Anthropology*, ed. F. Spencer. New York: Academic Press.

Little, Michael, and Paul T. Baker
1976. Environmental Adaptations and Perspectives. In *Man in the Andes*, ed. Paul T. Baker and M. Little. Stroudsburg, Pa.: Dowden, Hutchinson and Ross.

Little, M., and S. Friedman
1973. *Man in the Ecosystem*. University Park, Pa.: US/IBP.

Little, Michael, and G. Morren

1976. *Ecology, Energetics and Human Variability.* Dubuque, Ia.: William C. Brown.

Little, Michael, et al.

1984. Human Biology and the Development of an Ecosystem Approach. In *The Ecosystem Concept in Anthropology,* ed. E. F. Moran. Washington, D.C.: American Association for the Advancement of Science.

Lizot, Jacques

1977. Population, Resources and Warfare among the Yanomami. *Man,* n.s. 12: 497–517.

1980. La agricultura Yanomami. *Antropológica* (Caracas) 53: 3–93.

Longman, K. A., and J. Jenik

1974. *Tropical Forest and Its Environment.* London: Longman.

1987. *Tropical Forest and Its Environment.* 2d ed. New York: Longman/ Wiley.

Lopes, A. S.

1975. A Survey of the Fertility Status of Soils under Cerrado Vegetation in Brazil. Master's thesis, North Carolina State University.

Lopes, A. S., and F. R. Cox

1977. A Survey of the Fertility Status of Surface Soils under Cerrado Vegetation in Brazil. *Soil Science Society of America Journal* 41 (4): 742–747.

Love, T. F.

1977. Ecological Niche Theory in Sociocultural Anthropology. *American Ethnologist* 4: 27–42.

Lovejoy, T., R. Bierregaard, J. Rankin, and H. Schubart

1983. Ecological Dynamics of Tropical Forest Fragments. In *Tropical Rain Forest: Ecology and Management.* London: Blackwell.

Lowenstein, Frank

1968. Some Aspects of Human Ecology in South America. In *Biogeography and Ecology in South America,* ed. E. J. Fittkau et al. The Hague: W. Junk.

1973. Some Consideration of Biological Adaptation by Aboriginal Man. In *Tropical Forest Ecosystems in Africa and South America,* ed. Betty Meggers et al. Washington, D.C.: Smithsonian Institution Press.

Luizão, F. J., and H. O. R. Schubart

1987. Litter Production and Decomposition in a Terra Firme Forest of Central Amazonia. *Experientia* (Switzerland) 43: 259–265.

Lustig-Arecco, Vera

1979. Recursos naturais e técnicas de Caça. *Revista de Antropologia* (São Paulo) 22: 39–60.

Mabberley, D. J.

1992. *Tropical Rain Forest Ecology.* 2d ed. New York: Chapman and Hall.

MacArthur, Robert H.

1961. Population Effects of Natural Selection. *American Naturalist* 95: 195–199.

1965. Ecological Consequences of Natural Selection. In *Theoretical and Mathematical Biology*, ed. T. Waterman and H. Horowitz. New York: Blaisdell.

MacArthur, R. H., and E. Pianka.

1966. An Optimal Use of a Patchy Environment. *American Naturalist* 100: 603–609.

McCay, Bonnie

1981. Optimal Foragers or Political Actors? Ecological Analyses of a New Jersey Fishery. *American Ethnologist* 8: 356–382.

MacCluer, J. W., et al.

1971. Demographic Structure of a Primitive Population: A Simulation. *American Journal of Physical Anthropology* 35: 193–207.

McFalls, J. A., and M. H. McFalls

1984. *Disease and Fertility*. Orlando, Fla: Academic Press.

McKey, D., et al.

1978. Phenolic Content of Vegetation in Two African Rain Forests: Ecological Implications. *Science* 202: 61–63.

McNeil, M.

1964. Lateritic Soils. *Scientific American* 211: 96–102.

McNeill, J.

1988. Deforestation in the Araucaria Zone of S. Brazil, 1900–1983. In *World Deforestation in the 20th Century*, ed. J. Richards and R. Tucker. Durham, N.C.: Duke University Press.

Mahar, Dennis

1979. *Frontier Development Policy in Brazil: A Study of Amazonia*. New York: Praeger.

1988. *Government Policies and Deforestation in Brazil's Amazon Region*. Washington, D.C.: World Bank.

Marbut, C. F.

1926. The Soils of the Amazon Basin in Relation to Agricultural Possibilities. *Geographical Review* 16 (3): 119–142.

Marques, J., et al.

1977. Precipitable Water and Water Vapor Flux between Belém and Manaus. *Acta Amazônica* 7: 355–362.

Martin, M. Kay

1969. South American Foragers: A Case Study in Cultural Devolution? *American Anthropologist* 71: 243–260.

Martorell, Reynaldo

1980. Interrelationships between Diet, Infectious Disease and Nutritional Status. In *Social and Biological Predictors of Nutritional Status, Physical Growth and Behavioral Development*, ed. L. Greams and F. Johnston. New York: Academic Press.

1982. *Nutrition and Health Status Indicators*. LSMS Working Papers No. 13. Washington, D.C.: World Bank.

1989. Body Size, Adaptation and Function. *Human Organization* 48 (1): 15–20.

Martorell, R., et al.

1976. Protein-Calorie Supplementation and Postnatal Physical Growth: A Review of Findings from Developing Countries. *Arquivos Latinoamericanos de Nutrición* 26: 115–128.

1981. Maternal Stature, Fertility and Infant Mortality. *Human Biology* 53 (3): 303–312.

Mata, L. J.

1978. *The Children of Santa Maria Cauque*. Cambridge: Massachussets Institute of Technology Press.

May, P., et al.

1985. Subsistence Benefits from the Babassu Palm (*Orbignya martiana*). *Economic Botany* 39 (2): 113–129.

Maybury-Lewis, David

1967. *Akwé-Shavante Society*. Oxford: Clarendon Press.

Maynard Smith, J.

1978. Optimization Theory in Evolution. *Annual Review of Ecology and Systematics* 9: 31–56.

Medina, E., V. García, and E. Cuevas

1990. Sclerophylly and Oligotrophic Environments: Relationships between Leaf Structure, Mineral Nutrient Content, and Drought Resistance in Tropical Rain Forests of the Upper Rio Negro Region. *Biotropica* 22 (1): 51–64.

Medina, E., et al.

1978. Significance of Leaf Orientation for Leaf Temperature in an Amazonian Sclerophyll Vegetation. *Radiation and Environmental Biophysics* 15: 131–140.

Medina, José Toribio

1934. *The Discovery of the Amazon, According to the Account of Friar Gaspar de Carvajal*. Ed. H. D. Heaton. New York: American Geographical Society.

Meggers, Betty

1954. Environmental Limitations on the Development of Culture. *American Anthropologist* 56: 801–824.

1957. Environment and Culture in the Amazon Basin: An Appraisal of the Theory of Environmental Determinism. In *Studies in Human Ecology*. Washington, D.C.: Anthropological Society of Washington/Organization of American States.

1971. *Amazonia*. Chicago: Aldine.

1974. Environment and Culture in Amazonia. In *Man in the Amazon*, ed. Charles Wagley. Gainesville: University of Florida Press.

1975. Application of the Biological Model of Diversification to Cultural Distributions in Tropical Lowland South America. *Biotropica* 7 (3): 141–161.

Meggers, Betty, E. S. Ayensu, and W. D. Ducksworth, eds.

　1973. *Tropical Forest Ecosystems in Africa and South America*. Washington, D.C.: Smithsonian Institution Press.

Meireles, Denise M.

　1984. *Populações indígenas e a ocupação histórica de Rondônia*. Cuiabá: Departamento de História, Universidade Federal de Mato Grosso.

Melatti, J. C.

　1976. Corrida de toras. *Revista de Atualidade Indígena* 1: 38–46.

　1985. Enfermidades e contato interétnico. In Adaptação a enfermidade e sua distribuição entre grupos indígenas da bacia amazônica, ed. M. A. Ibañez-Nóvión and A. M. T. Ott. Rio de Janeiro: Univ. Fed. de Rio de Janeiro.

Métraux, A.

　1949. Warfare, Cannibalism and Human Trophies. In *Handbook of South American Indians*, ed. J. Steward, vol. 5. Washington, D.C.: Bureau of American Ethnology.

Miller, E.

　1987. Pesquisas arqueológicas paleoíndias no Brasil ocidental. In *Investigaciones paleoíndias al sul de la línea equatorial*, ed. L. Nuñez and B. Meggers. *Estudios Atacameños* 8: 36–61.

Milton, Katherine

　1981a. Distributional Patterns of Tropical Plant Foods as an Evolutionary Stimulus to Primate Mental Development. *American Anthropologist* 83: 534–548.

　1981b. Food Choice and Digestive Strategies of Two Sympatric Primate Species. *American Naturalist* 117: 496–505.

　1984a. Habitat, Diet and Activity Patterns of Free-Ranging Spider Monkeys (*B. aracnoides*). *International Journal of Primatology* 5: 491–541.

　1984b. Protein and Carbohydrate Resources of the Makú Indians of NW Amazonia. *American Anthropologist* 86: 7–27.

Miranda, V. C.

　1907. Os campos de Marajó e sua flora. *Boletim do Museu Paraense Emílio Goeldi* 5: 96–151.

Montagnini, F., and C. Jordan

　1983. The Role of Insects in Productivity Decline of Cassava on a Slash and Burn Site in the Amazon Territory of Venezuela. *Agriculture, Ecosystems and Environment* 9: 293–301.

Montgomery, E., and A. Johnson

　1977. Machiguenga Energy Expenditure. *Ecology of Food and Nutrition* 6: 97–105.

Moore, Dennis

　1984. Syntax of the Language of the Gavião Indians of Rôndonia, Brazil. Ph.D. diss., Department of Anthropology, Graduate Center, City University of New York.

Morais, M. B.

　1985. Estado nutricional de crianças índias do Alto Xingú e avaliação do perímetro braquial no diagnóstico da desnutrição protéico-calórica. Ph.D. diss., Escola Paulista de Medicina, São Paulo.

Moran, Emilio

1973. Energy Flow Analysis and *Manihot esculenta* Crantz. *Acta Amazônica* 3: 28–39.

1974. The Adaptive System of the Amazonian Caboclo. In *Man in the Amazon*, ed. C. Wagley. Gainesville: University of Florida Press.

1975. Pioneer Farmers of the Transamazon Highway: Adaptation and Agricultural Production in the Lowland Tropics. Ph.D. diss., Department of Anthropology, University of Florida.

1976. *Agricultural Development along the Transamazon Highway*. Bloomington: Center for Latin American Studies Monograph Series, Indiana University.

1977. Estratégias de sobrevivência: O uso de recursos ao longo da rodovía transamazônica. *Acta Amazônica* 7: 363–379.

1981. *Developing the Amazon*. Bloomington: Indiana University Press.

1982a. Ecological, Anthropological, and Agronomic Research in the Amazon Basin. *Latin American Research Review* 17: 3–41.

1982b. *Human Adaptability: An Introduction to Ecological Anthropology*. Boulder, Colo.: Westview Press.

1984. Levels of Analysis Shifting and Its Implications for Amazonian Research. In *The Ecosystem Concept in Anthropology*, ed. E. F. Moran. Washington, D.C.: American Association for the Advancement of Science.

1987. Socio-economic Considerations in Acid Tropical Soils Research. In *Management of Acid Tropical Soils for Sustainable Agriculture*, ed. P. Sanchez et al. Bangkok, Thailand: IBSRAM.

1989. Models of Native and Folk Adaptation in the Amazon. *Advances in Economic Botany* 7: 22–29.

1991. Human Adaptive Strategies in Amazonian Blackwater Ecosystems. *American Anthropologist* 93: 361–382.

Moran, Emilio, ed.

1983. *The Dilemma of Amazonian Development*. Boulder, Colo.: Westview Press.

1990. *The Ecosystem Approach in Anthropology: From Concept to Practice*. Ann Arbor: University of Michigan Press.

Moreira Neto, Carlos de A.

1988. *Índios da Amazônia: De maioria a minoria (1750–1850)*. Petrópolis: Vozes.

Mörner, Magnus, ed.

1965. *The Expulsion of the Jesuits from Latin America*. New York: Alfred A. Knopf.

Mueller-Dumbois, D. M., and H. Ellenberg

1974. *Aims and Methods of Vegetation Ecology*. New York: John Wiley.

Murphy, R.
  1960. *Headhunter's Heritage: Social and Economic Change among the Mundurucú Indians.* Berkeley: University of California Press.
Museu Paraense Emílio Goeldi
  1988. Salvamento arqueológico em Carajás. Relatório Preliminar.
Myers, Norman
  1991. Tropical Forests: Present Status and Future Outlook. *Climatic Change* 19: 3−32.
Myers, Tom
  1973. Toward the Reconstruction of Prehistoric Community Patterns in the Amazon Basin. In *Variations in Anthropology,* ed. D. Lathrap and J. Douglas. Urbana: Illinois Archaeological Survey.
  1981. Hacia la reconstrucción de los patrones comunales de asentamiento durante la prehistória de la cuenca amazónica. *América Indígena* 4 (7): 31−63.
  1983. Redes de intercambio tempranas en la hoya amazónica. *Amazonía Peruana* 4 (8): 61−75.
  1989. The Expansion and Collapse of the Omagua. Paper presented at the Wenner Gren conference Amazonian Synthesis, Nova Friburgo, Rio de Janeiro, June 2−10, 1989.
National Academy of Science (NAS)
  1972. *Soils of the Humid Tropics.* Washington, D.C.: National Academy of Science.
Neel, J. V.
  1974. A Note on Congenital Defects in Two Unacculturated Indian Tribes. In *Congenital Defects, New Directions in Research,* ed. D. T. Janerich et al. New York: Academic Press.
Neel, J., and F. Salzano
  1967. Further Studies on the Xavante Indians. *American Journal of Human Genetics* 19: 554−574.
Neel, J., et al.
  1964. Studies on the Xavante Indians of the Brazilian Mato Grosso. *American Journal of Human Genetics* 16: 52−140.
  1968. Further Studies of the Xavante Indians, IX: Immunologic Status. *American Journal of Tropical Medicine and Hygiene* 17: 486−498.
  1977. Man in the Tropics: The Yanomama Indians. In *Population Structure and Human Variation,* ed. G. A. Harrison. London: Cambridge University Press.
Nelson, Michael
  1973. *The Development of Tropical Lands.* Baltimore: Johns Hopkins University Press.
Nepstadt, D., et al.
  1990. Surmounting Barriers to Forest Regeneration in Abandoned, Highly Degraded Pastures: A Case Study from Paragominas, Pará, Brazil. In *Al-*

ternatives to Deforestation, ed. A. Anderson. New York: Columbia University Press.

Netter, A., and A. Lambert

1981. Iatrogenic and Environmental Factors in Human Reproduction. In *Research on Fertility and Sterility*, ed. J. Cortes-Prieto et al. Baltimore: University Park Press.

Netting, Robert

1968. *Hill Farmers of Nigeria*. Seattle: Washington University Press.

1969. Ecosystems in Process. In *Contributions to Anthropology: Ecological Essays*, ed. David Damas. Ottawa: National Museums of Canada.

1971. *The Ecological Approach to Cultural Study*. Reading, Mass.: Addison-Wesley Module in Anthropology.

1974. Agrarian Ecology. *Annual Review of Anthropology* 3: 21–56.

1976. What Alpine Peasants Have in Common: Observations on Communal Tenure in a Swiss Village. *Human Ecology* 4: 135–146.

1977. *Cultural Ecology*. Menlo Park, Cal.: Cummings.

Netting, R., et al.

1988. The Social Organization of Agrarian Labor. Paper presented at the annual meeting of the American Association for the Advancement of Science, Boston, February 11–15, 1988.

Neves, E. G.

1989. A Comparative Study of Upper Xingú and Upper Rio Negro Cultural Areas. Unpublished ms., Department of Anthropology, Indiana University.

Newman, M. T.

1960. Adaptations in the Physique of American Aborigines to Nutritional Factors. *Human Biology* 32: 288–313.

1962. Ecology and Nutritional Stress in Man. *American Anthropologist* 64: 22–33.

Newman, R., and E. Munro

1955. The Relation of Climate and Body Size in U.S. Males. *American Journal of Physical Anthropology* 13: 1–17.

Nicholaides, J. J., et al.

1983. Crop Production Systems in the Amazon Basin. In *The Dilemma of Amazonian Development*, ed. E. F. Moran. Boulder, Colo.: Westview Press.

1985. Agricultural Alternatives for the Amazon Basin. *Bioscience* 35 (5): 279–285.

Nietschmann, Bernard

1973. *Between Land and Water*. New York: Seminar Press.

Nimuendajú, Curt

1944. Mapa etnohistórico do Brasil e regiões adjacentes. Rio de Janeiro, IBGE (1981).

1946. *The Eastern Timbira*. Berkeley: University of California Press.

1949. Os Tapajó. *Boletim do Museu Paraense Emílio Goeldi* 10: 93–106.

Niswander, J., et al.
    1967. Further Studies on the Xavante Indians. *American Journal of Human Genetics* 19: 490–501.
Norgaard, Richard
    1981. Sociosystem and Ecosystem Coevolution in the Amazon. *Journal of Environmental Economics and Management* 8: 238–254.
    1984. Coevolutionary Development Potential. *Land Economics* 60 (2): 160–172.
Nye, P. H., and D. J. Greenland
    1960. *The Soil under Shifting Cultivation.* Technical Communication No. 51. Harpenden, U.K.: Commonwealth Bureau of Soils.
Oberg, K.
    1953. *Indian Tribes of Northern Mato Grosso, Brazil.* No. 15. Washington, D.C.: Institute of Social Anthropology.
Odum, Eugene
    1971. *Fundamentals of Ecology.* 3d ed. Philadelphia: Saunders.
Odum, Howard T.
    1971. *Environment, Power and Society.* New York: Wiley-Interscience.
Odum, Howard, and F. Pigeon, eds.
    1970. *A Tropical Rain Forest.* Springfield, Va.: U.S. Department of Commerce/Atomic Energy Commission.
Oliveira, A. E. de
    1988. Amazônia: Modificações sociais e culturais decorrentes do processo de ocupação humana. *Boletim do Museu Paraense Emílio Goeldi* 4 (1): 65–115.
Oliveira, A. E. de, and E. Galvão
    1973. A situação atual dos Baniwa, Alto Rio Negro, 1971. *O Museu Goeldi no Ano do Sesquicentenário* No. 29. Belém: MPEG Publicações Avulsas.
Oltman, R. E., et al.
    1964. Amazon River Investigations, Reconn. Measurements. *Geological Survey Circular* 486: 1–15.
Orlove, B.
    1977. *Wool, Sheep and Men.* New York: Academic Press.
    1980. Ecological Anthropology. *Annual Review of Anthropology* 9: 235–273.
Orlove, B., and D. Guillet
    1985. Theoretical and Methodological Considerations on the Study of Mountain Peoples: Reflections on the Idea of Subsistence Type and the Role of History in Human Ecology. *Mountain Research and Development* 5 (1): 3–18.
Padoch, Christine, and N. de Jong
    1987. Traditional Agroforestry Practices of Native and Ribereño Farmers in the Lowland Peruvian Amazon. In *Agroforestry: Realities, Possibilities and Potential,* ed. H. L. Gholz. Dordrecht: Nijhoff.

Palmore, J. A., and R. W. Gardner

1983. *Measuring Mortality, Fertility, and Natural Increase: A Self-Teaching Guide to Elementary Measures.* Honolulu: East-West Center Population Institute.

Parker, E.

1981. Cultural Ecology and Change: A Caboclo Várzea Community in the Brazilian Amazon. Ph.D. diss., Department of Geography, University of Colorado, Boulder.

1985a. The Amazon Caboclo: Historical and Contemporary Perspectives. *Studies in Third World Societies* Special Issue No. 32.

1985b. Caboclization: The Transformation of the Amerindian in Amazonia: 1615–1800. *Studies in Third World Societies* 29: xvii–li.

1992. Forest Islands and Kayapó Resource Management in Amazonia: A Reappraisal of the Apêtê. *American Anthropologist* 94: 406–428.

Parker, E., et al.

1983. Resource Exploitation in Amazonia: Ethnoecological Examples from Four Populations. *Annals of the Carnegie Museum* 52: 163–203.

Pearlman, Stephen

1980. An Optimum Diet Model, Coastal Variability and Hunter-Gatherer Behavior. In *Advances in Archeological Method and Theory*, ed. M. Schiffer, vol. 3. New York: Academic Press.

Penteado, Antonio Rocha

1974. Condições geo-ecológicas da Amazônia brasileira. *Revista do Museu Paulista* 21: 1–17.

Pesce, C.

1985. *Oil Palms and Other Oilseeds of the Amazon.* Algonoc, Mich.: Reference Publications.

Peters, J. F.

1980. The Shirishana of the Yanomami: A Demographic Study. *Social Biology* 27: 272–285.

Pianka, E. R.

1978. *Evolutionary Biology.* 2d ed. New York: Harper and Row.

Pinheiro, F. P.

1981a. Arboviral Zoonoses in South America: Bussuquara Fever. In *CRC Handbook Series in Zoonoses*, ed. J. Steele and G. Beran. Boca Raton, Fla: CRC Press.

1981b. Arboviral Zoonoses in South America: Mayaro Fever. In *CRC Handbook Series in Zoonoses*, ed. J. Steele and G. Beran. Boca Raton, Fla.: CRC Press.

Pires, J. M.

1973. *Tipos de vegetação da Amazônia.* Belém: Publicação Avulsa do Museu Paraense Emílio Goeldi 20: 179–202.

1978. The Forest Ecosystems of the Brazilian Amazon. In *Tropical Forest Ecosystems.* Rome: UNESCO.

Pires, J. M., and G. Prance
  1985. The Vegetation Types of the Brazilian Amazon. In *Key Environments: Amazonia*, ed. G. Prance and T. Lovejoy. Oxford: Pergamon Press.
Pires, J. M., et al.
  1953. An Estimate of the Number of Species of Trees in an Amazonian Forest Community. *Botanical Gazette* 114: 467–477.
Plattner, Stuart, ed.
  1974. *Formal Methods in Economic Anthropology*. Washington, D.C.: American Anthropological Association.
Porro, Antonio
  1989. Social Organization and Power in the Amazon Floodplain: The Ethnohistorical Sources. Paper presented at the Wenner Gren conference Amazonian Synthesis, Nova Friburgo, Rio de Janeiro, June 2–10, 1989.
Posey, Darrell
  1985. Indigenous Management of Tropical Forest Ecosystems: The Case of the Kayapó Indians of the Brazilian Amazon. *Agroforestry Systems* 3: 139–158.
  1986a. Etnoentomologia das tribus indígenas da Amazônia. In *Suma etnológica brasileira*, ed. B. Ribeiro, vol. 1. Petrópolis: Vozes.
  1986b. Manejo da floresta secundária, capoeiras, campos, e cerrados. In *Suma etnológica brasileira*, ed. B. Ribeiro, vol. 1. Petrópolis: Vozes.
Posey, D., and W. Balée, eds.
  1989. *Natural Resource Management by Indigenous and Folk Societies of Amazonia*. Advances in Economic Botany 7. New York: New York Botanical Garden.
Posey, D., et al.
  1984. Ethnoecology as Applied Anthropology. *Human Organization*. 43: 95–107.
Prance, G. T.
  1973. Phytogeographic Support for the Theory of Pleistocene Forest Refuges in the Amazon Basin, Based on Evidence from Dischapetalaceae and Lecythidaceae. *Acta Amazônica* 3: 5–28.
  1975. The History of the INPA Capoeira Based on Ecological Studies of Lecythidaceae. *Acta Amazônica* 3: 261–263.
  1977. The Phytogeographic Subdivisions of Amazonia and Their Influence on Selection of Biological Reserves. In *Extinction is Forever*, ed. G. Prance and T. Elias. New York: New York Botanical Garden.
  1978. The Origin and Evolution of the Amazon Flora. *Interciencia* 3 (4): 207–222.
  1986. Etnobotânica de algumas tribus amazônicas. In *Suma etnológica brasileira*, ed. B. Ribeiro, vol. 1. Petrópolis: Vozes.
Prance, G. T., ed.
  1976. Inventário florestal de um hectare de mata de terra firme km 30 da estrada Manaus–Itacoatiara. *Acta Amazônica* 6: 9–35.

1982. *Biological Diversification in the Tropics.* New York: Columbia University Press.

Prance, G., and T. Lovejoy, eds.

1985. *Key Environments: Amazonia.* London: Pergamon Press.

Pyke, G. H., H. Pulliam, and E. Charnov

1977. Optimal Foraging: A Selective Review of Theory and Tests. *Quarterly Review of Biology* 52 (2): 137–154.

RADAM

1972–1979. *Levantamento da região amazônica.* 12 vols. Rio de Janeiro: Ministério das Minas e Energia.

Ramos, Alcida

1990. *Memórias Sanumá: Espaço e tempo em uma sociedade Yanomami.* Brasília: Editôra da Universidade de Brasília.

Ramos, Alcida, P. Silverwood-Cope, and A. G. de Oliveira

1980. Patrões e clientes: Relações intertribais no Alto Rio Negro. In *Hierarquia e simbiôse: Relações intertribais no Brasil,* ed. A. Ramos. São Paulo: HUCITEC.

Rankin, Judy

1979. Manejo florestal ecológico. *Acta Amazônica* 9: 115–122.

Rappaport, Roy

1968. *Pigs for the Ancestors.* New Haven, Conn.: Yale University Press.

1971a. The Flow of Energy in an Agricultural Society. *Scientific American* 224 (3): 116–132.

1971b. The Sacred in Human Evolution. *Annual Review of Ecology and Systematics* 2: 23–44.

1984. *Pigs for the Ancestors.* Rev. ed. New Haven, Conn.: Yale University Press.

Rapport, D., and J. Turner

1977. Economic Models in Ecology. *Science* 195: 367–373.

Raven, P., and D. Axelrod

1975. History of the Flora and Fauna of Latin America. *American Scientist* 63: 420–429.

Redford, K., and C. Padoch, eds.

1992. *Conservation of Neotropical Forests.* New York: Columbia University Press.

Redford, K., and J. Robinson

1987. The Game of Choice: Patterns of Indian and Colonist Hunting in the Neotropics. *American Anthropologist* 89: 650–667.

Reichel-Dolmatoff, G.

1971. *Amazonian Cosmos.* Chicago: University of Chicago Press.

1976. Cosmology as Ecological Analysis: A View from the Rain Forest. *Man* 11: 307–318.

Reid, Howard.

1979. Some Aspects of Movement, Growth, and Change among the

Hupdu Makú Indians of Brazil. Ph.D. diss., Trinity College, Cambridge University.

Repetto, R., and M. Gillis, eds.

    1988. *Public Policies and the Misuse of Forest Resources.* New York: Cambridge University Press/World Resources Institute.

Ribeiro, B., and D. Ribeiro, eds.

    1986. *Suma etnológica brasileira.* 3 vols. Petrópolis: Vozes.

Ribeiro, Darcy

    1956. Convívio e contaminação: Efeitos dissociativos da depopulação provocada por epidemias en grupos indígenas. *Sociologia* (São Paulo) 18: 3–50.

    1967. Indigenous Cultures and Languages of Brazil. In *Indians of Brazil in the Twentieth Century,* ed. J. Hopper. Washington, D.C.: Institute for Cross-Cultural Research.

    1970. *Os índios e a civilização.* Rio de Janeiro: Civilização Brasileira.

Richards, Paul W.

    1952. *The Tropical Rain Forest.* Cambridge: Cambridge University Press.

    1973. The Tropical Rain Forest. *Scientific American* 229: 58–67.

Ricklefs, Robert

    1973. *Ecology.* Portland, Ore.: Chiron Press.

Ritchie, K. D., et al.

    1980. Calcium Leaching to Increase Rooting Depth in a Brazilian Savanna Oxisol. *Agronomy Journal* 32: 40–44.

Rizzini, C. T.

    1963. Nota prévia sôbre a divisão fitogeográfica do Brasil. *Revista Brasileira de Geografia* 25 (1): 1–64.

Robinson, J. G., and K. Redford, eds.

    1991. *Neotropical Wildlife Use and Conservation.* Chicago: University of Chicago Press.

Rodrigues, Aryon D'alla

    1986. *Linguas brasileiras.* São Paulo: Edições Loyola.

Rodrigues Ferreira, Alexander

    1885. Diário da viagem Philosóphica pela capitanía de São José do Rio Negro. *Revista do Instituto Histórico e Geográfico Brasileiro* 48 (1): 1–234.

Roett, R.

    1973. *Brazil: Politics in a Patrimonial Society.* Boston: Allyn and Bacon.

Rollet, J.

    1978. *Tropical Forest Ecosystems.* Paris: UNESCO.

Roosevelt, Anna C.

    1980. *Parmana.* New York: Academic Press.

    1987. Chiefdoms in the Amazon and Orinoco. In *Chiefdoms in the Americas,* ed. R. Drennan and C. Uribe. Washington, D.C.: University Press of America.

    1989. Natural Resource Management in Amazonia before the Conquest: Beyond Ethnographic Projection. *Advances in Economic Botany* 7: 30–62.

1991. *Moundbuilders of the Amazon: Geophysical Archeology on Marajó Island, Brazil.* San Diego, Cal.: Academic Press.

Roosevelt, A. C., et al.

1992. Eighth Millennium Pottery from a Prehistoric Shell Midden in the Brazilian Amazon. *Science* 254: 1621–1624.

Ross, Eric

1978. Food Taboos, Diet and Hunting Strategy: The Adaptation to Animals in Amazon Cultural Ecology. *Current Anthropology* 19: 1–36.

Ross, J. K.

1975. Social Borders: Definitions of Diversity. *Current Anthropology* 16: 53–72.

Ruddle, Kenneth

1973. The Human Use of Insects: Examples from the Yukpa. *Biotropica* 5 (2): 94–101.

Ruthenberg, Hans

1971. *Farming Systems in the Tropics.* London: Oxford University Press.

Sahlins, Marshall

1964. Culture and Environment: The Study of Cultural Ecology. In *Horizons in Anthropology*, ed. Sol Tax. Chicago: Aldine.

Sahlins, M., and E. Service

1960. *Evolution and Culture.* Ann Arbor: University of Michigan Press.

St. John, T. V.

1980. A Survey of Micorrhizal Infections in an Amazonian Rain Forest. *Acta Amazônica* 10: 527–533.

St. John, T. V., and C. Uhl

n.d. Micorrhizae in the Rain Forest at San Carlos de Río Negro, Venezuela. Unpublished ms.

Salati, Eneas

1985. The Climatology and Hydrology of Amazonia. In *Key Environments: Amazonia*, ed. G. Prance and T. Lovejoy. London: Pergamon Press.

Salati, E., ed.

1984. *Amazônia.* Brasília: Conselho Nacional de Pesquisas.

Salati, E., et al.

1978. Origem e distribuição das chuvas na Amazônia. *Interciencia* 3 (4): 200–205.

Saldarriaga, J., and D. West

1986. Holocene Fires in the Northern Amazon Basin. *Quaternary Research* 26: 358–366.

Salles, Vicente

1971. *O Negro no Pará.* Rio de Janeiro: Fundação Getúlio Vargas and Universidade Federal do Pará.

Salo, J., et al.

1986. River Dynamics and the Diversity of Amazon Lowland Forest. *Nature* 322: 254–258.

Salzano, F., and S. Callegari-Jacques

   1988. *South American Indians: A Case in Evolution*. New York: Oxford University Press.

Sánchez, Pedro

   1976. *Properties and Management of Soils in the Tropics*. New York: Wiley-Interscience.

   1977. Advances in the Management of Oxisols and Ultisols in Tropical South America. Proceedings of International Seminar on Soil Environment and Fertility Management in Intensive Agriculture, Tokyo, Japan.

   1981. Soils of the Humid Tropics. *Studies in Third World Societies* 14: 347–410.

   1987. Management of Acid Soils in the Humid Tropics of Latin America. In *Management of Acid Tropical Soils for Sustainable Agriculture*, ed. P. Sánchez, E. Stoner, and E. Pushparajah. Bangkok: IBSRAM.

Sánchez, P., and J. Benites

   1987. Low-Input Cropping for Acid Soils of the Humid Tropics. *Science* 238: 1521–1527.

Sánchez, Pedro, and S. W. Buol

   1975. Soils of the Tropics and the World Food Crisis. *Science* 188: 598–603.

Sánchez, P., and J. Salinas

   1981. Low Input Technology for Managing Oxisols and Ultisols in Tropical America. *Advances in Agronomy* 34: 279–406.

Sánchez, Pedro, et al.

   1974. Investigaciones en manejo de suelos tropicales en Yurimaguas, selva baja del Perú. Paper presented at Seminario de Sistemas de Agricultura Tropical, Lima, Peru, June 1–8, 1974.

   1982. Amazon Basin Soils: Management for Continuous Crop Production. *Science* 216: 821–827.

   1987. *Management Alternatives for Acid Soils of the Tropics*. Bangkok: IBSRAM.

Sanford, R. L., et al.

   1985. Amazon Rain-Forest Fires. *Science* 227: 53–55.

Saturnino, H. M., et al.

   1977. Sistema de produção pecuária em uso nos cerrados. In *IV simpôsio sôbre o cerrado*, ed. M. G. Ferri. São Paulo: Editôra Itatáia/Universidade de São Paulo.

Sauer, Carl

   1958. Man in the Ecology of Tropical America. *Proceedings of the Ninth Pacific Science Congress* 20: 104–110.

Schmidt, Max

   1951. Anotaciones sobre las plantas de cultivo y los métodos de la agricultura de los indígenas sudamericanos. *Revista do Museu Paulista* 5: 239–252.

Schmink, M., and C. Wood, eds.
  1984. *Frontier Expansion in Amazonia.* Gainesville: University of Florida Press.
  1992. *Contested Frontiers in Amazonia.* New York: Columbia University Press.
Schultes, R. E.
  1988. *Where the Gods Reign: Plants and Peoples of the Colombian Amazon.* Oracle, Ariz.: Synergetic Press.
Schultes, R. E., and R. F. Raffauf
  1990. *The Healing Forest: Medicinal and Toxic Plants of the Northwest Amazonia.* Portland, Ore.: Dioscorides Press.
Scudder, Thayer
  1962. *The Ecology of the Gwenbe Tonga.* Manchester, England: Manchester University Press.
  1973. The Human Ecology of the Big Projects: River Basin Development and Resettlement. *Annual Review of Anthropology* 2: 45–61.
  1975. Resettlement. In *Man-Made Lakes and Human Health*, ed. N. F. Stanley. London: Academic Press.
Seber, G. A. F.
  1986. A Review of Estimating Animal Abundance. *Biometrics* 42: 267–292.
Seeger, Anthony
  1982. Native Americans and the Conservation of Flora and Fauna in Brazil. In *Socio-economic Effects and Constraints in Tropical Forest Management*, ed. E. G. Hallsworth. New York: John Wiley.
Setz, Eleonore
  1983. Ecologia alimentar em um grupo indígena: Comparação entre aldéias Nambiquara de floresta e de cerrado. Master's thesis, Institute of Biology, Universidade de Campinas, São Paulo.
Seubert, C. E., et al.
  1977. Effects of Land Clearing Methods on Soil Properties on an Ultisol and Crop Performance in the Amazon Jungle of Peru. *Tropical Agriculture* 54: 307–321.
Shantzis, S. D., and W. W. Behrens
  1973. Population Control Mechanisms in a Primitive Agricultural Society. In *Toward Global Equilibrium*, ed. Dennis L. Meadows and D. H. Meadows. Cambridge, Mass.: Wright-Allen Press.
Shapiro, Judith
  1968. Tapirapé Kinship. *Boletim do Museu Paraense Emílio Goeldi* (Antropologia) 37.
Shoemaker, Robin
  1981. *Peasants of El Dorado.* Ithaca, N.Y.: Cornell University Press.
Silverwood-Cope, P.
  1972. A Contribution to the Ethnography of the Colombian Makú. Ph.D. diss., University of Cambridge.

Simões, M.

1978. Programa nacional de pesquisas arqueológicas na bacia amazônica. *Acta Amazônica* 7: 297–300.

1981. Coletores, pescadores Ceramistas do litoral do Salgado (Pará), Nota preliminar. *Boletim do Museu Paraense Emílio Goeldi* (Antropologia) n.s. 78: 1–26.

Simões, M., and F. Araújo-Costa

1987. Pesquisas arqueológicas no Baixo Rio Tocantins (Pará). *Revista de Arqueología* 4 (1): 11–28.

Simon, Pedro

1861. *The Expedition of Pedro de Úrsua and Lope de Aguirre in Search of El Dorado and Omagua, 1560–1561, Sixth Historical Notice of the Conquest of Tierra Firme.* London: Hakluyt Society.

Sioli, Harald

1950. Das Wasser in Amazonasgebiet. *Forsch. Fortschr.* 26: 274–280.

1951. Zum Alterungsprozess von Flussen und Flusstypen in Amazonas Gebiet. *Archiv für Hydrobiologie* 45 (3): 267–284.

1973. Recent Human Activities in the Brazilian Amazon Region and Their Ecological Effects. In *Tropical Forest Ecosystems in Africa and South America*, ed. Betty Meggers, E. Y. Ayensu, and W. D. Ducksworth. Washington, D.C.: Smithsonian Institution Press.

1975. Tropical River: The Amazon. In *River Ecology*, ed. B. Whitton. Oxford: Blackwell.

Sioli, Harald, ed.

1984. *The Amazon: Limnology and Landscape Ecology of a Mighty Tropical River.* Dordrecht: W. Junk.

Siskind, Janet

1973. *To Hunt in the Morning.* New York: Oxford University Press.

Smith, Eric A.

1981. The Application of Optimal Foraging Theory to the Analysis of Hunter-Gatherer Group Size. In *Hunter-Gatherer Foraging Strategies*, ed. B. Winterhalder and E. Smith. Chicago: University of Chicago Press.

1983. Anthropological Applications of Optimal Foraging Theory. *Current Anthropology* 24: 625–651.

1984. Anthropology, Evolutionary Ecology, and the Explanatory Limitations of the Ecosystem Concept. In *The Ecosystem Concept in Anthropology*, ed. E. F. Moran. Washington, D.C.: American Association for the Advancement of Science.

Smith, Nigel

1974a. Agouti and Babassu. *Orix* 22 (5): 581–582.

1974b. Destructive Exploitation of the South American River Turtle. *Yearbook of the Association of Pacific Coast Geographers* 36: 85–102.

1976. Transamazon Highway: A Cultural-Ecological Analysis of Settlement in the Lowland Tropics. Ph.D. diss., Department of Geography, University of California, Berkeley.

1978. Agricultural Productivity along Brazil's Transamazon Highway. *Agroecosystems* 4: 415–432.

1979. *A pesca no Rio Amazonas*. Manaus: Instituto Nacional de Pesquisas da Amazônia.

1980. Anthrosols and Human Carrying Capacity in Amazonia. *Annals of the Association of American Geographers* 70: 553–566.

1981. *Man, Fishes and the Amazon*. New York: Columbia University Press.

1982a. Colonization Lessons from the Rain Forest. *Science* 214: 755–761.

1982b. *Rainforest Corridors*. Berkeley: University of California Press.

Smole, W.

1976. *The Yanoama Indians: A Cultural Geography*. Austin: University of Texas Press.

Sombroek, W.

1966. *Amazon Soils*. Wageningen: Centre for Agricultural Publications and Documentation.

Sponsel, Leslie

1981. The Hunter and the Hunted in the Amazon: An Integrated Biological and Cultural Approach to the Behavior and Ecology of Human Predation. Ph.D. diss., Department of Anthropology, Cornell University.

1986. Amazon Ecology and Adaptation. *Annual Review of Anthropology* 15: 67–97.

Spruce, R.

1908. *A Botanist on the Amazon and Andes*. 2 vols. London: Macmillan.

Spuhler, J. N.

1959. Physical Anthropology and Demography. In *The Study of Population*, ed. P. Hauser and O. Duncan. Chicago: University of Chicago Press.

Stark, N.

1969. Direct Nutrient Cycling in the Amazon Basin. In *II Simposio y foro de biología tropical amazónica*. Bogotá, Colombia: Editorial Pax.

Stark, N., and C. Jordan

1978. Nutrient Retention by the Root Mat of an Amazonian Rain Forest. *Ecology* 59 (3): 434–437.

Stella, Donald

1976. *The Geography of Soils*. Englewood Cliffs, N.J.: Prentice-Hall.

Sternberg, H.

1975. *The Amazon River of Brazil*. Wiesbaden: Franz Steiner Verlag.

Steward, Julian

1936. The Economic and Social Basis of Primitive Bands. In *Essays in Anthropology Presented to A. L. Kroeber*, ed. Robert Lowie. Berkeley: University of California Press.

1938. *Basin Plateau Aboriginal Socio-political Groups*. Bulletin 120, Bureau of American Ethnology. Washington, D.C.: Smithsonian Institution.

1955. *Theory of Culture Change*. Urbana: University of Illinois Press.

1977. *Evolution and Ecology*. Urbana: University of Illinois Press.

Steward, Julian, ed.

1939–1946. *Handbook of South American Indians*. 7 vols. Washington, D.C.: Bureau of American Ethnology.

1948. *Handbook of South American Indians*. Vol. 3. Washington, D.C.: Bureau of American Ethnology.

Steward, J., and A. Métraux

1948. Tribes of the Peruvian and Ecuadorian Montaña. In *Handbook of South American Indians*, ed. J. Steward, vol. 3. Washington, D.C.: Bureau of American Ethnology.

Stigter, K.

1986. In Quest of Tropical Micrometeorology for On-Farm Weather Advisories. *Agricultural and Forest Meteorology* 36: 289–296.

Stini, William

1975. *Ecology and Human Adaptation*. Dubuque, Ia.: William C. Brown.

Stocks, Anthony

1983. Cocamilla Fishing: Patch Modification and Environmental Buffering to the Amazon Várzea. In *Adaptive Responses of Native Amazonians*, ed. R. Hames and W. Vickers. New York: Academic Press.

Stone, G., et al.

1990. Seasonality, Labor Scheduling and Agricultural Intensification in the Nigerian Savanna. *American Anthropologist* 92: 7–23.

Sturtevant, William

1964. Studies in Ethnoscience. *American Anthropologist* 66 (3), part 2: 99–131.

Sutton, S. L., T. C. Whitmore, and A. C. Chadwick

1983. *Tropical Rain Forest: Ecology and Management*. Oxford: Blackwell Scientific Publications.

Sweet, David

1974. A Rich Realm of Nature Destroyed: The Middle Amazon Valley 1640–1750. Ph.D. diss., History Department, University of Wisconsin.

Swift, M. J., ed.

1987. Tropical Soil Biology and Fertility. In *Biology International*. Special Issue 13. Report on the Third Workshop of the Decade of the Tropics/Tropical Soil Biology and Fertility Programme.

Swift, M. J., and J. M. Anderson

1989. Decomposition. In *Tropical Rain Forest Ecosystems: Biogeographical and Ecological Studies*, ed. H. Lieth and M. J. A. Werger. Amsterdam: Elsevier.

Takeuchi, M.

1960. The Structure of the Amazonian Vegetation: I. Savanna in N. Amazon. *Journal of Faculty of Science* (University of Tokyo) 7: 523–533.

1961. The Structure of the Amazonian Vegetation, II: Tropical Rain Forest. *Journal of Faculty of Science* (University of Tokyo), 8: 1–26.

Terborgh, J.

1971. Distribution of Environmental Gradients. *Ecology* 52: 23–40.

Thomas, Franklin
  1925. *The Environmental Basis of Society*. New York: Century.
Toledo, J. M., and E. A. S. Serrão
  1982. Pasture and Animal: Production in Amazonia. In *Amazonia: Agriculture and Land Use Research*, ed. S. Hecht. Cali, Colombia: Centro Internacional de Agricultura Tropical.
Tricart, J. L. F.
  1977. Tipos de planícies aluviais e de leitos fluviais na Amazônia brasileira. *Revista Brasileira de Geografia* 39: 3–39.
Trowbridge, F. L., et al.
  1987. Body Composition of Peruvian Children with Short Stature and High Weight for Height. *American Journal of Clinical Nutrition* 46: 411–418.
Turner, B. L., and P. D. Harrison
  1981. Prehistoric Raised-Field Agriculture in the Maya Lowlands. *Science* 213: 399–405.
Uhl, Christopher
  1980. Studies of Forest, Agricultural and Successional Environments in the Upper Rio Negro Region of the Amazon Basin. Ph.D. diss., Department of Botany, Michigan State University.
  1982. Recovery Following Disturbances of Different Intensities in the Amazon Rain Forest of Venezuela. *Interciencia* 7 (1): 19–24.
  1983. You Can Keep a Good Forest Down. *Natural History* 92: 69–79.
Uhl, C., and K. Clark
  1983. Seed Ecology of Selected Amazonian Successional Species. *Botanical Gazette* 144: 419–425.
Uhl, C., and C. F. Jordan
  1984. Succession and Nutrient Dynamics following Forest Cutting and Burning in Amazonia. *Ecology* 65: 1476–1490.
Uhl, C., and P. Murphy
  1981. Composition, Structure and Regeneration of a Tierra Firme Forest in the Amazon Basin of Venezuela. *Tropical Ecology* 22 (2): 219–237.
Uhl, C., and I. Vieira
  1989. Ecological Impacts of Selective Logging in the Brazilian Amazon. *Biotropica* 21 (2): 98–106.
Uhl, C., et al.
  1982a. Ecosystem Recovery in Amazon Caatinga Forest after Cutting, Cutting and Burning, and Bulldozer Treatments. *Oikos* 38: 313–320.
  1982b. Successional Patterns Associated with Slash-and-Burn Agriculture in the Upper Rio Negro Region of the Amazon Basin. *Biotropica* 14: 249–254.
Uriarte, Manuel J.
  1952. *Diario de un misionero de Maynas*. Serie A No. 7. Madrid: Instituto Santo Torigio de Mongrovejo.

Uricoechea, F.
    1980. *The Patrimonial Foundations of the Brazilian Bureaucratic State.*
    Berkeley: University of California Press.
Vandermeer, J. H.
    1972. Niche Theory. *Annual Review of Ecology and Systematics* 3:
    107–132.
Vayda, Andrew P.
    1974. Warfare in Ecological Perspective. *Annual Review of Ecology and
    Systematics* 5: 183–193.
    1976. *Warfare in Ecological Perspective.* New York: Plenum.
    1983. Progressive Contextualization: Methods for Research in Human
    Ecology. *Human Ecology* 11: 265–281.
Vayda, Andrew P., and B. McCay
    1975. New Directions in Ecology and Ecological Anthropology. *Annual Re-
    view of Anthropology* 4: 293–306.
Vayda, A. P., and Roy Rappaport
    1976. Ecology, Cultural and Noncultural. In *Human Ecology,* ed. Peter
    Richerson and J. McEvoy. North Scituate, Mass.: Duxbury Press.
Veríssimo, J.
    1895. *A pesca na Amazônia.* Rio de Janeiro: Livraria Clássica. New edition
    published 1970, Universidade Federal do Pará.
Vickers, William
    1975. Meat Is Meat: The Siona-Secoya and the Hunting Prowess-Sexual Re-
    ward Hypothesis. *Latinamericanist* (University of Florida Center for Latin
    American Studies) 11 (1): 1–5.
    1976. Cultural Adaptation to Amazonian Habitats: The Siona-Secoya of
    Eastern Ecuador. Ph.D. diss., Department of Anthropology, University
    of Florida.
    1979. Native Amazonian Subsistence in Diverse Habitats: The Siona-Secoya
    of Ecuador. *Studies in Third World Societies* 7: 6–36.
    1984. The Faunal Components of Lowland South American Hunting Kills.
    Interciencia 9 (6): 366–376.
    1988. Game Depletion Hypothesis of Amazonian Adaptation: Data from a
    Native Community. *Science* 239: 1521–1522.
Vieira-Filho, J. P. B.
    1977. O diabetes mellitus e as glicemias de jejum dos índios Caripuna e Pali-
    kur. *Revista da Associação Médica Brasileira* 23 (6): 175–178.
    1981a. O bócio entre os índios brasileiros. *Revista da Associação Médica
    Brasileira* 27: 285–287.
    1981b. Problemas de aculturação alimentar dos Xavantes e Bororo. *Revista
    de Antropologia* (São Paulo) 24: 37–40.
Viertler, Renate Brigitte
    1988. *Ecologia cultural: Uma antropologia da mudança.* São Paulo: Editôra
    Ática.

Viotti, Pe. Hélio Abranches
  1981. A Amazônia, a Companhía de Jesús e o Pe. João Daniel. *Anais da Biblioteca Pública Nacional* 101: 109–113.
Viveiros de Castro, E.
  1986. *Arawetée: Os deuses canibais.* Rio de Janeiro: Zahar.
Wagley, Charles
  1951. Cultural Influences on Population: A Comparison of Two Tupí Tribes. *Revista do Museu Paulista* 5: 95–104.
  1953. *Amazon Town.* New York: Macmillan.
  1977. *Welcome of Tears: The Tapirapé Indians of Central Brazil.* New York: Oxford University Press.
Wagley, C., ed.
  1974. *Man in the Amazon.* Gainesville: University of Florida Press.
Wallace, A. R.
  1853. *A Narrative of Travels on the Amazon and Rio Negro.* London: Reeve.
  1878. *Tropical Nature and Other Essays.* London: Macmillan.
Wallace, Anthony F. C.
  1956. Revitalization Movements. *American Anthropologist* 58: 264–281.
Wambeke, A. van
  1978. Properties and Potential of Soils in the Amazon Basin. *Interciencia* 3 (4): 233–242.
Weiner, J. S., and J. A. Lourie, eds.
  1969. *Human Biology: A Guide to Field Methods.* Oxford: Blackwell Scientific Publications.
Weinstein, Barbara
  1983. *The Amazon Rubber Boom, 1850–1920.* Stanford, Cal.: Stanford University Press.
Wellcomme, R. L.
  1976. Some General and Theoretical Considerations on the Fish Yield of African Rivers. *Fisheries Biology* 8: 351–364.
Went, F. W., and N. Stark
  1968. Mycorrhizae. *Bioscience* 18: 1035–1039.
Werner, Dennis
  1978. Trekking in the Amazon Forest. *Natural History* 87: 42–55.
  1983a. Fertility and Pacification among the Mekranotí of C. Brazil. *Human Ecology* 11: 227–245.
  1983b. Why do the Mekranotí Trek? In *Adaptive Responses of Native Amazonians,* ed. R. Hames and W. Vickers. New York: Academic Press.
Werner, Dennis, et al.
  1979. Subsistence Productivity and Hunting Effort in Native South America. *Human Ecology* 7: 303–315.
White, Gilbert, ed.
  1974. *Natural Hazards.* New York: Oxford University Press.

White, Leslie
   1943. Energy and the Evolution of Culture. *American Anthropologist* 45: 335–356.
   1949. *The Science of Culture*. New York: Free Books.
Whitehead, Neil Lancelot
   1988. *Lords of the Tiger Spirit: A History of the Caribs in Colonial Vene-zuela and Guyana, 1498–1820*. Providence, R.I.: Foris.
   1989. The Ancient Amerindian Polities of the Lower Orinoco, Amazon, and Guayana Coast: A Preliminary Analysis of Their Passage from Antiquity to Extinction. Paper presented at Wenner Gren conference Amazonian Synthesis, Nova Friburgo, Rio de Janeiro, June 2–10, 1989.
Whiting, John.
   1964. The Effects of Climate on Certain Cultural Practices. In *Explorations in Cultural Anthropology*, ed. W. Goodenough. New York: McGraw-Hill.
Whitmore, T. C., and J. A. Sayer, eds.
   1992. *Tropical Deforestation and Species Extinction*. New York: Chapman and Hall.
Whittaker, R. H.
   1970. *Communities and Ecosystems*. New York: Macmillan.
Whittaker, R. H., S. A. Levin, and R. B. Root
   1973. Niche, Habitat and Ecotope. *American Naturalist* 107: 321–338.
Whittaker, R. H., and G. E. Likens
   1975. The Biosphere and Man. In *Primary Productivity of the Biosphere*, ed. H. Lieth and R. H. Whittaker. New York: Springer-Verlag.
Whitten, Norman
   1978. Ecological Imagery and Cultural Adaptability. *American Anthropolo-gist* 80: 836–859.
Wilhelmy, H.
   1970. Amazonien als Lebens- und Wirtschaftsraum. *Staden Jahrbuch* 18: 9–31.
Wilken, G. C.
   1972. Modification of Microclimates by Traditional Farmers. *Geographical Review* 62: 544–560.
   1988. Minimum Climate Data for Comparative Analysis in Agriculture. Pa-per presented at annual meeting of the American Association for the Ad-vancement of Science, Boston, February 11–15, 1988.
Wilson, Edward O.
   1975. *Sociobiology: A New Synthesis*. Cambridge, Mass.: Belknap.
Winterhalder, Bruce
   1981a. Optimal Foraging Strategies and Hunter-Gatherer Research in An-thropology: Theory and Models. In *Hunter-Gatherer Foraging Strategies*, ed. B. Winterhalder and E. Smith. Chicago: University of Chicago Press.
   1981b. Foraging Strategies in a Boreal Environment: An Analysis of Cree Hunting and Gathering. In *Hunter-Gatherer Foraging Strategies*, ed. B. Winterhalder and E. Smith. Chicago: University of Chicago Press.

Winterhalder, B., and R. B. Thomas
  1978. *Geoecology of Southern Highland Peru: A Human Adaptation Perspective*. Occasional Paper 27/MAB Project 6. Boulder, Colo.: Institute of Arctic and Alpine Research.
Wissler, Clark
  1928. *The Relation of Nature to Man in Aboriginal America*. New York: Oxford University Press.
Wolf, J. M.
  1975. Water Constraints to Corn Production in C. Brazil. Ph.D. diss., Department of Agronomy, Cornell University.
Wood, C., and Wilson, J.
  1984. The Magnitude of Migration to the Brazilian Frontier. In *Frontier Expansion in Amazonia*, ed. M. Schmink and C. Wood. Gainesville: University of Florida Press.
Woodwell, G., ed.
  1984. *The Role of Terrestrial Vegetation in the Global Cycle. Scope*, vol. 23. New York: John Wiley.
World Health Organization (WHO)
  1976. Methodology of Nutrition Surveillance. Report of a Joint FAO/UNICEF/WHO Expert Committee. Technical Report Series 593. Geneva: World Health Organization.
  1979. *Measurement of Nutritional Impact*. Geneva: World Health Organization.
Worthington, E.
  1975. *The Evolution of the International Biological Program*. Cambridge: Cambridge University Press.
Wright, Robin
  1981. The History and Religion of the Baniwa Peoples of the Upper Rio Negro Valley. Ph.D. diss., Department of Anthropology, Stanford University.
Wright, R., and J. Hill
  1986. History, Ritual, and Myth: 19th Century Millenarian Movements in the Northwest Amazon. *Ethnohistory* 33 (1): 31−54.
Wust, Irmhild
  1988. A pesquisa arqueológica e etnoarqueológica na parte central do território bororo. *Revista de Antropologia* (São Paulo) 30.
  1989. Aspectos da ocupação pre-colonial em uma área nuclear Bororo entre os rios Vermelho e Garças, Mato Grosso. *Dédalo* (São Paulo) 1: 161−171.
Yesner, David
  1981. Archeological Applications of Optimal Foraging Theory: Harvest Strategies of Aleut Hunter-Gatherers. In *Hunter-Gatherer Foraging Strategies*, ed. B. Winterhalder and E. Smith. Chicago: University of Chicago Press.
Yost, J., and P. Kelley
  1983. Shotguns, Blowguns and Spears: The Analysis of Technological Effi-

ciency. In *Adaptive Responses of Native Amazonians*, ed. R. Hames and W. Vickers. New York: Academic Press.

Zarur, George

1975. *Parentesco, ritual e economia no Alto Xingú*. Brasília: Fundação Nacional do Índio (FUNAI).

1979. Ecological Need and Cultural Choice in Central Brazil. *Current Anthropology* 20: 649–653.

1986. Ecología e cultura: Algumas comparações. In *Suma etnológica brasileira*, ed. B. Ribeiro and D. Ribeiro. Petrópolis: Vozes.

Zucchi, A., and W. Denevan

1979. *Campos elevados e historia cultural prehispánica en los llanos occidentales de Venezuela*. Caracas: Universidad Católica Andrés Bello.

Index

Numbers in **boldface** indicate tables and illustrations.

Aborigines, 53
Achual Tipishca, 108
Agriculture, 41–46, 72, 73–74, 75–78, 77, 96–97, 98, 112, 118, 119–120, 126
Alfisols, 11–13, 12, 14, 66–67, 70, 71, 76, 124
Alluvial soils, 28
Amapá, 70
Amazon Basin Ecosystem, 19–24, 21
Amazon Development Agency (SUDAM), 151–154, 159
Amazon River, 27, 92
Amazon Valley, 2
Andes Mountains, 22, 87, 88, 90
Animal populations, 17
Araguaia River Basin, 100, 105, 119
Arawakan Wakuenai, 43, 46, 52–53, 54
Araweté, 71–72, 73
Area species, 15–18, 16
Aripuanā Reservation (Rondônia), 70
Aruacas, 4
Assuriní, 71–72, 73

Babaçú, 30, 69–70, 71, 78
Bamboo forests, 70
Bara Makú, 42, 48
Barro Colorado Island, 15, 17, 19
Belém–Brasília Highway, 148, 149
Belém (Brazil), 6, 28, 105, 157
Biomass, 14–15, 17, 18, 19, 20, 26, 27, 28, 29, 30, 31, 38, 39–40, 41, 43, 46, 60, 61, 62, 124, 164n.4
Biotopes, 89, 91–92, 91, 107–109, 108, 112, 113, 133
Birds, 60
Blackwater Ecosystems, 29–30, 35–55, 59, 62, 66, 131–132, 167n.1
Blackwater rivers, 22, 23, 24, 89, 91
Borneo (Malaysia), 38
Bororo, 127–128, 129, 132
Brazilian Plateau, 2, 22
Brazil nut forests, 70–71
Burning, 43–44, 73–75, 76, 98–99

Caatinga amazônica, 29–30, 38, 39, 42, 62, 63
Caboclos, 105, 111
Cana Brava (Tocantins), 135
Carajás Mountains, 67–68
Caripunas, 4
Casiquiare River, 47
Cattle ranching, 138, 154–155
Census, 7, 8
Ceramics, 3, 129–130
Clearwater rivers, 22, 23, 24
Climate, 9, 163n.2
Cocamilla, 108, 109, 111
Colonization, 148–151, 160–161
Cubeo, 52–53

Deforestation, 2, 9, 17–18, 58–59, 148, 151, 154, 156–157, 158–159
Development activities, 152–153, 159–160
Dolphins, 105–107, 106
Drought, 38, 39, 40, 44

Earth Summit, xiii, 32
Ecosystems, xiv, xv, 26, 163n.1. See also Amazon Basin Ecosystem, Blackwater Ecosystems, Humid Tropics Ecosystem, Upper Floodplain Ecosystem

Entomophagy, 46, 49–50
Epidemic disease, 2, 4–5, 5, 32–33,
    50, 51, 58, 81, 135–136, 151,
    167n.4
Estuary, 27, 95–96
Ethnoecology, 165–166n.8

Fauna, 17, 18–19, 40–41, 47,
    164n.5
First International Exposition of
    Amazonian Products, 157
Fishing, 24, 26, 37, 38, 41, 42–43,
    46, 47–49, 49, 53, 78–79, 79, 92,
    94, 97, 100–107, 106, 108–111,
    111, 126, 128, 130, 131, 166n.8
Fishing techniques, 100–104, 101,
    102, 103, 104, 109
Floodplain lakes, 92–94, 93, 99–
    100
Floodplains, xv, 4, 9, 21, 24–31, 61,
    85–115, 87
Floods, 38, 46
Flora, 14–18, 16, 24
Forests, 3, 9, 16–17, 18, 29, 30. See
    also Bamboo forests, Brazil Nut
    forests, Liana forests, Lowland for-
    ests, Montane forests, Upland
    forests
Foundation for Indian Protection
    (FUNAI), 32, 82

Gê, 124–125, 127, 129–130, 132–
    134, 158
Global warming, 2
Goeldi Museum (Belém), xvii, 27,
    164n.4
Goiás (Brazil), 151
Guainía River, 43, 47
Guajá, 69–70
Guiana Plateau, 22, 38

Handbook of South American Indi-
    ans, 119, 127
Herbivory, 17, 38, 41, 44
Horticulture, 134–135

Huallaga River, 87, 108
Human ecology, xv, 141–162,
    165n.6
Humid Tropics Ecosystem, 9–19, 10,
    20, 30
Hunting, 37, 46, 47, 53, 79, 79, 111,
    111, 118, 126, 128, 130–131,
    164n.5
Hupdu Makú, 42, 47

Içana River, 36, 38, 41, 43, 44, 52
Içá River, 4
Incipient Green, xvii
Insects, 19, 44, 49–50, 60, 78
Iriri Basin, 119
Itacoatiara, 98, 99, 100, 102, 102,
    103
Itá (Lower Amazon), 105

Jari Project, 159
Jari River Basin, 70
Javari River, 4
Juruá River, 118

Kaban (Suruí Indian clan), 82–83
Kalahari San, 53
Kamayurá, 105
Kanela, 132
Karajá, 100
Kayapó Gorotire, 70, 132, 133, 134
Kayapó Mekranotí, 128, 132–134
Kayapó, 7, 73, 127, 128, 129
Kuikuru, 14

Lake Coari (Middle Amazon), 98
Lakes, 109–110, 110
Lathrap, D., 86, 87–88
Leaffall, 62, 164n.4
Legal Amazon, 2–3, 3
Liana forests, 71–72
Llanos de Mojos, 86
Logging, 157
Lower Floodplain Ecosystem, 27, 28,
    90–95, 96–107, 109, 123
Lower Napo River, 4

Lower Rio Negro, 48, 52
Lower Tapajós Basin, 67, 71
Lower Tocantins Basin, 67, 70, 71, 76
Lower Xingú Basin, 67, 71, 76
Lowland forests, 60
Ludwig, Daniel, 159

Machado River, 107
Madeira River, 47, 69, 90, 94, 102, 107
Makú, 46, 47, 48, 49, 52, 54
Makuna, 42
Malacca (Malaysia), 38
Malaria, 151, 160
Management strategies, 147–148, **147**
Manaus (Brazil), 15, 19, 63, 67, 91, 105
Manaus River, 94
Manioc cultivation, 44–45, 46, 54, 70, 72–73, 75–76, 126, 127, 131–132
Marajó Island, 27, 94, 95
Maranhão (Brazil), 69, 70, 107
Marañón River, 87, 88
Marriage, 52–53, 83
Mato Grosso, 119, 151
Meggers, Betty, 14
Montane forests, 31, 62
Mortality, 7, 32, 50, 51, 58, 82, 135, 160

Nambiquara, 76, 126, 127
Neto, Moreira, 6
Nutrient cycling, 62–63, 73–75, 76, 80, 118
Nutrition, 50–51, 51, 83, 167 n.4

Oceanic evaporation, 21–22
Oligotrophy, 37, 39, 40–41, 42, 45, 46, 122
Omagua, 4, 28, 97–98
Orinoco River, 118
Oxbow lakes, 87, 89, **89**

Oxisols, 11–13, **12**, 36, 39, 42, 43, 46, 66–67, 76, 120, 121

Palms, 69–70, 95–96
Pará (Brazil), 151, 159
Parakanã, 127
Parintintin, 103
Peruvian Basin, 28
Pindaré River, 70
Pleistocene Era, 24, 118
Podzolic soils. *See* Spodosols
Population control, 81–82
Populations, native, xiv, xv, 2, 4–5, 6, 24, 29, 31–33, 37, 41–55, 60–61, 72–73, 86, 87–88, 97–98, 105, 112, 118, 123–124, 125–128, 143, 145–148, 158, 163 n.1, 167 n.4
Purús River, 89

Rainfall, 9, 10, 21, 22, 30, 40, 60, 62, 120
Ribeiro, Darcy, 7
Rio Negro Basin, 26, 36, 37, **37**, 38, 39, **39**, 41, 44, 45, 46, 47, 48, 50–51, **51**, 53, 54, 62
Rivers, 3, 87–88, **89**, 90–91, 96–97
Rondônia (Brazil), 5, 29, 32, 50, 58, 59, 67–68, 70, 119, 155, 157
Roraima (Amazon Basin), 38, 119, 122, 157
Rubber era, 6–7, **6**, 111–112

San Carlos de Río Negro (Venezuela), 39, 41, 45–46, 62, 63
Savannas, xv, 3, 9, 21, 26, 29, 61, 117–139, **119, 125**
Secondary succession, 27, 39, 45–46, 61, 80–81, 96
Serra da Mesa, 135
Serra do Cachimbo, 38
Settlement patterns, 51–54
Setz, Eleonore, 126
Siona-Secoya (Ecuador), 19
Social justice, 159–162

Social organization, 51–54, 81–82, 127, 129, 165 n.7

Soils, 11–14, 12, 13, 26, 27, 28–29, 30, 31, 40, 42, 43, 59–60, 61, 65–68, **66**, 72–75, **74**, 80, 89–90, 95–96, 97, 120–121, 122, **123**, 124, 126, 137–138, 148, 149, 163–164 n.3

Solimões (Brazil), 88, 92

Spodosols, 36, 38, 40, 42, 66

Steward, Julian, 60

Sumatra Island, 38

Suruí, 5, 7, 8, **8**, 32, 50, 58, 70, 76, 77, 78–79, 81–83

Swidden cultivation, 14, 31, 42, 43, 61, 75–76, 80, 118, 120, 126

Tapajós River Basin, 24, **26**, 90, 119

Tapirapé, 83, 105, 127

Tembé, 69–70

Temperatures, 9, 60, 75

Terra Firme Regions. *See* Upland forests

Tikuna, 88

Timbira, 127

Tocantins-Basin, 119

Transamazon Highway, 146, 149, 150

Trees, 16–17, 63–65, **64–65**, 80–81, 123

Tukanoan, 37, 42, 44, 45, 46, 48, 49, 50, 52, 53, 54

Tupí-Guaraní, 107

Tupí, 130

Uanano, 42, 43, 44, 48–49, 52–53

Ucayali River, 86, 87, 89, 112

Ultisols, 11–13, **12**, 66–67, 76, 120

United Nations Ecology and Development, xiii

Upland forests, xv, 4, 21, 24–31, 36, 57–84, 123–124, 125, 126, 128–129, 131–132

Upper Amazon, The (Lathrap), 86

Upper Floodplain Ecosystem, 27, 28–29, 88–90, 107–113

Upper Rio Negro, 48, 158

Upper Xingú Basin, 14, 42, 109

Urubú Ka'apor, 69, 107

Vargas, Getúlio, 148

Várzea. *See* Floodplains

Vaupés River Basin, 36, 37, 38, 41, 42, 44, 52

Vegetation, 21–22, 24, 25, 26, 29–30, 36, 38–40, **39**, **74**, 91–94, **93**, 96, 100, 121–123, **123**, 132, 164 n.4

Venezuelan Amazon, 18

Water cycling/recycling, 21–22, **22**, **23**

Waterlogging, 44

Whitewater rivers, 22, 23, 24, 89, 91, 94

Xavante, 130–132, 134, 135–136, **135**

Xinguano, 128, 129–130

Xingú River Basin, 26, 27, 90, 94, 95, 119

Yanomamo, 7, 49, 58

Yapú River, 42

Yupka, 49

Zonation, 98, 99, 112